SPEAK
SILENCE

SPEAK
SILENCE

Rhetoric and
Culture in Blake's
Poetical Sketches

Edited by
Mark L. Greenberg

Wayne State University Press • Detroit

Manufactured in the United States of America.

99 98 97 96   5 4 3 2 1

Library of Congress Cataloging-in-Publication Data

Speak silence : rhetoric and culture in Blake's Poetical sketches / edited by
    Mark L. Greenberg.
        p.   cm.
    Includes bibliographical references and index.
    ISBN 0-8143-1985-8 (alk. paper)
    1. Blake, William, 1757–1827. Poetical sketches.   2. Language and
culture—England—History—18th century.   3. English language—18th
century—Rhetoric.   4. Blake, William, 1757–1827—Technique.   5. Silence
in literature.   I. Greenberg, Mark L., 1948–   .
PR4144.P63S64   1996
821'.7—dc20   95-39561

For Erica and Alison

Contents

Contributors

VINCENT A. DE LUCA is late Professor of English at the University of Toronto

ROBERT F. GLECKNER is Professor of English at Duke University

MARK L. GREENBERG is Professor of Humanities at Drexel University and Director of the University Honors Program

NELSON HILTON is Professor of English at the University of Georgia

STUART PETERFREUND is Professor and Chair of the Department of English at Northeastern University

THOMAS A. VOGLER is Professor of English at the University of California, Santa Cruz

SUSAN J. WOLFSON is Professor of English at Princeton University

Preface

Some years ago a group of Blake scholars convened at a special session held during the Modern Language Association's national convention. We were there to celebrate, by engaging in criticism and debate, Blake's singular achievement in letterpress, *Poetical Sketches*.[1] Customarily brief papers were delivered, followed by unusually energetic and productive discussion. After the formal session had ended, the participants agreed with many of those in attendance that the ideas generated during the discussion deserved preservation in print and communication to the community concerned with the interpretation and teaching of Blake's art. We committed ourselves to gathering together revised and expanded versions of the conference papers, augmenting them with contributions by others engaged in the study of the *Sketches* but not present on the panel, and publishing them in a volume devoted to furthering our understanding of Blake's little book of poetic verses and prose poems.

The original panelists agreed, as well, about the importance of imparting to our readers a sense of the spontaneous interplay that had occurred at the conference while at the same time maintaining the carefully reasoned discourse of the particular arguments advanced there. The design of this book represents our attempt to do so, however imperfectly. Readers will find the essays printed here occasionally commenting on one another, thus reproducing portions of the original roundtable discussion. Both this volume's discursive Introduction and its polemical Afterword specifically engage the essays they frame, animating them anew, while also highlighting crucial interconnections and interprenetrations among them. Even the idea for an Afterword to be written by its particular author derived from our original commitment to capturing on these pages the discursive contours of our panel. Contributors to the volume recognized that in their written texts and during the panel discussion they often found themselves enmeshed in "conversation" with a scholar not physically present at the conference: Robert F. Gleckner, whose *Blake's Prelude: "Poetical Sketches"* was on everyone's mind.

---

1 Original discussants included Vincent A. De Luca, Mark L. Greenberg, Nelson Hilton, Stuart Peterfreund, Michael Phillips, and Thomas A. Vogler.

Why not transform such an engaging absence into a conversational presence? All the contributors enthusiastically endorsed the idea of my inviting Gleckner to have the last word, and we were delighted when he accepted our invitation. Written with characteristic grace and spiritual generosity, the Afterword demonstrates that when genuine intellectual "Opposition" occurs, it signifies "true Friendship." Gleckner's concluding rejoinder constitutes not only a "response" to the responses to *Blake's Prelude,* thus rounding out the volume. It also modifies and elaborates ideas Gleckner has previously published in light of the discussion presented here.

Apart from presenting polished essays on *Poetical Sketches,* then, this volume also invites the reader to witness the developmental process of specific ideas about Blake's early art—and its relation to his later works—as they solidify or dissolve. Between its covers we may see enacted in miniature the larger, ongoing dialogue that has characterized the progress of Blake studies during the second half of the twentieth century.

MLG

Introduction
Poetical Sketches: Critical Pivots and Pirouettes

MARK L. GREENBERG

Until recently, the warmest receptions of *Poetical Sketches* inevitably alloyed admiration with qualifications and even voiced serious reservations about the value of the work. Rhetorically, criticism has tended to pivot on questions of value, with generous appreciation yielding to reservations (or vice versa). This is true of the *Sketches'* earliest notices (by such writers as B. H. Malkin, Crabb Robinson, J. T. Smith, Alan Cunningham, Frederick Tatham, Alexander Gilchrist, and the Rossettis). And this tendency has continued well into the twentieth century, where particular attention to the perceived value of the work has been paid not only by such noted Blake detractors as T. S. Eliot but also by devotees, including Northrop Frye, Harold Bloom, David V. Erdman, and by those dedicated especially to interpreting the *Sketches,* including David Wagenknecht, Michael J. Tolley, Michael Phillips, Margaret Ruth Lowery, and Robert F. Gleckner. For a variety of reasons worth considering, the *Sketches* seems to invite—even demand—evaluative criticism. Concomitantly, discussions of evaluation and value, which seem inseparable from considerations of Blake's little book, expand naturally to invite ideas about its originality and origins, the contexts it claims, its language, influences on its author (however one defines these terms), the dynamic relations between and among works of art, and complexities involved with how and even why one interprets an artist's earliest work. While the essays gathered here press such issues vigorously, they too center on or return to matters of value—literally a pivotal issue that preoccupied even the earliest commentators writing on *Poetical Sketches.*

Consider contemporary and nineteenth-century accounts of the work with their sharply hinged views. John Flaxman, one of two principal patrons for the *Sketches* and perhaps its chief contemporary promoter, introduces a *"Pamphlet of poems . . .* the writings of a Mr. BLAKE" to the popular poet William Hayley as follows: Blake's "education," Flaxman apologizes, "will plead sufficient excuse to your Liberal mind for the defects of his work." Henry Crabb Robinson asserts firmly that the poems in *Poetical Sketches* are "of very unequal merit. The metre is usually so loose and careless as to betray a total ignorance of the art, whereby the larger part of the poems are rendered singularly rough and unattractive." "On the other hand," his evaluation veers, "there is a wildness and loftiness of imagination in certain dramatic fragments which testifies to genuine poetical feeling." Frederick Tatham, Blake's disciple and an early biographer, erects several evaluative fulcrums on which to balance the work. He grants that the *Sketches* are "succinct [,] original, fanciful & fiery but" his argument turns, "as a general criticism, it may be said that they are more rude than refined, more clumsy than delicate." Again, Tatham's evaluative poise suspends two opposing qualities possessed by this work: Blake's "blank verse is prose cut in slices, & his prose inelegant, but replete with Imagery."[1]

Alexander Gilchrist, author of the first and most influential full-length biography of Blake and a chief contributor to the mid-nineteenth-century Blake revival, observed that the *Sketches*, "did not even get so far as" to merit inclusion in the *Monthly Review's* "copious and explicit *Index* of 'books noticed' in that periodical, now quite a manual of extinct literature." After all, Blake's pamphlet is "now so rare," (Gilchrist observes in 1861) that he had to borrow a copy from a friend; there is "none . . . in the British Museum." Rhetorically, Gilchrist makes a virtue out of the *Sketches'* obscurity during Blake's lifetime and well into the nineteenth century; from such obscurity springs Gilchrist's program of comparative analysis that produces a highly positive valuation of lyrics found in the *Sketches*. First, Gilchrist contrasts these poems favorably with the "polished phraseology and subdued thought" that characterizes poetry written by Blake's contemporaries. "'Tis hard to believe these poems were written in the author's teens, harder still to realize how some of them, in their unforced simplicity, their bold and careless freedom of sentiment and expression, came to be written at all in the third quarter of the eighteenth century" (I, 23). Glancing ahead to an age of renewed poetic inspiration and execution, Gilchrist asserts as well a strong, positive association between Blake's early poems and lyrics that would be penned some years later by Cowper, Burns, Wordsworth, and Coleridge. Lyrics in *Poetical Sketches* deserve notice, Gilchrist argues, because they so clearly outshine other poems written during their poetically-depleted age and because they anticipate the style and substance of verse enacted by the early Romantics.

Dante Gabriel Rossetti was happy to encourage and even orchestrate such notice. Gilchrist's death in autumn, 1861 left the *Life of William Blake* unfinished (it was ultimately published in 1863; a second edition appeared in 1880). Rossetti, who agreed to edit (i.e., select, arrange, and "improve"). Blake's poems for the biography's second volume printed twenty-two pages of creatively-edited excerpts from the *Sketches:* eleven lyrics and almost ten pages of "selections" from "King Edward the Third."[2] His headnote to these selections balances admiration for the lyrics with glancing dismissal of its prose pieces. Taking his cue from Gilchrist's method in the biography's first volume, Rossetti engages in contextual evaluation of the lyrics contained in the *Sketches,* concluding robustly that "if we view them comparatively; in relation to Blake's youth when he wrote them, or the poetic epoch in which they were produced; it would be hardly possible to overrate their astonishing merit" (II, 1).

With much less enthusiasm Rossetti notices the volume's other contents. "Besides what is here given, there are attempts in the very modern-antique style of ballad prevalent at the time, and in Ossianic prose, but all naturally very inferior, and probably earlier" (II, 1). What readers could not have known as they read this was that from one of Blake's "very inferior" prose poems, "The Couch of Death," Rossetti appears already to have appropriated a significant number of specific features. These he incorporated into his own elegiac poem, "My Sister's Sleep," written in 1847 (it was published in 1850 in *The Germ*). The compositions bear striking resemblances: they share the same number of characters inhabiting similar, particularized situations; they share a common dramatic setting—the night vigil of a mother and a surviving sister at a child's death couch; they express the speaker's heightened awareness of auditory and visual phenomena; and they also depict intense psychological change resulting in a singular moment of mental transformation.[3] Perhaps conscious of his unacknowledged debt to Blake, "Rossetti regarded ["My Sister's Sleep"] with more than due disfavor" after publishing it in *The Germ* and for years objected to its being reprinted, according to his brother, William Michael (*Works of Dante Gabriel Rossetti,* 661). While Rossetti's casual dismissal of Blake's prose poems in *Poetical Sketches* was certainly in keeping with other nineteenth-century evaluations, in light of his blatant borrowing his critique now seems disingenuous. Like Rossetti's rejection of his own derivative composition, his criticism of Blake's "Ossianic prose" deflects attention from Rossett's creative appropriations from precisely those portions of Blake's work which Rossetti devalues. In short, Rossetti's critical comments tell us more about his embarrassment than about Blake's early writings.

For most non-appropriating readers, prominent features of the *Sketches* historically have encouraged conscious consideration of its value—or have sponsored unself-reflexive value judgments. The little book, as Susan Wolfson points out in the first sentence of the first essay in this collection, is itself primarily and immediately responsible for attenuating enthusiasm: "At first glance, *Poetical Sketches* averts critical attention." Wolfson invokes the work's title as marking a "provisional, even casual, composition, done in a few strokes." I would add that even the *typography* of the book's remarkably spare title page strikes a similarly humble pose, representing a marked contrast with late-eighteenth-century conventions. Margaret Ruth Lowery observed that the little volume lacks the "complexity of matter so frequently found" on title pages of contemporary books of verse (30). During this period, successful professional authors, printers, and booksellers enacted strategic programs for marketing their products. One of these programs involved transforming title pages into aggressive advertising instruments. Title pages were typically cluttered, attention-grabbing devices designed to tout the work and its author. Titles themselves tended to be highly descriptive, and were often long and involved commentaries on the work's contents, replete with numerous clauses and modifiers. Authors adorned their names with any degrees or honors they may have received and with other salient achievements to which they might lay claim. Epigrams from famous authors often appeared, and, of course, printers and booksellers boldly listed their names and the addresses of their shops. Contrast that practice with this:

POETICAL
SKETCHES

—

By W.B.

—

LONDON:

Printed in the Year mdcclxxxiii.

Blake's title page itself speaks silence. In Lowery's terms, here "all was simplicity itself, reserved, austere" (30). The reserve it graphically communicates constitutes another element contributing to tempered judgments of the work. It is worth keeping in mind, however, that typography may attempt to lead readers to conclusions that readers may not be willing to accept.

The interplay between the *Sketches*' typography and the volume's subsequent reception underscores the complex dynamic always characterizing acts of inscription and of reading. In *The Order of the Book*, Roger Chartier discusses how typography conditions a work's "register of references and its mode of interpretation" (11). The attenuated title page of *Poetical Sketches* and its truncated authorial presence, reducing the author's identity to two letters (virtually effacing "him"), conspire typographically to direct our reception of the text. Self-effacement is, of course, uncharacteristic of Blake, who etches his name prominently as "The Author & Printer" or as Printer at the beginning of each of his illuminated books. Beyond its spare title page, this little volume's unpretentious physical self-presentation— 72 pages, octavo, uncut and unsewn, printed in letterpress—also suggests modesty to a degree uncharacteristic of eighteenth-century books of poetry, or, for that matter, any of Blake's other, richly engraved and hand-detailed volumes. Perhaps a subtle politics of attenuation is at work here, sponsored by Blake's "supporters," if not by Blake himself? Whatever its origin, the ordering communicated by the typography of *Poetical Sketches* confronts "rebellious and vagabond" readers, in Chartier's phrase (viii), who subvert formal intentions, ignore or reject prescribed modes of reading, read between the lines, construct readings and textual relations that no author, printer, editor, or bookseller could possibly foresee, and in general act to thwart any measure of control that a book may try to enforce. Acts of independence certainly characterize the history of Blake's reception generally and that of the *Sketches* particularly. It is hardly overstatement to claim that the essays to follow describe the current horizon of readerly rebellion with respect to *Poetical Sketches.*

Rebellious readers certainly have been attracted by the anomalous character of this particular Blake work: his only unengraved, unilluminated *published* volume (*The French Revolution* having been typeset but never issued). Sophisticated readers of the *Sketches* acknowledge being conditioned not only by its peculiar letterpress printing, as we have briefly discussed, but also by experience and expectations learned and remembered from studying Blake's works produced in composite art. This sort of conditioning raises a number of important theoretical issues involving context and comparison. At the outset, the abundant *visualness* of Blake's purely verbal language in the *Sketches* displays a complex formal aesthetic that invites comparison with Blake's later graphics and attention to the cultural negotiations which they trace (a region explored deftly by Wolfson and Hilton). How much of what we "know" about Blake's other works finds its way "back" into our readings of the *Sketches?* Conversely, to what extent do we distort these early writings by locating in them embryonically artistic inclinations developed by a mature Blake? The little book presents other critical problems, as well.

A pervasive tendency in Blake studies has been to elucidate a particular figure, passage, or poem by ranging synchronically across all Blake's works in order to find compelling parallels and other interpretive "evidence." The remarkable coherence apparent in Blake's thought and designs certainly encourages glossing, and we all look to it for help. But especially in the case of the early and unengraved *Sketches*, we might do well to reconsider our tactics. Uncontextualized glossing actually ignores or attenuates changes in Blake's thought— and Blake's development as an artist—over some sixty years. Moreover, our growing awareness of the problems created by importing knowledge from particular iterations of Blake's other works should caution us regarding the accuracy and usefulness of this widespread practice. As Robert N. Essick, W. J. T. Mitchell, and Joseph Viscomi have shown us repeatedly, Blake's works in composite art often vary significantly from copy to copy both in overall design and in minute particulars. Glossing may actually gloss over deliberate and significant differences between and among various copies of a work; lack of precision in the source necessarily diminishes the usefulness of this practice for accurately illuminating the object of the gloss.

That tantalizing but problematic coherence apparent in Blake's opus, however, raises additional issues also explored in the essays here. How, contributors ask, may we describe the relationship between *Poetical Sketches* and the "body" of art attributed to Blake? How can it be said properly to "fit" within that body? To what extent are its relationships to Blake's other works attributable to the cleverness of Blake's many gifted readers? Then, of course, there is the related, expansive tendency to read these early poems not just as Blake's proto-myths but as proto-Romantic poems (a move encouraged by such early defenses as the one mounted by Gilchrist). Are such claims plausible? To what extent does such a burden distort these poems by unfairly raising our expectations of them? Moreover, given the remarkable outpouring of books and articles, periodicals, exhibits, conferences, and conference papers devoted to Blake during the last three decades (what has come to be known as "The Blake Industry"), we might well ask if all this enthusiasm itself might not result in overdetermining, overvaluing juvenilis that never would have received the culture's attention had it not been written by the late twentieth-century's "Blake." While this volume of essays challenges its readers to find answers for these questions themselves, a number of commentators writing here, including V. A. De Luca, Thomas Vogler, Susan Wolfson, and Stuart Peterfreund, offer their own detailed responses.

The evident derivativeness of many of these poems and prose sketches also has been a cause for praising or dismissing the young Blake. Every serious reader of the work agrees that in poetic and rhetorical structure, tone and other elements of "voice," phrasing, and imagery, the *Sketches* often echo the Bible, Shakespeare, Spenser, Milton, lyrics from Percy's *Reliques* and other Elizabethans, Jonson, Pope, Chatterton, and Macpherson's *Ossian,* to name just the most obvious precursors. Even Blake's experiments in form refer to prior formal strategies derived from previous poets. How are we to interpret such blatant "borrowing?" More importantly, the condition of such "influence" as we find here leads to questions of how we might interpret a work so firmly embedded in prior language and rhetorical fashioning. At an early age Blake appears to be a perceptive critic of poetic and political posturing in others, an adroit manipulator of voices, parody, style, and tropes. His youthful insights and abilities prompt us to consider how the young poet approaches form and themes in relation to earlier artistic achievements, about a young artist's negotiations with his precursors and his culture, and about how, viewed through this young artist's eyes, human character is constructed and, in some cases, deformed. Moreover, this discussion has opened to general analysis of the nature of context, voice, inscription, and imitation, and of poetic origins, originality, and attitude. Essays for this volume by Stuart Peterfreund, V. A. De Luca, Nelson Hilton, and Thomas Vogler engage these issues, as does Robert Gleckner's response. The issue of influence pervades literature written during Blake's lifetime and thereafter. It is worth keeping in mind that important theorists of influence writing during the past two decades, including Geoffrey Hartman, Walter Jackson Bate, and Harold Bloom, began their careers as students of writers active during the eighteenth and early nineteenth centuries (and in the case of Bloom, of course, with special attention to Blake).

Once past *Poetical Sketches'* attenuated title page, past its unpretentious format and size, our expectations for the volume are quickly diminished even further. Every full-length commentary on the *Sketches* (and most essays devoted to it) engage the books' notorious prefatory "Advertisement." It confronts readers with unconventionally excessive apologetics for what it calls an unrevised "production of untutored youth," containing some works written in Blake's "twelfth" year, and preserving "irregularities and defects . . . in almost every page" (ii).[4] Often cited, this might be the most inauspicious beginning for any book of verse by a major poet ever printed. The generally deprecatory "Advertisement" goes on to enact that rhetorical pivot that will come to characterize future receptions of the *Sketches.* It affirms that Blake's "friends" conscious of these poems' "irregularities and defects . . . have still believed that they possessed a poetic originality, which merited some respite from oblivion." Here, at the book's outset, *originality* as value is set against the otherwise flawed productions of an uneducated youth. We can trace to this brief prefatory notice the seemingly inexhaustible tendency to balance judgments of this work. We can trace to it, too, a consciousness of the idea that readers would ultimately determine the value of this obscure late-eighteenth-century volume, much as they have done and continue to do.

"Conscious of the irregularities and defects to be found in almost every page, his friends have still believed that they possessed a poetic originality, which merited some respite from oblivion. These their opinions remain, however, to be now reproved or confirmed by a less partial public." Thus concludes the "Advertisement" to Blake's first book of poetry. Of course, the Reverend Matthew (or whoever wrote those words) was right. The "public," the volume's subsequent readers, have in many ways given life to Blake's book, reproving or confirming the original patrons' judgments, even reproducing the dynamics of those judgments while reanimating the volume through fresh interpretations of it. The essays that follow continue in this critical tradition, one fostered and even predicted by a deceptively untraditional little book.

II

Forecasting the direction—if not the details—taken by the essays that follow suggests the range and depth of current responses to the issues outlined above, among others. Susan Wolfson's ambitious essay traces the poetics and politics of imaginative form in the *Sketches*. As well, she offers a perspicacious "forecast of later Romantic negotiations with formalism." Shrewdly eliding the apparent differences between Blake's singular published production in letterpress and his later illuminated art, she introduces Blake's composite verbal-visual rhetoric as a "route into," almost, ironically, a *forecast* of his early experiments with graphic form in the *Sketches*. Formalism in *Poetical Sketches*, she argues, is "inscribed as a reformation of conventional practices. . . ." Wolfson demonstrates that Blake purposefully introduced into his early poems unconventional stanza forms, irregular rhymes, dissonances in eye rhymes, and "patently unorthodox stops" to challenge aesthetic norms and the social foundations supporting them. The central portion of her essay directs our attention to Blake's deliberate typographical rhetoric evident throughout the *Sketches:* enjambement, the placement of particular words, the play of signifiers, the thetic display of phonemes and graphemes—pivot points of visual and semantic significance. Offering a wide-ranging phenomenology of typographical stylings in Blake's book, she highlights poignant asymmetries, graphic wreathing, verbal-and-visual balancing, and various subversions of conventional stanza forms. In similar fashion, Wolfson goes on to explore rhyme's reason. She argues for Blake's expert manipulation of rhyme to suggest bondage and freedom—an aesthetic device deliberately employed for political and social purposes. Placing these poems in the larger cultural context of England during the 1780s, Wolfson convincingly demonstrates how the poetics of *Poetical Sketches* expresses Blake's deep concerns about war, jingoism, and the nature of political power. For example, she analyzes Blake's blank verse as radical aesthetic, showing how some of the poems in blank verse trope the restrictiveness of their form; and she unpacks spoken ironies in "King Edward III" to reveal how they subtly undercut the characters speaking them, thus subverting the speakers' politics and social standing. Ultimately, Wolfson shows how Blake radically undercuts even his own aesthetic. In an imaginative move, she asks us to consider Blake's strategy of including prose poems along with those in verse within such a small book. She concludes that the deliberate formal contrast generated by juxtaposing versed with unversed (even unparagraphed) writing shows Blake "extending his elaborate performances of poetic form into their own effacement," which "may constitute the most radically experimental gesture of *Poetical Sketches.*"

Stuart Peterfreund begins his essay on originality in the *Sketches* by asserting that Blake himself wrote the "Advertisement" to *Poetical Sketches.* Such an audacious move, Peterfreund boldly argues, highlights the issue of originality and what it means for Blake, an issue, according to Peterfreund, that permeates the fabric of *Poetical Sketches.* Elaborating the two principal traditions available to poets writing during the late eighteenth century, the Hebraic and the Classical, Peterfreund shows that originality for Blake inheres in joining with and thus perpetuating the Hebraic strain in English verse. During Blake's age, the Hebraic in literature, characterized by strong metaphors, had become attenuated. Blake's project in *Poetical Sketches* represents a return to originality, reanimating what Blake understood literally to be the *origins* of Western poetry: the Bible. An important part of that project, Peterfreund argues, involves reasserting the priority of speech: "Blake's program for originality is a program to establish the proper priority of speech over phenomena, which is found in the Bible, and which fosters originality." Language thus becomes the contested critical ground here, what Peterfreund calls the "first step in this struggle toward aesthetic utterance and poetic originality." Peterfreund ultimately focuses his attention upon the season poems (as does Thomas Vogler in the following essay). For Peterfreund, they function dramatically: Blake's speakers enacting the struggles of "poetical character in the face of the Satanic temptation to classicize." Even as these poems trace speakers' struggles with the tendency to classicize, they also record the beginnings of Blake's lifelong project to "reattain the originality that precedes conventionality by invoking 'the Sublime of the Bible,'" as Peterfreund, citing Blake, puts it.

How, Thomas Vogler begins his essay, may we designate Blake's *originality* in a work so firmly embedded in prior language formulas and rhetorical fashioning? Vogler argues that to locate Blake's defining individual language also means that we must "locate Blake's work in a completely new context rather than as a moment in a series that is governed by prior organization and differentiation." Engaging Gleckner and Peterfreund, Vogler analyzes ideas of originality, context, pastiche, and irony that have regulated previous discussions of the *Sketches.* Moving beyond the precincts of Blake's book, Vogler also discusses the pertinence to it of postmodern treatments of irony and context. Focusing his discussion centrally on the season poems in *Poetical Sketches*, Vogler argues that they parody a number of prior, conventional compositions. Yet he questions whether Blake's poems move much beyond experimentation with voice and style, even speculating about the limits of such experimentation. Vogler's preoccupation with voice proves especially productive: Blake, he asserts, recognizes the "power and potential of [prior] voices as they are inscribed in and practiced within a systematized code of poetic discourse." Vogler then invites us to listen to the season poems as experiments in speech. Here Blake "tries on" different voices—different poetic styles—rather than breaking radically with tradition, even as he discloses his unease with that tradition. Vogler concludes his provocative piece by surveying Blake's complex responses to previous pastoral poems, attending especially to prior depictions of the sun and how Blake transforms them in the *Sketches*. A dazzling heliotropic excursion follows, in which Vogler leads us through four centuries of sun verse and concludes with a series of thoughtful questions regarding the nature of light, gold, and Blake's aesthetics in the season poems.

The dynamically changing states of mind depicted in the *Sketches* lead Vincent De Luca to conclude that Blake's early style, laden with tropes, demonstrates Blake's "aspiration to become a poet in the sublime mode." De Luca's essay discusses, as well, the "built-in attractions and dangers of this aspiration." Briefly surveying the spatial and temporal qualities that inhere in troping, especially as practiced by other late-eighteenth-century poets, De Luca elaborates "motifs of 'becoming,' of hurry, and of transformations from state to state" that characterize poems in the *Sketches*. Like the "troping style itself," he argues, such dynamics are "entirely suited to the aesthetic of the eighteenth-century sublime, for this aesthetic postulates sudden transformation of the mind, episodes in which we are rushed away from our proper selves." Yet De Luca also warns of the sublime's Janus-like operations: On the one hand, tropes efface spatial boundaries of every sort and thus conduce to a state of mental liberation—liberation even from the idea of bounds and bounding. On the other hand, troping also reduces and obscures, with the tropic style "always in danger of becoming en-tropic, an enactment and celebration of slippage, loss, and depletion, the grim corollaries of a vision of things that places transformation and instability at its center." The strong sense of melancholy that readers have experienced in the *Sketches* derives from this protean nature of troping. Tropes hasten the mind to contemplate what De Luca poetically calls "This dreaded yet delicious foretaste of doom." Reading Blake's book dynamically, De Luca traces a movement from the "lambent visionary pastorals" in its first half, to "death and the dark clashes of jagged powers" in the second half.

Such a movement is mirrored by the progress of individual poems in this reading, and we are asked to focus on "Mad Song" as central and pivotal in such an overall dynamic. De Luca charts the young Blake's oscillations between the rival attractions of the "Northern spell and the Biblical promise," a persistent, life-long rivalry that Blake will not reconcile until the "closing plates of *Jerusalem.*"

At the beginning of his minutely detailed explication, Nelson Hilton points out the historical basis for our close association of the autograph manuscript poem "then She bore Pale desire"—one of two poems called by Erdman "Further Sketches"—and the *Sketches* proper. At first, Hilton lineates Blake's fragment in a way that stresses the metrical basis of this early poem, while still faithfully following the word order in Erdman's standard text. This rendition offers a remarkable example of the power of typography, lineation, and graphic position to alter—even to determine—a "text." Hilton then offers a wide-ranging explication of Blake's language. In richly associative commentary on Blake's lines, Hilton frequently brings to bear apposite references to poets whose writings Blake had internalized: such contemporaries as Gray, Collins, Swift, and Watts, as well as the Bible, Spenser, Milton, and Shakespeare. Judiciously selected, complementary citations from the *OED* and Johnson's *Dictionary* enrich Hilton's encyclopedic method, revealing the networks of associations generated by Blake's polysemous language and other, equally allusive, methods of composition. Additionally, Hilton further layers our understanding of this poem by introducing appropriate autobiographical references. Shrewdly citing Blake's own letters and the psychoanalytic work of Melanie Klein, Hilton unfolds the subject of *envy* that is at the heart of this poem and that is explored by Blake himself in other *Sketches,* in certain of the *Songs,* and centrally in the prophecies. Envy, says Hilton (quoting Klein) is "at bottom 'directed against creativeness.'" Pondering Blake's own titanic struggle to combat destructive tendencies in himself deepens and complicates our understanding of this previously neglected "fragment." Hilton's essay resonates with the other approaches to the *Sketches* with which it joins in this volume.

Together, these chapters and portions of Robert Gleckner's Afterword analyze traditional elements in the *Sketches* in order to reveal how fully the young Blake had absorbed them and how deftly and deliberately he manipulated and transvalued them in his early, revolutionary experiments with language, voice, and rhetorical form. Like most sharply hinged receptions of the *Sketches,* Blake's work traces a series of unspoken evaluative pivots and pirouettes, his remarkably sophisticated rhetorical dance with priority. Even as the *Sketches* engages a body of previous poetry and poets, these readings argue, Blake's poems ultimately veer away from their precursors and from the politics and values of eighteenth-century culture encoded in such prior writings. Ideally, readers will also find in this collection a shared sense that while we can enhance our understanding of Blake's often tantalizing creations, we may have to acknowledge that at last we may be left with nothing less than a profound experience of their strangeness. I invite you to listen as these essays speak the silence that is not *Poetical Sketches* and the silence that is.

Notes

1. These passages are conveniently reproduced in Bentley, *Blake Records,* and may be found as follows: Flaxman, p. 27; Crabb Robinson, p. 453; Tatham, pp. 513–514.

2. Rossetti's selections appear on pp. 3–25. By comparison, he prints 45 pages of creatively-edited *Songs of Innocence and of Experience* and draws enough material from Blake's Notebook (which, at the time, Rossetti owned) to fill another 45 pages in the *Life's* second volume. For more on Rossetti's editorial techniques, see Dorfman and my own *Dante Gabriel Rossetti and William Blake,* chapter 5, and "The Rossettis' Transcription of Blake's Notebook."

3. For a full discussion of Rossetti's generous appropriations from "The Couch of Death," see my *Dante Gabriel Rossetti and William Blake,* pp. 238–240. Rossetti's poem may be found on pp. 165–166 of his *Works.*

4. Stuart Peterfreund, at the beginning of his essay for this volume, discusses the authorship of the notorious "Advertisement." Peterfreund's essay first appeared in an earlier form in *ELH* 52.3 (1985): 673–706; previously published portions are reprinted here by permission. Regardless of its origin, this prefatory apology no doubt proved an embarrassment for the twenty-six-year-old married engraver when it was issued—and continued to do so throughout his life. Its ineradicable connection with the volume may explain why Blake failed to market the work.

Works Cited

Bentley, G. E., Jr. *Blake Records.* Oxford: Clarendon P, 1969.

B[lake]., W[illiam]. *Poetical Sketches.* London: 1783; facsimile rpt. London: Noel Douglas Replicas, 1926.

Blake, William. *The Complete Poetry and Prose of William Blake.* Ed. David V. Erdman; commentary by Harold Bloom, newly rev. ed. Berkeley and Los Angeles: U Cal P, 1982.

Bloom, Harold. *Blake's Apocalypse.* Garden City: Doubleday, 1963.

Chartier, Roger. *The Order of Books: Readers, Authors, and Libraries in Europe between the Fourteenth and Eighteenth Centuries.* Stanford: Stanford UP, 1994.

Cunningham, Allan. *Lives of the Most Eminent British Painters, Sculptors, and Architects.* Bentley 476–507.

Dorfman, Deborah. *Blake in the Nineteenth Century: His Reputation as a Poet from Gilchrist to Yeats.* New Haven: Yale UP, 1969.

Eliot, T. S. "Blake," in *Selected Essays.* New York: Harcourt, Brace, 1950.

Erdman, David V. *Blake: Prophet Against Empire.* Princeton: Princeton UP, 1954.

Essick, Robert N., ed. *The Visionary Hand.* Los Angeles: Hennessey & Ingalls, 1973.

———. *William Blake Printmaker.* Princeton: Princeton UP, 1980.

Flaxman, John. "Letter to William Haley, 26 April 1784. Bentley, 27.

Frye, Northrop. *Fearful Symmetry: A Study of William Blake.* 1947. Princeton: Princeton UP, 1969.

Gilchrist, Alexander. *Life of William Blake, With Selections from His Poems and Other Writings.* 2 vols. London: Macmillan, 1880; "Selections," vol. 2, ed. Dante Gabriel Rossetti.

Gleckner, Robert F. *Blake's Prelude: "Poetical Sketches."* Baltimore and London: The Johns Hopkins UP, 1982.

Greenberg, Mark Lawrence. *Dante Gabriel Rossetti and William Blake.* doc. diss. Ann Arbor, MI: University Microfilms, 1978.

———. "The Rossettis' Transcription of Blake's Notebook." *The Library: Transactions of the Bibliographical Society* Sixth Series 4 (1982): 249–272.

———. "William Michael Rossetti's Transcription and William Bell Scott's Tracings from Blake's Notebook." *The Library: Transactions of the Bibliographical Society* Sixth Series 6 (1984): 254–270.

Lowery, Margaret Ruth. *Windows of the Morning: A Critical Study of William Blake's "Poetical Sketches," 1783.* New Haven: Yale UP, 1940.

Malkin, Benjamin Heath. *A Father's Memoirs of His Child.* Bentley 421–432.

Mitchell, W. J. T. *Blake's Composite Art: A Study of the Illuminated Poetry.* Princeton: Princeton UP, 1978.

Paley, Morton D., and Michael Phillips, eds. *William Blake: Essays in Honour of Sir Geoffrey Keynes.* Oxford: Clarendon P, 1973.

Phillips, Michael. "Blake's Corrections in *Poetical Sketches.*" *Blake Newsletter* 4 (1970): 40–47.

———. "Blake's Early Poetry." Paley and Phillips 1–28.

———. "The Reputation of Blake's *Poetical Sketches.*" *RES* 26 (1975): 19–33.

———. "William Blake and the 'Unincreasable Club': The Printing of *Poetical Sketches.*" *Bulletin of the New York Public Library* 80 (1976): 6–18.

Robinson, Henry Crabb. *Vaterlandisches Museum;* and "Reminiscences." Bentley 432–455; and 535–549, resp.

Rossetti, Dante Gabriel. *The Works of Dante Gabriel Rossetti.* Ed. William Michael Rossetti. London: Ellis, 1911.

Smith, John Thomas. *Nollekens and His Times.* Bentley 455–476.

Tatham, Frederick. MS. "Life of Blake." Bentley 507–535.

Tolley, Michael J. "Blake's Songs of Spring." Paley and Phillips, 96–128.

Viscomi, Joseph. *The Art of William Blake's Illuminated Prints.* Manchester: Manchester Etching Workshop, 1983.

———. *Blake and the Idea of the Book.* Princeton: Princeton UP, 1993.

Wagenknecht, David. *Blake's Night: William Blake and the Idea of Pastoral.* Cambridge: Harvard UP, 1973.

Sketching Verbal Form: Blake's *Poetical Sketches*

Susan J. Wolfson

Blake's privileging of writing makes him
less interesting to deconstruction because it
makes his work less resistant to its strategies.
Everything is open to view.   Paul de Man[1]

Lines and Outlines, Forms and Deformity

At first glance, *Poetical Sketches* averts critical attention. Not
only does the title mark a provisional, even casual, composition,
done in a few strokes, but its "Advertisement" begs indulgence for
"irregularities and defects . . . in almost every page" of this unrevised
"production of untutored youth" (ii). It is, moreover, one of Blake's
few unengraved, unilluminated volumes. Yet from the performative
charge of this debut, and from its shaping by an imagination already
engaged with visual art, there emerges a complex poetic formalism, one involving self-fashioning, poetic tradition, and the work
of cultural formation.[2] This very range is energized by the interac-
tion of opposing attitudes toward form: a political impatience with
any "bound or outward circumference of Energy" (*The Marriage of
Heaven and Hell,* Plate 4), and an artistic respect for form. "Nature
has no Outline: / but Imagination has," declares his epigraph for *The
Ghost of Abel* (*CPP* 270)—the epitome of a life-long conviction that
the "Reality" of "Every Thing . . . Is its Imaginative Form" (*CPP* 663–
64).[3] Notions of form, forms, Form, and formation are everywhere
limned in Blake's designs and illuminations, and the vocabulary itself
claims an important place in his lexicon.[4]

Poetical Sketches is an early stage of Blake's poetics and politics of "Imaginative Form," as well as a forecast of later Romantic
negotiations with formalism. "Under historical conditions of modernity," Donald Wesling argues, "poetry and commentators are alike

A later version of this essay will appear in *Formal Charges: The Shaping of Poetry in
English Romanticism*, by Susan J. Wolfson, forthcoming from Stanford University Press.
This chapter is used with the permission of Stanford University Press.

meshed in a contradictory structure of thought wherein the highest twin values are the corporeality and the transparency of the medium of language. Poetic form under these conditions is transparent yet insistent, at once a scandal and one of the central issues of post-romantic poetics" (*Chances* 12). That this "modern" condition is one of Romanticism itself is clear in Blake's *Sketches*, whose critical force in the pre-Revolutionary moment of "the Year MDCCLXXXIII"[5] concentrates on these tensed twin values. Blake is producing poetic form as a medium for a poet's voice; at the same time, his "sketches" provoke attention to form itself—its organization on the page and its status as a motivated and malleable construction, not only in the domain of the aesthetic but also in the habitual formations of self, nation, and history. These different formalisms bear different implications. At times, the forms that Blake uses to shape his poetic performance suggest the poet's complicity or entanglement in larger cultural practices; at other times, he mobilizes his forms to expose their contingency and potential for reform. *Poetical Sketches* may draw its artistry in lines of resistance to conventional forms; or it may ironize resistance itself as a conventional form of self-display. In all these events as well as in their aggregate, we see that Blake's formalism is no static aesthetic. It is an action that calls readers into a critical awareness of the work of form not only in poetic, but also in cognitive, social, and historical processes.

This rhetoric of form involves a textuality whose emergence John Hollander has described: the way "the look of the poem on the page had begun to assume a canonical importance, and patterns of versification and typographical arrangement to play a small but definite role in the history of form" (*VR* 268ff). *Poetical Sketches* is alert to this "look," and the later illuminated texts fully realize it, although here the actual visual art is so remarkable that the visual rhetoric of their scripts may recede from notice. It is worth reading some of these scripts, however, because the semiotics of their graphic designs are allied to the formalist experiments of *Poetical Sketches*.[6] This is a "composite art," Vincent De Luca argues, involving not just the interplay of visual and verbal but also the play of verbal *as* visual.[7] At its most extreme pitch, such as the "wall of words" engraved on the plates of *Jerusalem*, the verbal design assaults perception as an "agenc[y] in the sublime effect of the poetry itself" (91). In lesser events, too, the effect of mixing pictorial signifiers and alphabetic ones is to "induc[e] the eye to pictorialize the verbal portion of the plate," diverting attention "from a sequential pursuit of words and lines to a visual contemplation of the whole block of text as a single unit, a panel" (89–90). In both its presence and its form, Blake designs his scripts with a semantic beyond the semantics of words. This scriptive signifying operates in lines, in discrete words, even in syllables. This is why the usual editorial practice of "disregarding Blake's original line shape," contends the Santa Cruz Study Group, "does violence to the visual semiotics of Blake's printed page." Its case is a set of lines form Chapter II of *The Book of Urizen,* at the bottom of the left column of Plate 5 (typography approximate; see *IB* 187):

> *5. But no light from the fires, all wear*
> *   darkness ~*
> *In the flames of Eternal fury*
> *   ~ ~ ~ ~ ~ ~ ~ ~ ~ ~ ~ ~ ~ ~*
> *6. In fierce angusih & quenchlefs*
> *   flames*

Noting that letterpress editions (they cite Erdman's) typically straighten these lines to end with *darkness* and *flames,* the Study Group regrets the effacement of the way Blake arranged the words to read "up and down as well as across," the "vertical relationships imply[ing] a connection between 'no light / darkness,' 'darkness / flames,' and 'fierce / flames'" (306–7).

W. J. T. Mitchell sees this "graphic potential" even in the verging of letters on a "pictorial value" in which "the sensuous surface of calligraphic and typographic forms" suggests "symbolic values." On the title page of *The Marriage of Heaven and Hell,* for instance, the flowing and embellished script of *Marriage* (and, I'd add, of the linking *of* and *and*) against the large dark Roman capitals of *Heaven* and *Hell* shows Blake "literally embod[ying] in the calligraphic form of 'marriage' the symbolic marriage that his 'types' prefigure in the text" ("Visible" 83–84). Mitchell has less to say about *Urizen,* feeling that the design of its plates enforces an "increasing separation of textual and pictorial space" (its crowded two-column format, miming an open book, casts the text as "a strictly verbal, non-pictorial form" [*Composite* 110]). But Robert Essick has discerned an interesting event even in this form. At the bottom of the left-hand column of Plate 4 (Chap. I), appears this staggered sentence:[8]

> *6. Here alone I in books formd of me-*
> *   -tals*
> *Have written the secrets of wisdom*

As Blake's etching approached the center margin, Essick surmises, the constraints of his medium "dictated" a necessary hyphenation. Working with the fact that his books "are not just 'formd of me-/-tals'; they are formed *by* the very nature of those metals and the material processes he employed," Blake let his medium "express its own tendencies" with the syllabic form, *me-/-tals.* And by virtue of the fact that "words are composed of a sequence of phonemes and graphemes, any part of which may also be a word," his inscription "generates textual meanings": "An 'accident' resulting from an essential feature of Blake's method of publication has produced a word ('me') with its own associations and contributions to the *Book of Urizen*" (215–16).

The only adjustment I'd make to this subtle reading is to propose that the forming of *me-* is no accident at all but a deliberate choice informed by Blake's sense, so Eliot puts it, that "verse, whatever else it may or may not be, is itself a system of *punctuation*" in which "the usual marks . . . are differently employed" (*TLS* 687; his italics). Like enjambment, hyphenation can become a meaningful form. Plate 4 shows that Blake could have put all the letters of *metals* on his next line without leaving a conspicuous blank (his center margin is more erose than regular); or, having embellished other spaces, he could have done so here; or he could have used the customary hyphenation, "met-als." But releasing *me-* from *metals* yields distinct semantic advantages. On the most local level, the phoneme frames the line with a fleeting, but wittily punning, mirror of its preceding sign of self, "I": "Here alone I in books formd of me." This is a formalism of "Every word and every letter . . . studied and put into its fit place" (*Jerusalem* Plate 3; *IB* 282), in which "a Line or Lineament is not formed by Chance" but is "Itself & Not Intermeasurable with or by any Thing Else" (12 April 1827; *CPP* 783). Blake's literal forming of *me-* gains further semantic value across *The Book of Urizen* as an ironic limning of Urizen's self-involuted knowledge, his tendency to read himself into and in the form of his book. The peculiar phonemic event of *me-* shapes a brief graphic icon of the attitude imaged in the self-concentrated scribe on the title page—"a self-portrait of the artist as a solitary reader and writer of texts, a figure of the textual solipsist" (Mitchell, "Visible" 56).

In this formation of *me-* from the constraints of a preexisting material, Blake may seem to anticipate Derrida's deconstruction of the subject as "a function of language" ("Difference" 145–46), or even Barthes' dissolution of the author into the book that "is only a tissue of signs, an imitation that is lost, infinitely deferred" ("Death" 147).

Yet the writerly presence of Blake's hyphen, even as it distills its *me-* in a material script, also resists resigning all authority to the text. The idiosyncratic hyphenation shows how forms of writing can impress the self in writing in ways that paradoxically elude deconstruction by language, medium, or sheer textuality. The graphic expression of *me-* becomes a metagraphic formation of a poet seizing his line to assert new forms against received structures of grammar, syntax, and verbal integrity.

This visual rhetoric is already being exercised in *Poetical Sketches*, where conventions are deformed by poetic self-inscription. Blake confronts his readers with stanza forms that violate their paradigms ("An Imitation of Spencer"); quatrains and ballad stanzas that refuse rhyme or impose dissonant eye rhymes; rhythms and shifting caesurae that strain against or even defy conventional metrical patterns; and lines whose patently unorthodox stops aggravate an indulgence of enjambment that was already controversial in Neoclassical aesthetics:

> O thou, who passest thro' our vallies in
> Thy strength . . .
>
> ("To Summer")

> Smile on our loves; and, while thou drawest the
> Blue curtains of the sky . . .
>
> ("To the Evening Star")

> Rouz'd like a huntsman to the chace; and, with
> Thy buskin'd feet, appear upon our hills . . .
>
> ("To Morning")

> When the whirlwind of fury comes from the
> Throne of God . . .
>
> ("Prologue . . . King Edward the Fourth")

> "The narrow bud opens her beauties to
> "The sun, and love runs in her thrilling veins;
> "Blossoms hang round the brows of morning, and
> "Flourish down . . .
>
> ("To Autumn")

In the same year these sketches were printed, 1783, Dr. Johnson published his complaint about blank verse being "verse only to the eye." Blake's shaping of his line reverses the valuation, as if from Milton's own description of the "musical delight" of "sense variously drawn out from one Verse into another" he meant to show the visual potential of "sense" and "drawn out."[9] "The Style that Strikes the Eye is the True Style," Blake retorts to Reynolds (*CPP* 638), and he elaborates a remark of Berkeley to insist that "Forms must be apprehended by the Sense or the Eye of Imagination" (664).

Theorizing an implicit politics, Laura Riding and Robert Graves propose that "metre considered as a set pattern approved by convention . . . stand[s] for the claims of society," and "variations on metre[,] . . . the claims of the individual" (24). The allegory may be too schematic, but it is relevant to a poet given to claiming that "To Particularize is the Alone Distinction of Merit" (*CPP* 641). Some contemporary readers of the *Sketches*, such as Osbert Burdett, were "captivat[ed]" by the "faint irregularity . . . waving now toward and now away from the normal measure" (14). Others were not. Apologizing for the "imperfect form" of the poems, Gilchrist (Blake's biographer) itemizes their "hackneyed rhyme, awkward construction, and verbal repetition" (1:41). Crabb Robinson was also embarrassed: Blake's usual meter is "so loose and careless as to betray a total ignorance of the art, whereby the larger part of the poems are rendered singularly rough and unattractive" (Bentley 163). Whatever the reaction, it is clear that Blake's poetics, particularly his poetics of the line, challenge habitual contracts about poetic form. This challenge is most radical in the prose sketches at the back of the volume, forms not properly "poetic" at all, but posing a stylistic redefinition.

Yet throughout *Poetical Sketches*, Blake exerts variation against convention, and innovation against prescription, in ways that test the artist's forms against the authority of cultural and social forms. The master-term "Sketch," in this respect, bears into literary practice some of the social and performative aspects of the salon recitations that preceded the poems' circulation in print.[10] To claim authority as poems, the forms of Blake's "sketches" interplay tradition and individual talent, creating performances that are as skillful with tradition as they are self-consciously "modern." Well ahead of Eliot, Blake understood the projection of tradition by the modern moment—or even Michael Riffaterre's heightened formulation that the "norm is in effect deduced or even retroactively fantasized, from the text perceived as departure" (164). He even predicted de Man's deconstruction of "modernity" as itself historical: It is not only "the principle that gives literature duration and historical existence," it depends on history for its self-definition; indeed, the "more radical the rejection of anything that came before, the greater the dependence on the past" ("Literary Modernity" 162, 150). These involutions play into the formalism of *Poetical Sketches,* which uses tradition to ironize as well as legitimate the display of innovation.

Blake's formalist poetics gain semantic value not only in these turns with tradition but also in the way they compel a reader's involvement in the play of forms. This intertextual field of activity—both across literary history and within the volume's field of repetition, echo, and parody—is more important than the question of Blake's actual ordering of the sketches.[11] For rather than yielding a stable, unified image of the cryptic sketcher, "W.B.," the volume sketches various interactions. The correlative to this unnamed and unfixed authorial form is the sketcher's production of his reader, the intelligence in which these formal actions are registered and received.

Blank verse and the call to the reader's eye

Poetical Sketches repeatedly relates its aesthetic forms to issues of power—the power of poetic voice, of natural forces, of imagination, of social and political systems. The season poems at its front are a series of progressive experiments in poetic power that involve their reader in the play of its forms and at the same time encourage such a reader to reflect on the power and limitations of form itself. The reflection is important, because its issues will be replayed, with more darkly critical elaboration, in the social and political situations of later sketches.

In his initial test of poetic power, Blake casts the form of his verse line for apprehension by a reader's eye in a way that turns out to contribute to the authority of the poet's invocation. Here is the opening call of "To Spring," the first poem of this set:

> O thou, with dewy locks, who lookest down
> Thro' the clear windows of the morning, turn
> Thine angel eyes upon our western isle,
> Which in full choir hails thy approach, O Spring!
>
> (1–4)

In all the season poems, Geoffrey Hartman notes an "intensely vocative" poetics related to a "sense of poetical vocation." Jonathan Culler discerns a more specific self-constitution in apostrophe: "The object is treated as a subject, an *I* which implies a certain type of *you* in its turn. One who successfully invokes nature is one to whom nature might, in its turn, speak. He makes himself poet, visionary. Thus, invocation is a figure of vocation"; "voice calls . . . to dramatize its calling, to summon images of its power so as to establish its identity as poetical and prophetic voice."[12]

A casual phrase in this account, "in its turn," is a key to the production of a reading audience to complement these images of poetic power (*pace* Hollander's claim that this "poetry's discourse with itself" excludes "an audience or an active agent which might respond to the imperatives by clearly observable action" [*MG* 791]). With the turn of the line at the poem's first enjambment—"lookest down / Thro' the clear windows"—the reader's eye performs the action that the poet describes in imagination: at *down*, our eyes move down to the next line, the form of Blake's line making the preposition a directive for reading.[13] This readerly rhetoric invests the sketch with a kind of Barthesian "productivity"—a field "where the producer and reader of the text meet" and enter "into the play of signifiers" ("Theory" 36, 43). Such meetings, in Blake's text, lead to a potent fulfillment of the invocation at the very next point of enjambment: "turn / Thine . . . eyes." A reader's eyes must turn from one line to the next, thus releasing the poet's apostrophe from the fictive space of invocation into phenomenological agency. The *thou* invoked by the poet's voice is, referentially, the desired Spring, but in the action of his poetic line, it extends to readers, calling on them, in Wordsworth's phrase, to exert "a co-operating *power*" in the production of meaning (*Essay* [1815]; *PrW* 3:81). If, as Hartman writes, the "very energy of anticipation" in Blake's poetry enables it to "envision what it calls for" (ibid. 195), Blake's shaping of poetic form plays an important part by involving the reader in this envisioning.

The turn of verse to the next stanza expands the formalist agency of this invocation to evoke a sensation of a response from Spring itself. The new stanza proceeds from the close of the first on the assurance that a

> full choir hails thy approach, O Spring!
>
> The hills tell each other, and the list'ning
> Vallies hear; all our longing eyes are turned
> Up to thy bright pavillions: issue forth,
> And let thy holy feet visit our clime.

> (4–8)

The poetics of stanza two deftly draw the object of the call into the climate of the call. As *O Spring!* completes the syntax and closes the form of the first stanza, this terminal position pivots visually and syntactically as a transition into the next stanza's elaboration. Blake enhances this linking with the faint ad hoc rhyme of a split, interstanzaic couplet: *Spring/list'ning,* a chime that resonates semantically as an anticipatory joining of desire and event, of Spring and its expectation. This formal harmony, strengthened by the next line's *longing,* is sustained by a larger design of correspondence that the full syntax of "all our longing eyes are turned / Up to thy bright pavillions" brings into view. In a chiasmus extended across the first two stanzas, Blake mirrors his initial call to a "*thou* . . . who lookest *down*" to "*turn* / Thine angel *eyes up*on" in the image of "*our* longing *eyes* . . . *turned* / *Up.*" The second image does not merely describe desire but shapes a reciprocal poetic form to evoke its object. And the enjambment of both syntaxes tropes a further reciprocal turn of a reader's eye, an event intensified by the cross-lingual Latin punning of its key word, *turn,* on the visual formation that marks poetry itself: the turn of the verse line (*versus: turning*)[14]

Line endings, Christopher Ricks shows in his remarkable reading of Wordsworth, "can be a type or symbol or emblem of what the poet values, as well as the instrument by which his values are expressed" (91), and they often use the blank space of the page as visual punctuation. Such blanks become the expectant vacancy into which Blake's call "issue[s] forth" in stanza two (7), and in stanza three they pose anticipatory suspenses on the actions invoked by the enjambed syntaxes:

> Come o'er the eastern hills, and let our winds
> Kiss thy perfumed garments; let us taste
> Thy morn and evening breath; scatter thy pearls
> Upon our love-sick land that mourns for thee.
>
> (9–12)

"The eye puts a cheat upon the ear, by making us imagine a pause to exist where there is only vacancy to the eye," objected an eighteenth-century critic, John Walker, to the way Milton's enjambments break the coincidence of syntax and metrical lines (255–56). Where Walker makes an interesting point without realizing it, Blake's enjambments motivate such pauses and vacancies as part of his "verse to the eye."

The visual punning is the counterpart of a simultaneous verbal punning. In stanza three above, the homonym of *morn* and *mourns*

(11–12) alogically implies that the latter will vanish into the former, a melodious plot carried forth by the phonics at the start of the next, and last, stanza:

> O deck her forth with thy fair fingers; pour
> Thy soft kisses on her bosom; and put
> Thy golden crown upon her languish'd head,
> Whose modest tresses were bound up for thee!
>
> (13–16)

Pour draws forward the sound of *morn* and *mourns* through *forth* to pause at an expressive enjambment of languorous delay, before the poem subsides in a harmonious metrical flow whose design bears as much on the poetry of "To Spring" as on its call to "Spring." Naming an audience bound up for Spring, Blake also binds his poetical pattern: "golden crown" chimes a distant rhyme with the first line's "lookest down"; the last *For thee!* recalls the initial *O thou* (as well as repeating itself in line 16 and echoing *forth* in 7 and 14); "let out winds / Kiss" mirrors "pour / Thy soft kisses"; the "dewy locks" of the first imagining of Spring are matched to the "modest tresses" of the waiting land. To apprehend these correspondences of reading is to see poetic form itself mobilized into a syntax for what its voice summons.

No wonder that the next poem, "To Summer," begins by repeating this vocative rhetoric and its appeal to correspondent readerly actions:

> O thou, who passest thro' our vallies in
> Thy strength, curb thy fierce steeds, allay the heat
> That flames from their large nostrils! thou, O Summer,
> Oft pitched'st here thy golden tent, and oft
> Beneath our oaks hast slept, while we beheld
> With joy, thy ruddy limbs and flourishing hair.
>
> (1–6)

This petition does not call to absence, but to a fiercely rushing presence that it would arrest. When Frederick Tatham called Blake's blank verse "prose cut in slices," he noted, even if he didn't appreciate, an important effect.[15] These odd, prosey cuts enlist reading as an agent of arrest, halting the passage of the eye and its pursuit of the syntax.

This arrest is also scripted by Blake's several repetitions. After the reiterative halting of the opening vocative, a term of temporal recurrence, *oft*, recurs to hold Summer's golden tent in the verbal frame of the line:

> thou, O Summer,
> Oft pitched'st here thy golden tent, and oft
> Beneath our oaks hast slept, while we beheld . . .
>
> (3–5)

Beneath and *beheld* form a similar linear frame, tightening it with the etymological link of *beheld* to "holding." These tropings of frames anticipate the anaphora that Blake extends across the interstanzaic space to draw lines of sumptuous containment:

> Beneath our oaks [thou] hast slept, while be beheld
> With joy, thy ruddy limbs and flourishing hair.
> Beneath our thickest shades we oft have heard
> Thy voice, when noon upon his fervid car
> Rode o'er the deep of heaven; beside our springs
> Sit down, and in our mossy vallies, on
> Some bank beside a river clear, throw thy
> Silk draperies off, and rush into the stream:
> Our vallies love the Summer in his pride.
>
> (5–13)

At the start of this sequence, "Beneath . . . // Beneath . . . oft" (5–7) not only repeats but forms a chiasmus with "Oft . . . oft / Beneath" (4–5) to contain "Summer." As Blake modulates this prepositional design into syntaxes of *beside*, he assists the poetics of delay by binding the line of "Our vallies love the Summer in his *pride*," a surplus of this singular seven-line stanza, to a soft but semantically important pattern of rhyme.

Emerging from these holding patterns, and beginning with a sustained anaphora drawn from and incorporating this surplus line, the last stanza casts a network of phonic containments,

> Our bards are fam'd who strike the silver wire:
> Our youth are bolder than the southern swains:
> Our maidens fairer in the sprightly dance:

> We lack not songs, nor instruments of joy,
> Nor echoes sweet, nor waters clear as heaven,
> Nor laurel wreaths against the sultry heat.
>
> (14–19)

Blake's rhymes go beyond promising this laurel wreath; they shape a phonic version of it: his final *heat* chimes with *sweet*, a chord that echoes in *wreaths*, which in turn joins the chord of *beneath*; *heat*, moreover, rejoins its own *heat* at the end of line 2—drawing in a wreath of verbal attributes to hold the poetry of summer.

In "To Autumn" Blake takes this self-harvesting further by having the poem draw on the words and imagery of "To Summer," even repeating its three-stanza form:

> O Autumn, laden with fruit, and stained
> With the blood of the grape, pass not, but sit
> Beneath my shady roof, there thou may'st rest.
> And tune thy jolly voice to my fresh pipe;
> And all the daughters of the year shall dance!
> Sing now the lusty song of fruits and flowers.
>
> (1–6)

In the next stanza, the poet seems to propose a script for the song that he petitions:

> "The narrow bud opens her beauties to
> "The sun, and love runs in her thrilling veins;
> "Blossoms hang round the brows of morning, and
> "Flourish down the bright cheek of modest eve,
> "Til clust'ring Summer breaks forth into singing,
> "And feather'd clouds strew flowers round her head.
>
> "The spirits of the air live on the smells
> "Of fruit; and joy, with pinions light, roves round
> "The gardens, or sits singing in the trees."
>
> (7–15)

But what we discover at line 16 is that the song proposed is already realized: "Thus sang the jolly Autumn as he sat." By a sleight of verse form, Blake has transformed invocation into event, vocative into response.[16] *Provocatively*, Blake does not close "To Autumn" with Autumn's song, but with its situation in the impending bleakness it must sustain:

> he sat
> Then rose, girded himself, and o'er the bleak
> Hills fled from our sight; but left his golden load.
>
> (16–18)

The adjectival weight produced by the enjambment of "bleak / Hills" aptly anticipates similar effects in the poem this image prefigures, "To Winter":

> The north is thine; there hast thou built thy dark
> Deep-founded habitation.
>
> (2–3)

In a punning grammar, the terminal *dark* first weighs in as a substantive (a metonym for Winter) before the next line shows that it modifies *habitation*. The effect is to intensify the sense of this season as one in which the contingent and the attributive usurp substance— so much so that the terminal word of the next stanza's first line, "He hears me not, but o'er the yawning *deep* / Rides heavy," tricks reading: "yawning deep" seems a double adjective for some as-yet-undesignated perilous expanse. The shock of the predicate, "Rides heavy," is that the seeming attribute is really the substance, the condition of a Winter sublime and of the paralyzing depth of imagination that it evokes.

"To Winter" presses the question of unforming and deforming even further by inverting and subverting the rhetoric of the previous three poems. Most obviously, the poet's call is not for advent, stay, and song, but for refrain, restraint, and retraction: "O Winter! bar thine adamantine doors." Robert Gleckner carefully shows how this poem echoes and deforms the previous season-poems to turn their generative invocations into a "parodic antimyth" (70) wherein poetic power cancels itself, projects its undoing and ruin. "To Winter" thus looms as the shadow text of all invocation, imagining an audience moving without regard for how it is called. But it also counters this force by closing with an image of the cyclical negation of negation: "till heaven smiles, and the monster / Is driv'n yelling to his caves beneath mount Hecla." As a sign by form to sustain this anticipation, Blake visibly sketches "To Winter" in the pattern of "To Spring": a four-quatrain poem (the others have three longer stanzas).

Seasons need no poet for their advents and passings, and Blake's invocations know as much. These are ultimately tropes of audience, petitions answered by a supportive reader. In "To the Evening Star," Blake romances this reading by invoking an ideal of benignly "glimmering eyes" against the threat of more antagonistic glares:

> Thou fair-hair'd angel of the evening,
> Now, while the sun rests on the mountains, light
> Thy bright torch of love; thy radiant crown
> 4 Put on, and smile upon our evening bed!
> Smile on our loves; and, while thou drawest the
> Blue curtains of the sky, scatter thy silver dew
> On every flower that shuts its sweet eyes
> 8 In timely sleep. Let thy west wind sleep on
> The lake; speak si[l]ence with thy glimmering eyes,
> And wash the dust with silver. Soon, full soon,
> Dost thou withdraw; then the wolf rages wide,
> 12 And the lion glares thro' the dun forest:
> The fleeces of our flocks are cover'd with
> Thy sacred dew: protect them with thine influence.

This blank-verse sonnet struck Gilchrist as a "poetic power and freshness quickening the imperfect, immature *form*" (25, his italics); but the form is more accomplished than he recognizes, for it is "imperfect" in tacit reference, and resistance, to sonnet tradition. Not only does its most impressive enjambment, "let the wind sleep on / The lake" (8–9), occur exactly at the point where traditional sonnet form would close a unit, but its only gesture toward end-rhyme is a repetition of *eyes*, as if insisting on "verse to the eye."

These subtle reforms constellate "To the Evening Star" into an experimental poise against the unsettling vulnerabilities of its temporal imagination ("Soon, full soon"). Note how the unusual anaphoric positioning of the very first rhyme, *Thou* . . . / *Now*, uses its forming across the line in tacit resistance to the impending dark close by evoking the transition of light for which the poet petitions— its sound expanding into *mountains, crown, our, our, thou, flower, thou,* and counterpointed in the interwoven harmonies of *while . . . smile . . . Smile . . . while . . .* silence, and *sky, thy, eyes, timely*. This extravagant phonotext involves several semantically resonant enjambments. Aptly, the first of these verses for the eye has to do with vision:

> . . . while the sun rests on the mountains, light
> Thy bright torch . . .

The cut not only exploits the blank space after light but also suspends grammar to make *light* seem adjectival to *mountains* (as if these looked light rather than heavy and dark) or adverbial to *rest*, as if it meant *lightly*. Our discovery that *light* is part of an imperative predicate is an emergence on the level of syntactic understanding that corresponds to the transfer of light for which the poet calls (and seems himself to spark with the quick rhyme of *"light /* Thy *bright"* across the turn). The shifting syntax—first seeming to image sun-lightened mountains, then petitioning evening starlight—evokes the subtle visual shifts of twilight, wherein forms shimmer in different aspects of perception. Indeed, evening is the brief coincidence of both kinds of light: "the theme is evening," writes Hartman, "but Blake's poetical energy has transformed it into an emblem of dawn" ("Discourse" 227).

This patent aesthetic transformation becomes the subject as well as the form of the next phase of invocation to the star:

> Smile on our loves; and, while thou drawest the
> Blue curtains of the sky, scatter thy silver dew
> On every flower that shuts its sweet eyes
> In timely sleep. Let thy west wind sleep on
> The lake; speak si[l]ence with thy glimmering eyes . . .
>
> > (5–9)

Here Blake's cuts apply a formal, as opposed to grammatical, punctuation to lines whose rhymes, usually terminal in sonnets, are soft internal soundings: *smile/while; Blue/dew; sleep/sleep* (this last also pulling in *sweet* and *speak*). The linear frame of *Blue . . . dew* in the midst of these is especially effective for its momentary stay against the pressure of syntactic, and temporal, flow: the containment by rhyme forms a delicate pause in the progress of evening, and Blake protracts the effect with its alexandrine, a formal surplus to trope the invocation for the expansive scattering.

The deviation of these forms is evident in the editorial supervision they provoked. Eric Partridge admires Blake's "daringly weak verse-endings" (ix), but Dante Gabriel Rossetti thought the "frequent imperfections in the metre . . . best to remove" (2:1). When he assembled the *Sketches* for Gilchrist's *Life*, he decided to help Blake out by emending lines 5–6 thus:

> Smile on our loves; and whilst thou drawest round
> The curtain of the sky, scatter thy dew . . .

Lost hereby are both the semantically charged alexandrine and the internal rhyme, *smile/While* (about which Blake cared enough to restore by hand from a misprinted *whilst*). Swinburne keeps both this rhyme and *Blue/dew* when he quotes these lines; but he, too, meddles, undoing Blake's containment of the line by the *Blue/dew* rhyme, and further regularizing the meter:

> Smile on our loves; and while thou drawest round
> The sky's blue curtain, scatter thy silver dew . . .

(p. 11)

Not only does Swinburne follow Rossetti in revising Blake's "the / Blue" cut but, confronting the "incredible chaos" of most of the volume's blank verse, he endorsed efforts such as Rossetti's "in righting [its] deformed limbs and planing off [its] monstrous knots" (11).[17] The refinements efface Blake's formal play, not only against sonnet form but also against a line's necessary containment by grammar. Not the least of the effects of "Let the west wind sleep on / The lake," for instance, is the way the enjambment opens into the page's space beyond the line's end as a visual protraction of the call to the wind to *sleep on;* not just the evening star but the page itself is asked to "speak si[l]ence." When at the turn of the line, the syntax gives *on* a local habitation, this continuation does not so much revoke the dreamy protraction of "sleep on" as it leaves us, in Hollander's sensitive reading, with a "phantom image," a "blurred superposition of the two syntactic alternatives" (*VR* 115).

Hartman is sufficiently captivated by the paradox of "speak si[l]ence" to call this figure one of "the strongest, most startling" in all of Blake for its intimation of "presence, not absence" ("Discourse" 227). This presence, he concedes, is a precarious moment, for the invocative present shifts into "Soon, full soon, / Dost thou withdraw." There is, moreover, an unsettling double force in this action. As an intransitive verb, *withdraw* names the benign star's vanishing; but as a curtailed transitive, it turns this vanishing into a disclosure, a veil withdrawn to reveal a Miltonic counterworld in which "the wolf rages wide, / And the lion glares," and against which the weak dactyl of the poem's very last word, *influence*, sounds only a cautious hope. Blake's repetition of "while thou drawest . . . scatter thy silver dew" in "Dost thou withdraw . . . cover'd with / Thy sacred dew" evokes two economies and shows their relation: one of protected, shepherded flocks aligned with human loves, and the other of lurking predators. His enfolding of these apprehensions is more forceful for having been anticipated by the slightly unstable, benignly expanded syntaxes shaping the prayer all along.

The Figurings of Rhyme

Rhyme, Hollander and Wimsatt help us see, is a double force, allying sound and sense, figure and reference, but also restricting how lines have to end. In *Poetical Sketches* this doubleness pits self-assertiveness against external restraints. "A literary text," argues Richard Poirier, "generates itself . . . only by compliance with or resistance to forms of language already available to it," and although the "impulse to resist, or at least to modify, is necessarily stronger than is the impulse to comply . . . the two factors coexist in a sort of pleasurable agitation" (29). Blake's rhymes frequently turn the question of compliance or resistance into heightened alternatives. Sometimes rhyming corresponds to forms of harmony (love, dance, song), but sometimes it figures entrapment by artifice and enforcement by law. While "Love and harmony" plays the signifying of rhymes to fantastic excess (every line a rhyme or nearly so), other songs problematize rhyme as a suspect aesthetic illusion. And still others ironize Milton's troping of release from rhyme as "liberty" from "bondage"—an irony, I will show later, that plays a critical part in the political subtext of the later blank-verse sketches.

We see a prediction in the lurid ballad "Fair Elenor." It is unrhymed, but this is hardly liberty, as the flatly declarative sentences of its first stanza reveal:

> The bell struck one, and shook the silent tower;
> The graves give up their dead: fair Elenor
> Walk'd by the castle gate, and looked in.
> A hollow groan ran thro' the dreary vaults.

Supplanting rhyme is a pattern of deadening terminal repetitions, internal echoes, and stark homophones splayed out across the verse: *silent-silent; pale-pale-pale; sighing-sighs; death-death; gate-gate; wretch-wretch-wretched; vaults-vaults; feet-feet; arms-arms-arms; dreary-ear-fear-fear-fear; dead-dead-dead-head-dead-shed*—the random but persistent return of their tones evoking a sense of terror from inescapable forces. Within the tale, Elenor is "Amaz'd" by events over which she has no control; within the verse, she is caught in a maze of words that resound lethally and relentlessly, but with no predictability. By the last stanza, this verbal accumulation has taken possession of the poem in a thematically resonant way:

> She sat with dead cold limbs, stiffen'd to stone;
> She took the gory head up in her arms;
> She kiss'd the pale lips; she had no tears to shed;
> She hugg'd it to her breast, and groan'd her last.
>
> (69–72)

Using a sudden shift into anaphora, whose vertical axis of repetition at once alludes to and writes a more constricting version of the rhyme-forms they displace, Blake enforces a kind of paralysis from which there is no recovery.

Troping *with* rhyme, Blake makes his only *Sketch* in couplets, "Blind-Man's Buff," a wicked satire of Dryden's argument that one of the "advantages which Rhyme has over Blanck Verse" is that it "Bounds and Circumscribes" an "Imagination" that might run "Wild and Lawless" (*RL* 101). Reversing the order-keeping of Dr. Johnson's claim that poetry that does not strike "the ear" but is verse "only to the eye" loses its distinction ("Milton" 192–93), Blind-Man's Buff, a children's game of all ear and no eye, invites actions so sadistic and "lawless"—and often in "cheat" of the rules of the game—that the poet-reporter is impelled into a summary call for new laws:

> Such are the fortunes of the game,
> And those who play should stop the same
> By wholesome laws; such [:] all those
> Who on the blinded man impose,
> Stand in his stead; as long-agone
> When men were first a nation grown;
> Lawless they liv'd—till wantonness
> And liberty began t'increase;
> And one man lay in another's way,
> Then laws were made to keep fair play.
>
> (60–70)

But if, as a call for the law and order of fair play, these lines are sound enough as social allegory, the symbolic corollary of their form is less certain. In reminding us that victim and tormentor may change positions, this voice of sober distress still speaks in the popular tetrameter measure of children's rhymes. If this writes a parodic criticism of the children's less-than-innocent games, it also casts their local mischief, tricks, and blood-letting confusions as a formal mimicry and rehearsal of worldly plays of power.

The first two of the volume's set of eight rhymed "Songs"—"How sweet I roam'd" and "My silks and fine array"—address these darker plots of law and power by deploying their rhyme-forms to tell stories of capture by delusive art and showing how, as Hollander puts it, "the instrument of rhyming, and the sort of linkage it enforces, becomes allegorized as bondage" (*MG* 184). These sketches bear more than the "demonstrably simple derivativeness and passive relationship to other songs" that Gleckner sees (55); their patterns are too cagey:

> With sweet May dews my wings were wet,
>   And Phoebus fir'd my vocal rage;
> He caught me in his silken net,
>   And shut me in his golden cage.

This is stanza 3 of "How sweet I roam'd" (9–12), about its singer's capture by the "prince of love." Is it "simply . . . a first account of the movement from Innocence into Experience with the deceptions of nature as the responsible agent" (Bloom 10)? Or does what Alicia Ostriker calls its "ironic smoothness" (39) evoke the agency of art as well? It is not just that a rapacious personification, Phoebus, is distilled out of the more naturally amorphous "sunny beams" on which the prince of love seemed to glide (3–4); it is Blake's tight rhymes at the moment of capture. Half the end rhymes of the first two are slightly off:

> How sweet I roam'd from field to field,
>   And tasted all the summer's pride
> 'Till I the prince of love beheld,
>   Who in the sunny beams did glide!
>
> He shew'd me lilies for my hair
>   And blushing roses for my brow;
> He led me through his gardens fair
>   Where all this golden pleasures grow.

The atonalities of *field/beheld* and *brow/grow* open up the links of rhyme in this part of the song. But in stanza three the rhymes spring shut with the seductive traps of silken "net" and golden "cage." A singer "caught" by love sings in verse caught by rhyme, "the icon in which the idea is caught" (Wimsatt, "One Relation" 165). The rhymes of the last stanza reflect and report this plight:

> He loves to sit and hear me sing,
>   Then, laughing, sports and plays with me;
> Then stretches out my golden wing,
>   And mocks my loss of liberty.
>
> (13–16)

"I" had agency only in stanza 1, about the era before love; by stanza 2 this self has become an object, *me*, ruled by *He:* "He shew'd me," "He led me" (5, 7). And the pattern is set: "He caught me . . . / And shut me" (11–12); "He loves to . . . hear me sing, / . . . sports and plays with me" (13–14). This rule is not only of grammar but a function of how *me* is claimed by *He* in a sinister bind of rhyme. The only variance from this strong governor is a ruefully asymmetrical chiming of *me* with the *liberty* that has been lost.

The relation of poetic form to self-possession is the critical issue of another lover's lament, "My silks and fine array." To Cleanth Brooks, the "discipline of form"—not just poetic form but also "ritual performance"—controls emotion, "mak[ing] it precise and deft, graceful and yet resonant" (*CEA* 6). I find the effects less certain than this, seeing Blake's poetics ironizing the control by form, but what is clear is that Blake has made a reading of form the focus of this question. This song begins,

> My silks and fine array,
>   My smiles and languish'd air,
> By love and driv'n away;
>   And mournful lean Despair
> Brings me yew to deck my grave:
>   Such end true lovers have.
>
> (1–6)

This singer describes two performances, or forms of social display: a past one of "fine array" and "languish'd air" and a present one of self-dramatizing "Despair." Part of what makes Brooks see form as "discipline" is his sense of how the present, despairing "languishment in earnest" (5) takes the form of a "more serious kind of play" (6). Yet his deeper intuition, if not his argument, is his verging on saying that emotion is not so much articulated in this form as produced and agitated by it: as the singer turns despair into a "performance," she "rehearses" its "set steps . . . in anticipation," treating them "as if they were known and recognized gestures" (5). If this is discipline, it is so with a vengeance, a form that subsumes what it invests—and Blake's own play of form projects the subtle emergence of this power.

We see this effect especially in the rhymes with which Blake subverts the lady's own display. As she speaks of how her affected "smiles and languish'd air" are betrayed to the mourning of a "true" lover, a spectral *you* in "yew to deck my grave" and a telling, though buried, rhyme with its summary in "Such end *true* lovers have" evoke the core of her lament: there is no *you*, even in apostrophe, only this emblem of grief and its trace of love lost. The faintly personified love in line 3 is part of this trace: as external force, it turns the self-possessive *my*s of 1 and 2 over to the defeat of "my grave." Blake supplements this event with a syntactic pressure that (despite his semicolon at the end of 3) makes line 4—"And mournful lean Despair"—seem conjunctive, as if "Despair" were in league with love's action. Blake repeats this effect in the first line of the next stanza, "His face is fair as heav'n" (7): while *His* turns out to refer to the jilter, its liminal position, initially and aptly, gives it antecedence in *love* and *Despair.* The fatal trajectory of the song is driven as much as by these anarchic poetics as by its singer's ritualizing, and the conclusion is a figure of their involution:

> When I my grave have made,
>   Let winds and tempests beat:
> Then down I'll lie, as cold as clay,
> True love doth pass away!
>
> (15–18)

The rhyme pattern interacts with treacherous repetitions: "I my grave have made" answers the poem's first couplet rhyme, *grave/have* (5–6), tightening its fated linkage into fatal action, while the singer's earlier self-regard in the fate of "true lovers" (in this same couplet) echoes in, and as, the final alien abstraction of a fugitive "True love."

Blake heightens the issue of whether form controls or cooperates with anarchic powers in "Mad Song." This singer's voice is

an alternative to surrender, but not without other ambiguities: if it
invests its art as resistance to larger social and psychological imposi-
tions, Blake's poetics of form also show such how resistance can be
drawn into other forms of compulsion. L. C. Knights takes up one
side of this question, arguing that the declarative emergence of "I" in
the final stanza—

> After night I do croud,
>   And with night will go;
> I turn my back to the east
>
> (19–21)

—exposes this voice of "distressed and distressing consciousness [as]
in fact willed. The speaker exults in his desperat[ion]" (388). Yet this
reading of *will* is strained by the form of the stanza's actual close:
"For light doth seize my brain / With frantic pain" (23–24). A syntax
of self gripped by forces (light and pain) that it cannot control and a
verse gripped by tight rhymes and meter spell the compulsion in this
will, with the peculiar verb *croud* ("murmur dovelike") adding to the
sensation of pure instinct. Even the singer's boasting—

> My notes are driven:
> They strike the ear of night,
> They make mad the roaring winds
> Make weep the eyes of day . . .
>
> (12–15)

—raises the question of whether "Mad Song" refers to his notes or
the wind's roar. That the endwords *night* and *winds* refuse rhyme
(not even flirting with the consonance of *dawn/scorn; vault/fraught;
heaven/driven*) underscores the contest of natural force and human
song. This is impressed at the very start by a flux of aural and visual
forms (in which winds plays a part) against the pattern of rhyme
and meter:

> The wild winds weep,
>   And the night is a-cold;
> Come hither, Sleep,
>   And my griefs infold;
> But lo! the morning peeps
> Over the eastern steeps . . .
>
> (1–6)

The alliterations undo the forms of the very words, letting the sound of *winds weep* blend into *winds sweep.* This sweep of sound soon infolds *peeps* and *steeps,* words with which the singer images the dawn that will presumably relieve the torments of the windy night. The rueful irony played by the sounds is that day will offer no relief, only perpetuation. The note of day, "But lo!" (5), is absorbed into this flux, its sound returning to the end rhymes in the last, nightbound stanza:

> Like a fiend in a cloud
>   With howling woe,
> After night I do croud,
>   And with night will go.
> I turn my back to the east,
> From whence comforts have increas'd;
> For light doth seize my brain
> With frantic pain.
>
>   (17–24)

The twice-toned *night* chimes chiefly with its repetitions: "the night is a-cold" (2), "the ear of night" (13). It finally gets another chord in an internal rhyme with the *light* in the penultimate line (23), but this release only tightens what Gleckner nicely terms the "cyclicity of a perverted eternity" (51), a perversion that is also the work of the verse.

The perversion of verse form on the stage of self-fashioning is most fully displayed in *Poetical Sketches* by "An Imitation of Spencer." Dr. Johnson urged poets away from this elaborate and archaic stanza form,[18] but Blake liked the challenge of simultaneous homage and defiance. His apprentice work convinced him that, *pace* the cult of "original genius," imitation and copying were important exercises: "Imitation is Criticism," he refutes Reynolds (*CPP* 643). His imitation of Spenser works out this criticism by violating its model at almost every turn: its stanzas are, variously, eight, nine, or ten lines; none obeys the Spenserian rhyme scheme and only two end in an alexandrine. Such practices make conservatives impatient, but Blake's "perversity" is a strategic performance, for this is the first of the *Sketches* to focus explicitly on tradition and verse convention, using imitation as a critical review.[19]

The second stanza promotes this critical imitation with a parody of the practices of "modern peers": a debased poet, "brutish Pan," and a debased critic, the quantifying Midas, deal only in "tinkling sounds . . . Sound without sense . . . tinkling rhymes, and elegances terse." Blake's descent of tinkling rhymes enacts what Milton's head-note to *Paradise Lost* scorned (with his own parodic jingle) as "the jingling sound of like endings": Apollo's nervous *verse* (11) is debased by "Folly's leesing *nurse*," its *curse*, Midas's *worse* and *terse* (13, 14, 18). Blake sets the first stanza of his "Imitation" to a sketch of new arrangements:

> Golden Apollo, that thro' heaven wide
>   Scatter'st the rays of light, and truth's beams!
> In lucent words my darkling verses dight,
>   And wash my earthy mind in thy clear streams,
>   That wisdom may descend in fairy dreams:
> All while the jocund hours in thy train
> Scatter their fancies at thy poet's feet;
>   And when thou yields to night thy wide domain,
> Let rays of truth enlight his sleeping brain.
>
> (1–9)

He petitions the god of poetry in verse that subverts even as it honors Spenser's form. The stanza still rhymes: two triple rhymes including two couplets on the Spenserian plan. But the unrhymed end-words are the thematically potent ones. The most wayward of these end-words is *feet* (7), with a punning that extends to metrics, and whose syntactic form, "thy poet's feet," allows a reference to both Apollo and his earthly disciple. *Wide* (1) and *dight* (3) half tease at a match *(id/di)*, but Blake resists the lock, keeping his first terminal word free and refusing the formal dictation implied by *dight*, a cognate of "dictate" (arrange or compose). The unrhyme of *dight*, itself Spenserian diction,[20] is a patent reform set exactly where it should (but does not) complete the first rhyme of a Spenserian stanza (3). The freedom of *wide* from rhyme gets further semantic value from the way it leads into the open space of the page, as if this were part of a composite figure for the "heaven wide," or "wide domain" (9) from which the poet seeks his forms.

Actually, Blake does rhyme *dight*—not by dictation, but with a scattering for internal rhymes by *light* (2) into *night* and the absorption (verbally as well as thematically) of *light* by *enlight* (8–9), as if to imitate Apollo's scattering of light. The rhyme plays beyond this stanza to endow its sketchings of form with a mythopoetic value. When the poet addresses Mercurius as a figure of "airy flight" (21), not only does *flight* continue to scatter the rhyme of *light,* but as it does so, it extends Apollo's "rays of light" (2) into the sound of "rays of flight," an "assist [to] lab'ring sense" (35) performed by the poet's witty agency of imitation.

Politics in rhyme, blank verse, and the poetics of prose

Blake's "Imitation" sets contingency against formula and invention against repetition, with past models inflecting but not prescribing present practice. It is an exercise that is primarily aesthetic but, as we have seen, not exclusively so. In the historical pieces of *Poetical Sketches* Blake turns this formal sketching to broader cultural concerns. "Gwin, King of Norway," *King Edward the Third,* "Prologue, Intended for a Dramatic Piece of King Edward the Fourth," and "Prologue to King John" are not only about conflicts in the eras of these kings; they are also tuned to England in the 1780s, when the empire was suffering erosions of royal power and prestige at home, being weakened abroad by rebellions and then full-scale war with America, and drawn into new conflicts with its long-standing enemies, Spain, and especially France.[21]

In "Gwin," Blake works the ballad form into a dialectic, evoking its traditional status as cultural language, but also exploiting the recent emergence of the *literary* ballad to direct a reading of its forms toward ideological critique. The ballad opens as a caution to "Kings" about the consequences of tyranny, epitomized in Gwin, oppressor of the "nations of the North," and then moves into its central drama, a peasant uprising led by "Gordred the giant," who slays Gwin in battle. David Erdman is right about the content: it expresses the "intense, even propagandistic abhorrence of war-making kings" spelled by the compound adjective—the way such kings unleash fury and slaughter not just in their own war-making but in the actions they compel in others (*Prophet* 18). Not only Blake's content but also his formalist poetics imprint this abhorrence, deploying their resources to convey the contamination that Erdman names.

This political analysis, a demonstration of how victims of tyranny will turn violent because the economy of power offers no alternative to the positions of tyrant and victim, registers almost immediately in Blake's parallel images and verbal repetitions. The tyrannical "Nobles" who "feed upon the hungry poor" (5–6) engender a violent politics of revolt: "furious as wolves" (27), the poor become "lions' whelps, roaring abroad, / Seeking their nightly food"

(19–20). Noble arrogance produces its own dark legacy: "let ten thousand lives / "Pay for the tyrant's head" (31–32), shout the poor, now "numerous sons of blood," as they roll "like tempests black" (17–18) to meet Gwin and "his host as black as night" (55). *Black* covers both sides. This reproduction of violence also operates subverbally, in the way Blake exploits puns latent in the name *Gordred* (which me may have converted from Chatterton's "Godred Crovan" for the sake of such effects[22]). The alarm sounded by Gwin's watchmen, "Arouse thyself! the nations black, / 'Like clouds, come rolling o'er!" (35–36) bears the visual and perhaps phonic latency of *rolling gore,* a flood led by Gordred and rhymed aptly in this stanza with its mighty antagonist, "Gwin . . . of Nore" (34). This latency soon erupts as "fields of gore" (46), and echoes in the report that "Earth smokes with blood, and groans, and shakes, / To drink her children's gore" (73–74). Allied with blood, in fact, *Gordred* releases not only *gore,* but *Gore-dread* and its nearly redundant cause, *gored red—* the second word distilled in the image of the battle's "red fev'rous night" (84).

In this phonic and semantic field, the *gore*-rhyme *war,* as word and event, impends with near inevitability. And once it sounds in Blake's verse (62), the reproduction of violence emerges as the dominant political trope: "The armies stand, like balances / Held in th'Almighty's hand" (66). Blake takes a Miltonic and Homeric image of divine, even cosmic, supervision and converts it to a simile for political inevitability.[23] that "th'Almighty" figures in his ballad only in a simile (and with an internal pun on military "might") depletes moral theology.[24] Indeed, the poem's unsimilized theology is an undiscriminating "god of war . . . drunk with blood" (93), the wargore that unites the sons of Gordred and of Nore in forces that act with the indifferent violence of nature:

> And now the raging armies rush'd,
> Like warring mighty seas;
> The heavens are shook with roaring war,
> The dust ascends the skies!
>
> (69–72)

As sound and action, *warring* subtends "roaring war" with a cognitive punning that exploits the phonic resonance and from stanza to stanza keeps alliance with *gore:*

> Earth smokes with blood, and groans, and shakes,
>   To drink her children's gore,
> A sea of blood; nor can the eye
>   See to the trembling shore!
>
>   (73–76)

In a *sea* where, punningly, the eye can *see* only blood, distinction of factions is overwhelmed in the common chaos of destruction:

> And on the verge of this wild sea
>   Famine and death doth cry;
> The cries of women and of babes.
>   Over the field doth fly. . . .
>
>   (77–80)

> Now death is sick, and riven men
>   Labour and toil for life;
> Steed rolls on steed, and shield on shield,
>   Sunk in this sea of strife!
>
>   (89–92)

"By the time Godred cleaves Gwin's skull," remarks Gleckner, "the social and political 'meaning' of that victory has paled to insignificance—even irrelevance. . . . Visionary history inheres in the 'vale of death' and the 'river Dorman' as the loco-descriptive symbols of the universal battle's 'sea of blood'" (119).[25]

This common fate is also conveyed by the drama of Blake's similes. Before the summary formulation of "The armies stand, like balances / Held in th'Almighty's hand" (66), similes suggest an affective, if not a moral, balance. In the figures of Gordred's "sons of blood" advancing "Like rushing mighty floods," and "Like clouds come rolling o'er" (24, 36), and of Gwin's troops, which "Like clouds around him roll'd" (60), the same vehicle serves, reinforced by the same stanzaic position of a last line. Over the course of the ballad and battle, Blake moves this parallelism into a semantic figure. First, and again with the force of syntactic repetition, he encompasses both armies not even with the same, but with one common, simile, intensified by a redoubling of tenor and vehicle: "And now the raging armies rush'd, / Like warring mighty seas." Tenors and vehicles merge: the armies rush and rage like seas, which themselves are imaged at war.

This involution then yields to stark equivalence: the battlefield is not just "like" a sea which is itself a battlefield; sea and battlefield merge: "A sea of blood," a "wild sea," a "sea of strife" (75, 77, 92). This transformation is completed as the metaphor is finally, and literally, overwhelmed by its vehicle, "sea," which emerges in the ballad's final stanza as a universal force, obliterating distinction between tenor and vehicle and, with this erasure, between the armies themselves:

> The river Dorman roll'd their blood
>   Into the northern sea;
> Who mourn'd his sons, and overwhelm'd
>   The pleasant south country.

(113–16)

The "human forces actually become what they formerly were merely like," observes Vincent De Luca; "they are enveloped in the element and annihilated by it" (77). This envelopment is more haunting for the way the stanza's weak rhymes release another chord in which *Dorman, northern, mourn'd* absorb and eerily reverberate the sounds of *war, gore, Nore,* and *Gordred.* Blake's poetics of rhyme and related repetitions do not imply the moral or political equivalence of oppressors and desperate subjects; but they do suggest how extreme political imbalances will press toward equalizing parallels, if only, but massively, in mutually annihilating violent action.

Repetition, in both formal and political registers, writes the political text of *King Edward the Third.* Formerly, it recalls the blank-verse invocations ("O thou") that open the volume. In literary tradition, the situation of its scenes—Crécy before the battle of 1346—recalls the Shakespearean stage of English wars with France. And history impinges on Blake's moment of writing via particular linguistic signs that provoke awareness of the same antagonisms in contemporary British tensions with France. The trajectory of this history, extending from Edward's reign to Blake's day, defines the sketch's political perspectivism. Edward the Third generates his line in English history, even as their Shakespearean characters engender Blake's; and all these royal and dramatic precedents, as Erdman carefully demonstrates, resonate in Blake's historical moment in the conduct of King George the Third.[26]

Blake evokes this history of repetitions in the macro-form of this sketch, its open-endedness. It consists of six scenes: invocations, conversations, debates, and a "war song" all in the hours before the battle. The sketch's stopping short of the battle and its British victory does not, as is usually supposed, render it a "fragment." Nowhere does Blake term *King Edward* such; nor is there any typographical sign to denote an unfinished text.[27] Its suspense is a formal determination, not a symptom of an incomplete venture. Although Blake's readers know that the English prevailed at Crécy, as they would in another cycle of history at Harfleur and Agincourt under Edward's descendant, Henry the Fifth, Blake's refusal to evoke these outcomes functions semantically as a refusal of the nationalistic satisfactions such conclusions might supply. He diverts his reader's attention, instead, into various critical perspectives on the motivations and self-interests that impel England's history of military adventurism.

This critical perspective has a counterpart in the other formalism of this sketch, its use of blank verse, a measure deeply saturated in tradition and, more specifically, Milton. Ever since Dryden and Milton, the form had provoked highly charged political language of "liberty" on the positive side or "wantonness" and "luxury" on the other—in any event, the opposite of "constraint." That the issue was alive in Blake's day is clear in Kames's summoning of the same discourse: "the peculiar advantage of blank verse is, that it is at liberty to attend the imagination in its boldest flights" (Mills ed. 316).[28] Yet as early as 1804, Blake was raising the stakes. Energized by the revolutions in America and France that were alarming conservatives all over Europe as an apocalypse of wanton lawlessness, he launched a revolutionary poetics in *Milton* that outdid Milton, expressing a heroic contempt for any "tame high finisher of . . . paltry Rhymes; or paltry Harmonies" (41:9–10). The sneer at "paltry Harmonies" gives no quarter even to blank verse, for it too, as Morris Eaves puts it, is read as one of the "uniform systems of execution owned by the culture, or by poetic tradition" (159); the parodic Miltonic headnote of *Jerusalem*—"of the Measure, in which / the following Poem is written"—calls it bondage, an institutional prescription that can only hinder a "true Orator":

> I consider'd a Monotonous Cadence like that used by Milton & Shakespeare & all writers of English Blank Verse, derived from the modern bondage of Rhyming; to be a necessary and indispensible part of Verse. But I soon found that in the mouth of a true Orator such monotony was not only awkward, but as much a bondage as rhyme itself. . . .

Poetry Fetter'd, Fetters the Human Race! Nations are
Destroy'd, or Flourish, [in] proportion to their Poetry!

(Plate 3)

This is no momentary hyperbole; it is part of an expanding orbit of
casting innovative poetic style as a mark of political vision. The blank-
verse poetics of the *Sketches* are Blake's first critical review of Milton's
tropes of liberty. The season poems play a part, applying the form to
lyrics and quasi-sonnets and testing its susceptibility to reform.[29]
In *King Edward the Third,* Blake plays the other side, employing
the measure to trope its restrictions, a prelude to his declaration of
independence from it in *Jerusalem.*

If, in Miltonic legacy, the measure signals "ancient liberty" re-
covered from the bondage of inculcated practice, in *King Edward*
Blake performs another turn by leaguing the apparent freedom of
the line with a motivated rhetoric, a recurring imperialist cant of
"Liberty." The way the design of the line tropes the orderings of self-
interest that underwrite English claims stirs as the subtle contradiction in King Edward's opening exhortation to his subjects:

> O thou, to whose fury the nations are
> But as dust!
>
> . . . .
> Let Liberty, the charter'd right of Englishmen,
> Won by our fathers in many a glorious field,
> Enerve my soldiers; let Liberty
> Blaze in each countenance, and fire the battle.
> The enemy fight in chains, invisible chains, but heavy;
> Their minds are fetter'd; then how can they be free,
> While, like the mounting flame,
> We spring to battle o'er the floods of death!
> And these fair youths, the flow'r of England
> Venturing their lives in my most righteous cause,
> O sheathe their hearts with triple steel, that they
> May emulate their fathers' virtues,
> And thou, my son, be strong; thou fightest for a crown . . .

(1–21)

This rhetoric convinces Damon that the sketch is an expression of
Blake's youthful, "uncritical patriotism" (228–29), Schorer that it
is "an extended defense of war and national interests" (165), and

Frye that it is "simply 'Rule Britannia' in blank verse" (*Fearful* 180). Indeed, we hear it again as the King exhorts "just revenge for those / Brave Lords, who fell beneath the bloody axe at Paris" (1.43–45) and proclaims "our right to France" (3.72), and as the Bishop, in a business council at home, refers to English merchants as "sovereigns / Of the sea" and claims this as a Heaven-given "right" (2.78–80). Yet Blake's very multiplication of this rhetoric in several venues makes its transparent cant as much an issue as its claims.

As a *poetic* rhetoric, moreover, its formalism is subtly subversive. Predicting the cry of *Jerusalem*—"Poetry Fetter'd, Fetters the Human Race!"—Blake motivates the fettered poetry of *King Edward*. Despite its "natural" cadence, the visible form of the line sets the claims of liberty at odds with the poetics of liberty and its not-quite-invisible chain of special interests. Blake's formalism, mingling manipulative eloquence in the pulse-quickening form of verse, is both politicized and rhetoricized: by exposing the formal design in Edward's language of liberty, he implies similar designs in other languages, including those of history and national ideology. And he intensifies this critical regard with a semantics of rhyme in the midst of this blank verse: the chime of *Liberty/enemy/heavy/free* (11–14). Edward's own rhetoric links the middle words to the "fetter'd" minds of France and the first and last to England; but in Blake's verse, one chord joins all. These phonics signify what the sketch exposes at large: British minds, fettered by political and moral self-justification, are less free than they imagine. The chain includes even Edward's blithe description of "Liberty" as a "charter'd" English "right" (9). This claim would chime for a reader in the 1780s with emerging critiques of the tyranny veiled in ideologies of "charter'd" rights—including Blake's bitter song, a decade later, on London's "charter'd" streets and "charter'd Thames."[30]

Blake's formalist exposure of chartering forecasts the staging of patent economic self-interest in scene 2. As Edward exhorts his army, his son at home, the Duke of Clarence, celebrates the swirling activity of chartered English business, imagining that from abroad, his father

> sees commerce fly round
> With his white wings, and sees his golden London,
> And her silver Thames, throng'd with shining spires
> And corded ships; her merchants buzzing round
> Like summer bees, and all the golden cities
> In his land, overflowing with honey . . .

(2.9–14)

Frye finds the "most puzzling feature" of these lines and the sketch as a whole to be the frank admission "that economic ambitions are the cause of the war. Industry, commerce, agriculture, manufacture and trade are the gods directing the conflict"—gods sufficiently "worthy of worship" that "there seems to be no use looking for irony" (180). Erdman finds any irony at best "hidden" (69).[31] But irony presses forth in the next scene when the Prince's minstrel, Sir John Chandos, reacting to his patron's claim of the "genuine spirit of Liberty" within every "genuine Englishman" (3.189–90), observes,

> Teach man to think he's a free agent,
> Give but a slave his liberty, he'll shake
> Off sloth, and build himself a hut, and hedge
> A spot of ground; this he'll defend; 'tis his
> By right of nature.
>
> (3.195–99)

The irony of this curriculum is in its disparity of form and content: free agency as a subject of instruction; liberty harnessed to the interests of royal power; such interests presented as a "right of nature." Is Sir John speaking in tones of liberal idealism or just political pragmatism? The question develops a more sinister ring in the rhetoric of the King's rejoinder, "O Liberty, how glorious art thou! / I see thee hov'ring o'er my army . . . I see thee / Lead them on to battle" (204–7), where liberty itself is conscripted to "my" army and a war to secure English commercial hegemony.[32] To underscore the shifty illusions of liberty, Blake bends the formalist poetics of his verse into an insistently critical mirror of the ruling powers. As the Prince announces—

> my blood, like a springtide,
> Does rise so high, to overflow all bounds
> Of moderation; while Reason, in his
> Frail bark, can see no shore or bound for vast
> Ambition
>
> (3.234–38)

—Blake's enjambment displays the disease of ambition: if the suspension of *vast* at the end of the line romantically tropes blank space as a visual pun for the unbounded field that the Prince imagines for the enterprises of ambition, the weakness of *bounds* in syntax and sensibility makes an opposite point about this costly intemperance.

An important shift in the poetics of form occurs in scene 4. After sixteen lines, the sketch seemingly sets aside the aesthetics of historical verse drama for prose—specifically, a dialogue between Sir Thomas Dagworth and the Blake-informed voice of "William his Man" in which the mobilization of military enterprise by ambition receives its sharpest commentary. Yet the suggestion of a turn from the rhetoric and aesthetics of illusion to the discourse of frank critique is complicated by the return of the artist in this scene: we hear that Chandos has composed a "war-song" that has so pleased his Prince (who has an affection for the genre) that he has "made [him] a 'squire"—a reward that inspires another such song from Chandos "about all us that are to die, that we may be remembered in Old England" (44–50). Scene 6, the last is the unmediated script of the minstrel performing this war-song. A composition in blank pentameter stanzas, it displays what has always been the implicit, if unacknowledged, artificiality of the line. With this patent formation of stanzas and song, Blake's sketch concludes by presenting the formalization of war into poetry—and reflexively, implying that national "history" too is an aesthetic formation.

In the aesthetics of desire borne by this "war-song," *war* is, significantly, the only rhyme, a sounding intensified by its status within the *Sketches* as a repetition: the opening line, "O sons of Trojan Brutus, cloath'd in war," chiming with "Heated with war" (10) and then "covered with gore" (11), repeats the key rhymes of "Gwin." The repetition is enhanced by a host of other verbal and imagistic repetitions whose cumulative effect is to make the line of Brutus in England seem merely one more warpath. Again we hear of "thunder," of "Rolling dark clouds," of a "sickly darkness," of the "wrath and fury" of "wild men, / Naked and roaring like lions," of "savage monsters rushing like roaring fire," of "red lightning . . . furious storms" and a "molten raging sea" (2–31). Even as the song advances a vision of eventual prosperity, its language bears marks of this past violence: the promise that "plenty shall bring forth, / Cities shall sing, and vales in rich *array* / Shall laugh, whose fruitful laps bend down with fullness," refigures "the firm *array* to battle" (46–48, 25 cf. 13); the prospect of "Cities" recalls the city in ashes that produced Trojan Brutus; and the summary icon of Liberty bears the legacy of violence recorded in the singer's opening stanzas:

"Liberty shall stand upon the cliffs of Albion,
"Casting her blue eyes over the green ocean;

"Or, tow'ring, stand upon the roaring waves,
"Stretching her mighty spear o'er distant lands;
"While with her eagle wings, she covereth
"Fair Albion's shore, and all her families."

(55–60)

Everything here is a repetition: Liberty's blue eyes mirror a genetic history of "eyes" that "glare against the stormy fires / Heated with war"; the roaring waves of her domain evoke the memory of the "roaring" armies of the invading fathers (22, 26, 27); and the iconography of the mighty spear, its imperial(ist) thrust, and the eagle, reinscribe the "spears" of the fathers and their spoil of "mighty dead" (34–35), as well as the aggressive "empire"-building that has them roaming "Like eagles for the prey" (42–45). There is a further, and ultimately more potent, range of repetition: in a sketch that opened with the King's manipulative rhetoric of Liberty, the same language is replayed, now fully contextualized in the history of violence that it sustains and perpetuates.

Two contiguous war-songs in *Poetical Sketches* expand this formalist critique by displaying the line in a visionary mode that discloses repetition, both conceptual and verbal. The first, following *King Edward the Third*, is the sonnet-like "Prologue [for] King Edward the Fourth." Blake's grim joke is that "the Fourth" is not Edward the Third's son (who predeceased his father by a year), but a king born almost a century after Crécy. The thwarted succession is scarcely felt, however, for the term of continuity between the two sketches is a perpetual, incorrigible English thirst for war, reaching not just across generations but across centuries. The "Prologue" gives this language a succinct, ritualistic form, in which repetitions not only echo previous sketches and war literature, but suggest the frustrating repetitions of history itself:

O For a voice like thunder, and tongue
To drown the throat of war!—When the senses
Are shaken, and the soul is driven to madness,
Who can stand? When the souls of the oppressed
Fight in the troubled air that rages, who can stand?
When the whirlwind of fury comes from the
Throne of God, when the frowns of his countenance
Drive the nations together, who can stand?
When Sin claps his broad wings over the battle,

And sails rejoicing in the flood of Death;
When souls are torn to everlasting fire,
And fiends of Hell rejoice upon the slain,
O who can stand? O who hath caused this?
O who can answer at the throne of God?
The Kings and Nobles of the Land have done it!
Hear it not, Heaven, thy Ministers have done it!

(1–16)

The echo of the opening chorus of *Henry V* amplifies the indictment:
the allusion to Shakespeare's (ostensibly) nationalistic history, located between Blake's two Edwards and again with France as enemy,
is yet one more parody of the enthusiasms that mobilize military
violence. The repetition is that of history itself, summarized emphatically in the repetitive syntactic and verbal form of "When . . .
who can stand?" The stunning modulation of this formula in line 13,
where the invocation shifts into an interrogation of agency—"O who
hath caused this?"—yields a pair of declamations in which "Kings and
Nobles" and Heaven's Ministers are indicted together. Blake turns the
couplet charge of the final lines in this slightly expanded sonnet into
a repetition that exceeds the semantic linkage of a couplet. Erdman
wonders about the "inconsistent theology" (29): if the Kings and
Nobles who invest themselves as Heaven's Ministers represent an
affront to the "Throne of God," what about this Throne being the
origin and authorizing "drive" of their violence (6–8)? As in "Gwin,"
the ambiguity has a critical point: in a theological register, it indicts
God as a creator of violence; in a political register, it indicts earthly
tyrants for self-justification as heavenly ministers. And in the self-
reflexive irony of the sketch, the charge potentially implicates the
poetic agency too, a "madness" of anger and distress that longs for
an efficacious thunder of its own.

This poetic agency emerges in "A War Song to Englishmen,"
whose master trope is also repetition, the reiterated injunction, "Prepare, prepare," that forms and issues a drumbeat for battle. Erdman
suspects that this song was "intended for the second War Song of the
Chandos minstrel" and disjoined from *King Edward* by "a typographical mischance" (*CPP* 848; *Prophet* 69); but its position in the volume,
after the short prose sketch "Prologue to King John," produces a more
unsettling possibility. Following the "Prologue [for] King Edward
the Fourth," "Prologue to King John" wends from tyranny to a
summary prophecy for Albion reborn: "Her sons shall joy as in the

morning! Her daughters sing as to the rising year!" This is its last line; then follows the second "War Song," with the devastating effect of suggesting that while Albion "may . . . smile again, and stretch her peaceful arms, and raise her golden head, exultingly," in the larger trajectory of her history, her daughters will always be singing her sons off to war.

This unhappy prophecy haunts the three prose-poetry sketches at the back of the volume. All turn to a sometimes specified, sometimes emblematic historical past, and all are cast into a form of writing, prose, a disjunctive heterogeneity that expresses Blake's critical confrontation with the role of poetic form in conveying the pressures of historical awareness in the present moment. These sketches swell the page with words, declining even a shaping by paragraphs. In a field of "poetical" sketches, this contingent textual organization gains effect from the semantic charge of formal difference. The prose line conveys the illusion of an unprescribed outpouring of voice, a force of visionary information uncontainable by poetic form. Blake's refusal, not just of poetic form but of standard prose form, is made to seem the expressive necessity of a primary, unmediated voice of prophesy and political emergency, the ultimate "organic" form. That he should produce this contradiction—extending his elaborate performances of poetic form into their own effacement—may constitute the most radically experimental gesture of *Poetical Sketches*.

Notes

1. Quoted by W. J. T. Mitchell, "Visible Language" 91.

2. Critics usually put these poems into some historical narrative, either reading them backwards, in relation to literary history, or forwards, as prefigurations of "later Blake." Their relation to literary history has received detailed attention. As Robert Gleckner (who, after Margaret Lowery, gives the fullest account) comments, the "early interest and wide reading in English poetic tradition is abundantly evident" (1), with "one text allusively challenging another" (7); indeed, the volume may be read "as a series of essays on (not exercises in) the idea of imitation, a revealing mental fight with . . . predecessors out of which emerged Blake's unshakable conviction that true imitation is criticism" (148). Joseph Wittreich sees Blake moving "decidedly beyond a poetry of allusion, creating a poetry of contexts" (73). The "immense power of assimilation" that T. S. Eliot sees in this "boy of genius" ("Blake" 276) also fuels the genius of the man, whose assimilation includes even his own early work: Gleckner shows how often the "phrasing and imagery of the *Sketches* reappears . . . in later contexts, a habitual self-quotation and intracanonical allusiveness that one comes to perceive quickly as a staple of Blake's mythopoeic method" (10); in Northrop Frye's succinct statement, *Poetical Sketches* gives "the main outlines of Blake's archetypal myth," the "major themes" of the canon in "embryo" (182).

3. For all his complaints about the tyranny and littleness of imposed rules, Blake respects craft as much as art: "Mechanical Excellence is the Only Vehicle of Genius," he annotated Reynolds's Discourse I (*CPP* 643). Anne Mellor gives a full study to Blake's critical negotiations with "the nature and value of form": even as he was "rejecting as a Urizenic tyranny the outline or 'bound or outward circumference,' " Blake was developing a visual mode that was "above all a matter of outline, of an image realized almost entirely through a strong, clear, bounding line" (xv-xvi).

4. Of the hundreds of words tabulated in Erdman's *Concordance, form* is 34th in frequency, and multi-syllabic words beginning with this syllable fill eight pages (1:739–46)—a tally that does not include the plural, the verbal conjugations, or morphemes such as *deformed, unformed, transformed.*

5. The title page reads: "POETICAL SKETCHES. // By W. B. // London: Printed in the year MDCCLXXXIII" (*CPP* 408).

6. The usual line on the visual aspects of *Poetical Sketches* does not concern this graphic quality, but treats what Blake's contemporary, Osbert Burdett, described as the "pictorial quality" of the poetic figures (12). With these "pictorial qualities" also in mind, Lowery admires the way Blake's "visual imagery" compels "his readers' eyes to follow his" (196–98).

7. The term "composite art" is best known from Mitchell's title; he cites prior usages by Frye and Jean Hagstrum (3). The visual aspect of Blake's poetic forms is also suggested by Roman Jakobson's remarks on the "plastic geometricity" (8) of grammatical and rhyme patterns in "Infant Sorrow" (*Songs of Experience*): the "symmetry and palpable interplay" of these structures form a verbal art of "mythological power and suggestiveness" (10). Mitchell analyzes Blake's "tendency to treat writing and printing as media capable of full presence," especially in "the material character of the printed word in his illuminated books" ("Visible" 51, 80). More recently, Aaron Fogle has written perceptively on "morphemic patterning" in "London" (237–38).

8. This text is briefly noted by the Santa Cruz Blake Study Group (308) and Nelson Hilton ("Becoming Prolific" 420). See Plate 4[B] (*IB* 186).

9. See Johnson's "Milton" (193) and Milton's headnote to *Paradise Lost.* A superb study of blank verse in this aspect is John Hollander's " 'Sense variously drawn out': On English Enjambment" (*VR* 91–116).

10. That this sense of "performance" to an audience was habitual for Blake (despite his limited production of work for public sale) is evident even in private marginalia. At the front of his copy of Reynolds's *Discourses,* he writes, "The Reader must Expect to Read in all my Remarks on these Books Nothing but Indignation & Resentment" (*CPP* 636)—as if imagining an audience were necessary to energize any commitment of opinion to paper. While OED gives no citation of a performative sense of *sketch* in the eighteenth century, the Advertisement for *Poetical Sketches* evokes it in its appeal to "a less partial public" than the poet's friends. Because Blake did not market the volume, this "public" was not a social fact until the 1860s, when the Pre-Raphaelites published and publicized *Sketches.* In 1863, Dante Gabriel Rossetti selected ten lyrics and passages of *King Edward* for Gilchrist's *Life* (2:3–16), and in 1868, Richard Herne Shepherd scrupulously edited Pickering's reprinting of the entire volume from the 1783 typeset. Before then, its readership was limited chiefly to a coterie, with a few poems occasionally finding wider publication. For an account of the volume's reputation before the 1860s, see Michael Phillips's careful research in "The Reputation of Blake's *Poetical Sketches.*"

11. There is no manuscript authority for the sequence in the printing arranged by Blake's patrons, the artist John Flaxman and Reverend Mathew. Lowery thinks that Blake had no part in preparing the volume for or seeing it through press (31), and Phillips guesses that Flaxman was the supervisor ("Early Blake" 13). Blake's role was to assemble the unbound printed sheets: he "folded the sheets of his poems and hand-stitched them

in plain blue-gray wrappers" and presented these volumes to friends and acquaintances throughout his life; both the nature and the relatively small number of his corrections suggest, moreover, that he was pleased with the faithfulness to his original (Phillips, "Blake's Corrections" 41, 43).

There have been various attempts to thematize the printed volume's ordering. The classical trajectory of a poet's career is routinely traced: pastoral lyrics and love songs succeeded by epic and visionary pieces. Erdman refines this arc into a movement "from laughing songs . . . to grim prophesies" (17). Elaborating, James McGowan sees a progress from "calm and confident lyric artistry, cosmic in scope (the season-day poems), to the uncertainties of increasing involvement in the secular world (the love songs), to the terrors of political chaos during a time of war and of the responsibility to be a public artist (the political pieces), to a state of discontent and frustration" in the prose sketches (143); but he (like others) notes a few aberrations (133). Construing an ideal sequence, John Ehrstine does Blake the favor of rearranging the contents "on the basis of complexity" to show a "growing thematic awareness" (3): he begins with "To the Muses" and ends with the seasons poems, inverting even this set to conclude, optimistically, with "To Spring."

12. I quote from Geoffrey Hartman, "Blake" (193) and Jonathan Culler, "Apostrophe" (142). Hartman is concerned with how the invocations individualize a cultural preoccupation with the "Progress of Posey" in England and the West. Phillips, reading a code more biographical than cultural, finds in these exercises a "record of self in relation to its increasing sense of poetic vocation" ("Early Poetry" 2). All note a concern with vocation: the "prophetic or speaking out and the invocational or calling upon," remarks Hartman, "are more important than the conventional subject" (193). The chief concern is with "poetic tradition," suggests Culler: "devoid of semantic reference, the O of apostrophe refers to other apostrophes and thus to [their] lineage and conventions" (143).

13. A similar event occurs in "Imitation of Spencer," where the call to Mercurius—"And thou, Mercurius, that . . . laden with eternal fate, dost go / Down, like a falling star" (24–25)—exploits the turn of the line to mime the action described.

14. Punning on this etymology, Spenser's Perigot tells Colin, "How I admire ech turning of thy verse!" ("August" 191). Wordsworth puns similarly, with the graphic enhancement of enjambment, when he speaks in *The Prelude* of how "forms" infused with "Visionary Power" may, "through the turnings intricate of Verse, / Present themselves as objects recognis'd, / In flashes, and with a glory scarce their own" (1805, 5: 625–30).

15. Quoted in G. E. Bentley (215); Mark Schorer reacts similarly when he remarks that "the first seven poems in *Poetical Sketches,* while broken into stanzas, are unrhymed, and their cadences, as in 'To the Evening Star,' are more like those of the rhythmical prose passages at the end of the book than they are like the normal cadences of the iambic line they purport to emulate" (350).

16. Thanks to Joseph Accioli for sharp conversation about this effect.

17. In his preface, Shepherd "firmly protest[s] against the dangerous precedent" of Rossetti's editorial license: although he credits Rossetti's "genius and rare critical perception" and concedes the value of his emendations in "remov[ing] or ton[ing] down" "much ruggedness of metre and crudeness of expression," he complains of the "unwarrantable" intrusion of "tampering with [the] author's text" (ix). Swinburne and Rossetti derided Shepherd as an unimaginative drudge, but when Dante Gabriel's brother, William Michael Rossetti, assembled his edition, he accepted Shepherd's authority.

18. The stanza is "difficult and unpleasingly tiresome to the ear by its uniformity, and to the attention by its length," and its archaic diction "disfigure[s] their lines" with bad rhymes: "If it be justly observed by Milton, that rhyme obliges poets to express their thought in improper terms, these improprieties must always be multiplied, as the difficulty of rhyme is increased by long concatenations" (*Rambler* No. 121; 4:285).

19. To Lowery the poem lacks "mastery" (90–91); Alicia Ostriker sees only juvenile arrogance in Blake's flouting of his model ("reluctant to obey the simplest rules of his craft" [35]); "Blake at his worst technically," says Gleckner (16); Ehrstine can't get past clumsy "metrics and diction" (64), and Schorer decides that Blake's refusal to be "correct" renders the poem "of no consequence *except* as it shows the young poet's impatience, even when he is deliberately imitating a formal pattern, with the structures of the pattern" (350). But both Phillips and Hollander see a point in the "perversity": for Phillips, it signals "disquiet within the convention" and a desire to "modulate the form in new ways" (3); for Hollander, "conscious formal perversity" is a master-trope: "every stanza is 'defective' if taken from one point of view, or 'adapted' if from another" (*VR* 205).

20. E.g., *The Faerie Queene*: "the hall . . . With rich array and costly arras dight" (1.4.6); "ere he could his armour on him dight" (1.7.8); "Alma . . . to her guests doth bounteous banket dight" (2.11.2); "the Priests were damzels, in soft linnen dight" (4.10.38); "he . . . bids him dight / Himself to yeeld his loue" (6.2.18); "*Spring,* all dight in leaues of flowres" (7.7.28). For Blake, *dight* is a conscious archaism; after wide medieval usage, it was nearly obsolete in the eighteenth century before revival by Romantic poets and their nineteenth-century heirs (OED D: 352).

21. See Erdman's admirable account of how Blake addresses these poems to the urgencies of his immediate historical situation (*Prophet* 14–19). Part of my discussion in this section appears, in somewhat different form and context of argument, in *Aesthetics and Ideology,* ed. George Levine (New Brunswick: Rutgers University Press, 1994).

22. For the echoes of Chatterton in this ballad, see Lowery 177–82.

23. At the end of *Paradise Lost* Book 4, Milton writes that, in the face-off between Satan and "th'Angelic Squadron," all creation might have "gone to rack, disturb'd and torn / With violence of this conflict, had not soon / Th'Eternal to prevent such horrid fray / Hung forth in Heav'n his golden Scales . . . // Wherein all things created first he weigh'd" (994–99) and which now show the futility of Satan's resistance. Merritt Hughes's note details the Homeric precedents that Milton was remembering in this image (301).

24. See also William Keach's brief but trenchant analysis of how "Gwin" and *King Edward the Third* focus attention on the images of violence that animate Blake's representation of revolutionary energy as a collective social conflict ("Blake" 26–28).

25. To John Holloway, the fact that this sketch opens with "O thou" exposes the "patriarchal pastoralism" of the season poems, which open in the same key. His concern is with literary rather than social radicalism, but Erdman shows that even the most favorable prose histories available to Blake described Edward's reign as "filled with aggressive wars, cruel executions, and hypocritical manifestos" (65 ff), and linked the victory at Crécy to the siege of Calais (where Edward prevailed, but with great cruelty and with disastrous losses on his side), the Black Death which ravaged England soon after, and the perpetual conflicts of the Hundred Years' War (63).

26. Because the drama is left in suspense, readers tend to think the sketch "unfinished" and call it a "fragment": see Crabb Robinson's initial remark of this kind (1811; rpt. Bentley 163), followed (inter alia) by Damon (228), Lowery (112), Erdman (18, 56, 63–64, 83), Bloom (*CPP* 969), and Gleckner (96). For an illuminating critique of the "reception protocols" in both the publication and the reading of the "fragment" genre, see Marjorie Levinson's *The Romantic Fragment Poem,* especially her first two chapters.

27. After Milton's headnote to *Paradise Lost,* Dryden's debates in *Essay of Dramatick Poesie* and his own statement in the dedication of *The Rival Ladies,* and Johnson's complaints in "Milton," a political vocabulary continued to inflect commentary on blank verse— well into the nineteenth century, after its canonicity was secured and was even being challenged by freer verse. In his study of English prosody, George Saintsbury evokes a politics of blank verse when he suggests that it joins "the claims of Order and Liberty . . . as in no other metrical form" (1:345). William Morris perhaps had such analyses in

mind when, coyly summoning the law to restrain the illusory freedom of this form, he suggested that "the use of blank verse as a poetic medium ought to be stopped by Act of Parliament for at least two generations" (quoted by Theodore Watts-Dunton 248).

28. For the most part, unrhymed lyrics before Blake, notes Hartman, "were obvious imitations of the classics of paraphrases of the Psalms, so that Blake's choice of verse may signify an 'ancient liberty recover'd' and evoke prophetic portions of both traditions" ("Blake" 194). If we accept Anthony Easthope's plausible claim that the "ascendancy of pentameter" as *the* English meter relegated "older accentual metre to a subordinate or oppositional position . . . the appropriate metre for nursery rhymes, the lore of schoolchildren, ballad, industrial folk song" (65), Blake resists this formal order (and Milton's investment in it) in two ways. After *Poetical Sketches* he rejects pentameter, and by *Songs of Innocence and of Experience*, he is mobilizing "low" forms as vehicles of political, philosophical, and aesthetic critique. Even so, he is haunted by what he resists. In the atmosphere of "real experimentation" in the *Sketches*, Hollander sees the "move toward freer accentualism" interacting with "a commitment to a traditional-sounding accentualism," and in *Jerusalem*, "a kind of traditional modality of meter" resembling "a transformed equivalent of the freest kind of blank verse" (*VR* 205, 208–9).

29. During the 1780s, the language of "chartering" was focusing ever sharper critical discussion. By 1792, Paine was insisting in *The Rights of Man* that "it is a perversion of terms to say that a charter gives rights. It operates by a contrary effect, that of taking rights away. Rights are inherently in all the inhabitants; but charters, by annulling those rights in the majority, leave the right, by exclusion, in the hands of a few. . . . [T]he only persons on whom they operate, are the persons whom they exclude" (458). Even his opponent, Burke, was noting the "fallacious and sophisticated" perversion of the rhetoric of "chartered rights," distinguishing public instruments such as the Magna Carta from the charters awarded to commercial interests: "*Magna Charta* is a Charter to restrain power, and to destroy monopoly: the East India Charter is a Charter to establish monopoly, and to create power. Political power and commercial monopoly are not the rights of men. . . . These Chartered Rights . . . suspend the natural rights of mankind." Paine's condemnation is noted by Erdman (*Prophet* 276–77), and Burke's remarks, from a document of 1784 abstracting his speech on the East India Bill, are quoted by Heather Glen (382n.62).

30. This perception notwithstanding, Erdman does suggest that "Blake's early intellectual growth is in part the story of his learning to see the larger web of commerce and war within which 'peace' was often mere hallucination" (ibid. 4), and he was one of the first readers of Blake to see the massive ironies of the sketch as a whole.

31. David Simpson notes that by the turn of the century such arguments were being promoted as a political expedient against unrest. Recanting his early support of enclosure, Arthur Young, for example, recognized that if a man is allowed to "love his country the better even for a pig" (i.e., given land sufficient to keep a pig), he will feel that he "has a stake in the country," and therefore will be reluctant "to riot in times of sedition" (Simpson *Wordsworth* 78; Kenneth MacLean 23). Simpson (ibid.) also cites *The Anti-Jacobin's* support for this idea: such ownership "tends to connect more firmly the links of the social chain; and to encrease that attachment to *home,* which is the source of much individual comfort and of infinite public good" (3 [1799]: 458–59). And Erdman refers to the Ode of the Bard of Albion (William Whitehead), published 4 June 1778, "urging British troops to fight in France to 'guard their sacred homes'" (*Prophet* 70).

32. It is revealing of Blake's formal challenge that many readers try to recuperate these sketches as versions of (Blakean) blank verse. Ehrstine compares the general cadences of these prose sketches to that of blank verse (32); tuning more finitely, Phillips remarks that in diction, elevation of style, and diversity of rhythm, "Samson" resembles the blank verse of *Samson Agonistes* ("Early Poetry" 18). W. M. Rossetti even casts "Prologue to King John" and "Samson" in blank verse for his edition; Jack Lindsay, to demonstrate the general debt of eighteenth-century prose rhythms to *Paradise Lost* and Blake's

particular "bondage" to Miltonic measures, experimentally casts the opening lines of "Samson" in blank verse (18); and Lowery—either inattentively, or pointedly but without explanation—prints the second part of the youth's lament in "The Couch of Death" ("My hand is feeble . . .") in the form of a blank-verse sonnet (70).

Works Cited

Barthes, Roland. "The Death of the Author" ("La mort de l'auteur"). 1965. Tr. Stephen Heath. *Image-Music-Text.* London: Fontana, 1977. 142–48.

———. "The Theory of the Text." ("Théorie du Texte," *Encyclopedia Universalis* Paris, 1968–75; 15:1013–17]). Tr. Ian McLeod. *Untying the Text: A Post- Structuralist Reader.* Ed. Robert Young. London: Routledge & Kegan Paul, 1981. 31–45.

Bentley, G. E., Jr. *William Blake: The Critical Heritage.* London and Boston: Routledge & Kegan Paul, 1975.

B[lake], W[illiam]. *Poetical Sketches.* London: 1783; facsimile rpt. London: Noel Douglas Replicas, 1926. Cited as *PS.*

Blake, William. *The Complete Poetry & Prose of William Blake.* Ed. David V. Erdman. Garden City, NY: Anchor/Doubleday, 1982. Cited as *CPP.* Quotations follow this edition; the text of *Poetical Sketches* incorporates Blake's various corrections and emendations of the 1783 printing.

———. *The Illuminated Blake.* Annotated by David V. Erdman. Garden City, NY: Anchor/Doubleday, 1974. References to plates follow this publication, cited as *IB.*

Bloom, Harold. *Blake's Apocalypse.* Garden City, NY: Doubleday, 1963.

Brooks, Cleanth. "Current Critical Theory and the Period Course." *The CEA Critic* 7/7 (Oct. 1950): 1, 5, and 6 (cols. 3–4).

Burdett, Osbert. *William Blake.* New York: Macmillan, 1926.

Culler, Jonathan. "Apostrophe." *The Pursuit of Signs: Semiotics, Literature, Deconstruction.* Ithaca: Cornell UP, 1981. 135–54.

Damon, S. Foster. *A Blake Dictionary: The Ideas and Symbols of William Blake.* 1965; New York: E. P. Dutton, 1971.

De Luca, Vincent Arthur. *Words of Eternity: Blake and the Poetics of the Sublime.* Princeton: Princeton UP, 1991.

De Man, Paul. "Literary History and Literary Modernity." *Blindness and Insight: Essays in the Rhetoric of Contemporary Criticism.* 1971; 2nd rev. ed. Minneapolis: U of Minnesota P, 1983. 142–65.

Derrida, Jacques. "Difference." *Speech and Phenomena and other Essays on Husserl's Theory of Signs.* Tr. David B. Allison. Evanston: Northwestern UP, 1973. 129–60.

Dryden, John. *Of Dramtick Poesie, An Essay.* 1668. *The Works of John Dryden.* 19 vols. Ed. H. T. Swedenberg, Jr. Berkeley and Los Angeles: U of California P, 1961–79. Vol. 17. Ed. Samuel Holt Monk (1971): 1–81.

———. "To the Right Honourable Roger Early of ORRERY" (Dedicatory epistle to *The Rival Ladies*). 1694. *The Works of John Dryden*, Vol. 8., ed. John Harrington Smith and Dougald MacMillan (1967):95–102. Cited as *RL.*

Easthope, Antony. *Poetry as Discourse.* London and New York: Methuen, 1983.

Eaves, Morris, *William Blake's Theory of Art.* Princeton: Princeton UP, 1982.

Ehrstine, John W. *William Blake's POETICAL SKETCHES.* Washington: Washington State UP, 1967.

Eliot. T. S. "Blake." *Selected Essays, 1917–1932.* New York: Harcourt Brace, 1932. 275–80.

———. Letter to the editor, *TLS* 27 (September 1928): 687.

Erdman, David V. *Blake: Prophet Against Empire.* Princeton: Princeton UP, 1954.

———, ed. *A Concordance to the Writings of William Blake.* 2 vols. Ithaca: Cornell UP, 1967.

Essick, Robert N. "How Blake's Body Means." Hilton and Vogler 197–217.

Fogle, Aaron. "Pictures of Speech: On Blake's Poetic." *Studies in Romanticism* 21 (1982): 217–42.

Frye, Northrop. *Fearful Symmetry: A Study of William Blake.* 1947; Princeton: Princeton UP, 1969.

Gilchrist, Alexander. *The Life of William Blake, "Proctor Ignotus." With Selections from His Poems and Other Writings.* 2 vols. London and Cambridge: Macmillan, 1863; "Selections" ed. Dante Gabriel Rossetti, vol. 2.

Gleckner, Robert F. *Blake's POETICAL SKETCHES.* Baltimore: John Hopkins UP, 1982.

Glen, Heather. *Vision & Disenchantment: Blake's SONGS & Wordsworth's LYRICAL BALLADS.* Cambridge: Cambridge UP, 1983.

Graves, Robert, and Laura Riding. *Contemporary Techniques of Poetry: A Political Analogy.* London: Leonard and Virginia Woolf, 1925.

Hartman, Geoffrey H. "Blake and the Progress of Poesy." 1969; rpt. *Beyond Formalism: Literary Essays, 1958–70.* New Haven: Yale UP, 1970. 193–204.

———. "The Discourse of a Figure: Blake's 'Speak Silence' in Literary History." *Languages of the Unsayable: The Play of Negativity in Literature and Literary Theory.* Ed. Sanford Budick and Wolfgang Iser. New York: Columbia UP, 1989. 225–40.

Hilton, Nelson. "Becoming Prolific Being Devoured." *Studies in Romanticism* 21 (1982): 417–24.

——— and Thomas A. Vogler, eds. *Unnam'd Forms: Blake and Textuality.* Berkeley: U of California P, 1986.

Hollander, John. *Melodious Guile: Fictive Pattern in Poetic Language.* New Haven: Yale UP, 1988. Cited as *MG.*

———. *Vision and Resonance: Two Senses of Poetic Form.* New York: Oxford UP, 1975. Cited as *VR.*

Holloway, John. *Blake: The Lyric Poetry.* London: Edward Arnold, 1968.

Jakobson, Roman. "On the Verbal Art of William Blake and Other Poet-Painters." *Linguistic Inquiry* 1 (1970): 1–23.

Johnson, Samuel. "Milton." *Lives of the English Poets.* 1783. Ed. George Birbeck Hill. 3 vols. Oxford: Clarendon, 1905. 1:84–200.

———. "The dangers of imitation. The impropriety of imitating Spenser." *The Rambler* 121 (14 May 1751). *The Yale Edition of the Works of Samuel Johnson.* Vols. 3–5. Ed. W. J. Bate and Albrecht B. Strauss. New Haven: Yale UP, 1969. 4:280–86.

Kames, Henry Home, Lord. *Elements of Criticism.* 1762; rpt. as *Elements of Criticism by Henry Home, Lord Kames.* Ed. Abraham Mills. New York: Mason Bros., 1857.

Keach, William. "Blake, Violence, and Visionary Politics." *Representing the French Revolution: Literature, Historiography, and Art.* Ed. James A. W. Heffernan. Hanover: UP of New England, 1992. 24–40).

Knights, L. C. "Early Blake." *Sewanee Review* 79 (1971): 377–92.

Leavis, F. R. "Justifying One's Valuation of Blake." Paley and Phillips 66–85.

Levinson, Marjoie. *The Romantic Fragment Poem: A Critique of a Form.* Chapel Hill and London: U of North Carolina P, 1986.

Lindsay, Jack. "The Metric of William Blake." *POETICAL SKETCHES by William Blake.* London: Scholartis P, 1927. 1–20.

Lowery, Margaret Ruth. *Windows of the Morning: A Critical Study of William Blake's* POETICAL SKETCHES, *1783.* New Haven: Yale UP, 1940.

MacLean, Kenneth. *Agrarian Age: A Background for Wordsworth.* 1950; Hamden, CT: Archon, 1970.

McGowan, James. "The Integrity of Blake's *Poetical Sketches:* A New Approach to Blake's Earliest Poems." *Blake Studies* 8 (1979): 121–44.

Mellor, Anne Kostelanetz. *Blake's Human Form Divine.* Berkeley: U of California P, 1974.

Milton, John. *Paradise Lost.* Ed. Merritt Y. Hughes. New York: Macmillan, 1986.

Mitchell, W. J. T. *Blake's Composite Art: A Study of the Illuminated Poetry.* Princeton: Princeton UP, 1978.

———. "Visible Language: Blake's Wond'rous Art of Writing." *Romanticism and Contemporary Criticism.* Ed. Morris Eaves and Michael Fischer. Ithaca: Cornell UP, 1986. 46–86.

Ostriker, Alicia. *Vision and Verse in William Blake.* Madison and Milwaukee: U of Wisconsin P, 1965.

OED. Oxford: Oxford UP, 1971.

Paine, Thomas. *The Rights of Man.* In *Two Classics of the French Revolution.* New York: Anchor/Doubleday, 1973. 267–515.

Paley, Morton D., and Michael Phillips, eds. *William Blake: Essays in Honour of Sir Geoffrey Keynes.* Oxford: Clarendon, 1973.

Partridge, Eric. "Introduction." POETICAL SKETCHES *by William Blake.* London: Scholartis P, 1927. ix–xxiv.

Phillips, Michael. "Blake's Corrections in *Poetical Sketches.*" *Blake Newsletter* 4 (1970): 40–47.

———. "Blake's Early Poetry." Paley and Phillips 1–28.

———. "The Reputation of Blake's *Poetical Sketches.*" *RES* 26 (1975): 19–33.

Poirier, Richard. *The Renewal of Literature: Emersonian Reflections.* 1987; New Haven: Yale UP, 1988.

Reynolds, Joshua. *The Works of Sir Joshua Reynolds.* Ed. Edmond Malone. 2nd ed. 3 vols. London: Cadell and Davies, 1798.

Ricks, Christopher. "A Pure Organic Pleasure from the Lines." 1971; rpt. *The Force of Poetry.* Oxford and New York: Oxford UP, 1987. 89–116.

Riffaterre, Michael. *Semiotics of Poetry.* Bloomington: Indiana UP, 1978.

Rossetti, William Michael, ed. *The Poetical Works of William Blake, Lyrical and Miscellaneous.* Aldine edition; London: Bell, 1874.

Saintsbury, George. *A History of English Prosody.* 3 vols. London: Macmillan, 1910.

Santa Cruz Blake Study Group. "What Type of Blake?" *Essential Articles for the Study of William Blake, 1970–1984.* Ed. Nelson Hilton, Hamden, CT: Archon, 1986. 301–33.

Schorer, Mark. *William Blake: The Politics of Vision.* 1946; rpt. New York: Random House, 1959.

Shepherd, Richard Herne, ed. POETICAL SKETCHES *By William Blake. Now first reprinted from the Original edition of 1783.* "Preface": vii–xiv. London: Basil Montagu Pickering, 1868.

———. *The Poems of William Blake, Comprising* SONGS OF INNOCENCE AND EXPERIENCE *Together with* POETICAL SKETCHES *and Some Copyright Poems not in any other collection.* London: Basil Montagu Pickering, 1874.

Simpson, David. *Wordworth's Historical Imagination: The Poetry of Displacement.* London and New York: Methuen, 1987.

Spenser, Edmund. "August," *The Shepheardes Calendar. Complete Poetical Works of Edmund Spenser.* Ed. R. E. Neil Dodge. Boston and New York: Houghton, Mifflin, 1908.

———. *The Faerie Queene.* Ed. Thomas P. Roche, Jr. Middlesex, England: Penguin, 1978.

Swinburne, Algernon Charles. *William Blake: A Critical Essay.* London: John Camden Hotten, 1868.

Tatham, Frederick. "Life of Blake." ?1832; selections rpt. Bentley 213–19.

Watts-Dunton, Theodore. *Old Familiar Faces.* London, 1916; Freeport, NY: Books for Libraries Press, 1970.

Wesling, Donald. *The Chances of Rhyme: Device and Modernity.* Berkeley: U of California P, 1980.

Wimsatt, W. K., Jr. "One Relation of Rhyme to Reason." *The Verbal Icon: Studies in the Meaning of Poetry.* Lexington: U of Kentucky P, 1954. 153–66.

Wittreich, Joseph A., Jr. *Angel of Apocalypse.* Madison: U of Wisconsin P, 1975.

Wordsworth, William. "Essay, Supplementary to the Preface" [of 1815]. *The Prose Works of William Wordsworth.* Ed. W. J. B. Owen and Jane Worthington Smyser. 3 vols. Oxford: Clarendon P, 1974. 3: 62–84.

———. *The Thirteen-Book "Prelude".* Ed. Mark L. Reed. 2 vols. Ithaca: Cornell UP, 1991.

The Problem of Originality and Blake's *Poetical Sketches*

Stuart Peterfreund

Introduction

The assumption, current since the publication of J. T. Smith's *Nollekens and His Times* (1828), has been that Blake did not write the Advertisement to *Poetical Sketches* (1783). It has been accounted the malicious handiwork of the Reverend A. S. Mathew, putting the cultural *parvenu* Blake in his place.[1] Some have thought it the handiwork of John Flaxman, who may have overseen the arrangement and printing of Blake's volume,[2] or perhaps the handiwork of some unspecified third party.[3] But Blake himself is as likely the author of the Advertisement as these others. Moreover, its tone is not so much condescending as satirical. The Advertisement attacks the eighteenth-century consensus esthetic,[4] as well as the subgenre of the advertisement itself. This subgenre is a virtually indispensable element in the genre of the "original" book. Advertisements appear not only in the first edition of *Lyrical Ballads* (1798) and Shelley's *Posthumous Fragments of Margaret Nicolson* (1810), but in earlier works with which Blake was certainly familiar, such as *Ossian* (1762–63) and Chatterton's *Miscellanies* (1769; 1778).[5]

Blake's Advertisement raises the issue of originality. What Blake means by this term will be discussed below. But at this point it is important to demonstrate that Blake is indeed responsible for the Advertisement. First, there is the matter of presentational norms. If *Poetical Sketches* lacks an introductory comment by Blake, it is virtually his only completed imaginative work so lacking. In *An Island in the Moon* (1784–85) and thereafter, Blake frames his texts with an argument, introduction, preface, or preludium that serves as a "door" into the work.[6]

Reprinted from *ELH* 52 (1985): 673–705 with the permission of Johns Hopkins University Press.

Then there is the matter of generic norms. *Poetical Sketches* is a send-up of the "original" book and all of its conventions. Whether the Advertisement sounds a note of "creative parody"[7] or signals the beginning of an "anatomy"[8] of originality, the remarks have a predictable place usually occupied by a predictable individual—the volume's author under the guise of a persona. Macpherson's introductory remarks are *in propria persona* because he transfers the authorial fiction to the character of Ossian, but Chatterton more predictably assumes the guise of "A. E.," as Shelley does the guise of "John Fitzvictor." Since the author of the "original" book is clearly not a Dryden, Pope, or Johnson, such an advertisement must acknowledge this fact with suitable humility and claim the reader's attention on different grounds, having to do with authenticity, spontaneity, immediacy, or the like.

Finally, there is the matter of echoes. The salient paragraph of the Advertisement is the second, which presents the central problem of the volume, one Blake returned to repeatedly. "Conscious of the irregularities and defects to be found in almost every page, his friends have still believed that they [i.e., "these sheets"] possessed a poetic originality which merited some respite from oblivion. These their opinions remain, to be now reproved or confirmed by a less partial public."[9]

The implication is that "irregularities and defects" are breaches of decorum and high finish that undercut originality. Originality, it would seem, is characterized by an abundance of such decorum and high finish—the perfect tulip without numbered streaks, the high mimetic rather than the expressive ideal.[10] However, the validity of the speaker's claims is questionable when they are compared with the claims made by Blake, *in propria persona*, in *Public Address.* Here Blake asserts that originality is dependent upon the streaks of the tulip because the artist, be it Maker or maker, creates distinct and articulated forms rather than generalized ones. ("Original Invention," Blake argues, cannot "Exits without Execution Organized & minutely Delineated & Articulated either by God or Man[.] I do not mean smoothed up & Niggled & Poco Piud [but] (and all the beauties pickd out [but] & blurrd & blotted but) Drawn with a firm (and decided) hand at once [*with all its Spots & Blemishes which are beauties & not faults*] like Fuseli & Michael Angelo Shakespeare & Milton") (p. 576).

Blake here develops "an idea of correctness that includes incorrectness, an idea of finish that includes a lack of finish in the usual eighteenth-century sense of the term, roughness as well as smoothness."[11] But to suggest, as Morris Eaves does, that this idea is iconoclastic is to lose sight of what Blake means by "Original Invention," where he gets his idea of it, and how Blake applies the concept after identifying it as a problem in *Poetical Sketches* and beyond.

Hebraism, Metaphor, and Originality

For his definition of Blakean originality, Eaves turns to the conclusion of *Jerusalem*, with its conversation "in Visionary forms dramatic" (p. 256, pl. 97.28). Originality, according to Eaves, "is an act of imagination in a community where any one expression of individuality complements or coexists with many other expressions of other individualities."[12] But this definition subverts the very ideology it is supposed to rescue. "Expression of individuality" does not take place in utopia or neutral space for Blake. Locale, whether biblical, imaginative, or contemporary, is nearly always specified in Blake's poetry. At the end of *Jerusalem* the locale is the one announced in the preface to *Milton*—"Jerusalem / In Englands green & pleasant Land" (pl. 1.15–16). Such an expression of originality can *only* take place in this locale, according to Blake. By failing to heed this stipulation, Eaves makes the sort of ideological mistake Jerome J. McGann has recently warned against.[13]

Jerusalem in England's green and pleasant land is an essential prerequisite for originality, not an incidental locale. Specifically, originality is dependent upon making Jerusalem the indwelling principle in Albion's bosom, where it supplants other possibilities such as Athens or Rome. Blake's position on this matter, far from iconoclastic, is in fact only an extension of a position maintained by a number of commentators during the eighteenth century.

As Harold Fisch has demonstrated, Jerusalem is already *in* Albion—at least in the sense that there is a Hebraic strain in English literature—from the seventeenth century onward.[14] In the succeeding century, discussions of originality often focus on the affinities between the Hebraic and the English. By the English tradition most commentators intend an English nativist line, which includes Spenser and Shakespeare and reaches its apotheosis in Milton. A hallmark of originality in either tradition is strong metaphor, which constitutes the mystery and otherness in the world by finding an analogy drawn from lived experience with which to humanize that otherness. A lack of originality is often marked by the presence of weak personification, which merely ornaments the already-constituted world by applying additional likening and humanization to a non-human something that has already been constituted. While most of the commentators on the English nativist tradition see the attenuation of figural power and waning of originality as the wages of "progress," some think that there are ways to revitalize metaphor and restore originality.

The constitutive role played by strong metaphor in the Hebraic literary tradition is noted by two of the principal English Hebraists of the eighteenth century—William Warburton and Robert Lowth. In *The Divine Legation of Moses Demonstrated* (1738–41), Bishop Warburton locates the beginnings of metaphor in the "*most* ancient *Hieroglyphic* Writing" of the Hebrews. " . . . [W]hen Men first thought of *recording their* Conceptions, the Writing would be, of course, the very Picture which was before painted in the Fancy, and from thence delineated in Words: And long afterwards . . . figurative Speech was continued out of Choice. . . ."[15] And in *Lectures on the Sacred Poetry of the Hebrews* (1787), Bishop Lowth argues that the genius of Hebraic metaphor's originality is its ability to render the unknown in terms of the experientially known—the ability to find old ways to say new things and thereby make those new things apprehensible to the community to which the metaphor is directed.

> [A] principal use of metaphors is to illustrate the subject by a tacit comparison; but if, instead of familiar ideas, we introduce such as are new, and not perfectly understood; if we endeavour to demonstrate what is plain by what is occult, instead of making a subject clearer, we render it more perplexed and difficult. . . . The Hebrews not only deduce their metaphors from familiar, or well-known objects, but pursue one constant tract or manner in the accommodation of them to their subject.[16]

Lowth's comments suggest the scenario by which the originality and figurative power of the Hebraic tradition were subverted. Instead of following in the tradition of vision and originality by attempting to find old ways to say new things, subsequent poets attempted "to demonstrate what is plain by what is occult"—to find new ways to say old things. The result was wit rather than vision and originality, personification rather than metaphor, mystification rather than clarity. These subsequent poets mark the next stage of what Gleckner calls "westering poetic genius."[17] The locus of poetry shifts westward across the Mediterranean, from the biblical to the classical world. The result is the attenuation of figural power and originality. Warburton talks of how,

> when figurative Speech was continued out of Choice, and adorned with all the invention of Wit, as among the *Greeks* and *Romans;* and that Genius of the *most ancient Hiero-glyphic* Writing again revived for Ornament in *Emblems* and *Devices,* the Custom of their Poets and Orators in personalizing [i.e., personifying] every Thing, filled their *Coins,* their *Arches,* their *Altars,* &c. with all kinds of imaginary Beings.[18]

Warburton in essence describes the rise of the classicizing tendency. When metaphor was no longer a primary human constitutive tool, the visionary line yielded pride of place to the classical. The logocentric world ordered by metaphors disavowed a figural basis and began to take on the appearance of the Derridean "always already."[19] To get a sense of what Warburton means, one might consider Isaiah 34–35, a favorite passage of Hebrew poetry for Blake, as well as for Lowth, who notes its figurative power.[20] Classical writers imitate the metaphors of the passage instead of Isaiah the man, who made those metaphors by means of a "firm perswasion" that "discover'd the infinite in every thing" (*The Marriage of Heaven and Hell,* pl. 12). The result is that Isaiah's powerful vision of the dominion of Edom, with the wrath of God turned against all the nations (34:2), is trivialized to something like the plague of Apollo, visited upon the Greeks in the *Iliad* when Agamemnon refuses to give Achilles his justly won spoils, most especially the beautiful Briseis (*Iliad* 1.59–392).

Though the classicizing tendency might have weakened the Hebraic tradition, the problem diagnosed by Lowth and Warburton would not be significant if it were restricted to the period in which it first arose. But the classicizing tendency and the culture that sponsored it are deeply implicated in the rise, progress, and establishment of eighteenth-century European culture, literature, and values—especially those of the English nativist tradition. The subversion of the Hebraic tradition by the classicizing tendency is the co-optation of one dead language and literature by another. But its effect on the English nativist tradition is in Blake's time a difficult "live" problem. To repudiate the classicizing tendency outright is to repudiate many of the accomplishments of the eighteenth century. Yet to own the existence of such a tendency within the culture is to acknowledge the likelihood that it may yet do to the English nativist tradition what it had already done to the Hebraic. Thus, while writers on the English nativist tradition recognize the constitutive power of strong metaphor as the means of humanizing otherness, and while they recognize the deleterious effects that come to pass when writers cease constituting in this manner and begin merely reconstituting the metaphors of others, they do not always express the desire to reattain originality. And when they do, that desire is as often as not weakened or deflected by other considerations.

For example, William Duff, in *An Essay on Original Genius . . . in Poetry* (1767), recognizes the importance of metaphor in creating an original style. But Duff thinks that the world once constituted by metaphor is forever constituted. Originality is as much a matter of circumstance—of being there first—as it is of talent, "especially in a modern age. Many of the most splendid images of Poetry have already been exhibited, and many of the most striking characters in human life have been delineated, and many of the most beautiful objects of nature, such as are obvious, have been described by preceding Bards." For Duff, the progress of civilization compensates for the loss of originality: "It is, that though the progress of Literature, Criticism, and Civilization, have contributed to unfold the powers and extend the empire of Reason . . . yet the art of original Poetry, to an excellence in which the wild exuberance and plastic force of Genius are the only requisites, hath suffered, instead of having gained, from the influence of the above-mentioned causes. . . ."[21]

James Beattie is even more accepting than Duff is. Even though Beattie argues, in *Essays on Poetry and Music* (1779), that "Tropes and Figures are often necessary to supply the unavoidable defects of language," and even though he knows that metaphor "may be made to seize our attention and interest our passions almost as effectually as if it were an object of outward sense," Beattie is not particularly concerned about the attenuation of figural power in his own time. He claims that "no author equals Shakespeare in boldness and variety of figures," discourses at length on the power of Milton's metaphor in *Paradise Lost* 2.1013 ("To spring upward, like—a pyramid of fire"), then finds Gray's figures "equal . . . in propriety" to those of Milton, "though not in magnificence."[22] Yet Beattie draws no inference from this last comparison, nor does he attempt to argue that figural attenuation may be justified in the name of progress.

Beattie's apparent equanimity arises from his view that original genius is the anomaly, the classicizing tendency the norm. It

is arguable that in Beattie's lexicon the word *originality* is an entry
that is starred or under erasure, since he views poetry as an unending
continuity of poets imitating the composition and not the man. In *Of
Memory and Imagination* (1783), in his "Remarks on Genius," Beattie
notes that, "Among contemporary poets, we may sometimes observe
a similarity of genius; which is probably occasioned by their imitating
one another." From this observation, he generalizes to the claim that
"all good poets imitate one another more or less: and I am not sure
whether Homer himself has not in some things condescended to
imitate Hesiod. But in the workings of a great genius, even when he
imitates, nay when he is only a translator, there is always something
peculiar and extraordinary."[23]

John Aikin disagrees by implication. In *An Essay on the Application of Natural History to Poetry* (1777), Aikin begins by posing a
problem: "No literary complaint is more frequent and general than
that of the insipidity of Modern Poetry." And the cause he ascribes is
that sort of imitation typical of the classicizing tendency, by means of
which poets imitate other texts and not other poets, and as the result
of which figural attenuation occurs, with constitutive metaphor giving
way to ornamental personification. To document the "perpetual repetition of the same images, clad in almost the same language," Aikin
traces a figure that originates in Shakespeare's *Macbeth* as "The shard-
born beetle with his drowsy hums," resurfaces in Milton's "Lycidas"
as "the gray-fly [that] winds her sultry horn," and reappears again in
Gray's "Elegy Written in a Country Church-Yard" as "Save where the
beetle wheels her droning flight." Despite his derivativeness, Gray's
appropriation of the figure is accounted superior to that of Collins,
who frames the sort of fanciful personification disliked so strongly
by Johnson. In his "Ode to Evening," Collins talks of a place

> where the beetle winds
> His small but sullen horn,
> As oft he rises midst the twilight path
> Against the pilgrim borne in heedless hum.[24]

Aikins' advice under the circumstances is to turn away from
literature and back to scientific nature. "[T]he votary of Science is
continually gratified with new objects opening to his view," Aikin
reflects, in terms that anticipate Keats's sonnet on Chapman's Homer,
and echo Edward Young's advice about how best to imitate Homer:
"Tread in his steps to the sole fountain of immortality; drink where he

drank, at the true *Helicon*, that is, the breast of nature."[25] But from Blake's point of view, this is a dangerously seductive program for rescuing poetic originality. The problem with the "nature" of Young is an obvious one: it is both classicized as the Helicon, home of the Muses, and personified as a mother figure, replete with nurturing breast. But discovering and following "nature," as Aikin's "votary of Science" does, is hardly a satisfactory alternative. Science presumes nature as its object—as what is there in the first place, prior to the language that describes it or the experiments that unmask its workings—without admitting any doubt as to whether the nature in question pre-exists the language in question. And yet, as Edmund Husserl demonstrates, the mathematization of nature occurs at the cost of ignoring the fact that the nature thus mathematization is not self-evidently "out there," but is instead a creation of language itself, albeit a language of the trivium rather than the quadrivium.[26] The self-evident truth of the Pythagorean theorem rests on eighteen axioms and enabling premises which create the geometric universe that theorem inhabits.[27] And even Newton's *Principia* is irreducible to a purely mathematical basis in truth, as Blake knew and as Gödel was later to demonstrate mathematically.[28]

Blake's Ontology and Program of Originality

In the biblical model, speech precedes phenomena. The speech act "let there be light," illocutionary rather than perlocutionary in its effect, manifests the force that causes the observer of the speech act to report the phenomenon of light.[29] Similarly, the prophetic formula "it shall come to pass" creates the conditions of awareness that structure subsequent phenomena. Attempting to deny this sequence or blur the initial sequence of causation leads to the sort of murkiness one glimpses at the outset of *The [First] Book of Urizen,* where Urizen's willful silence is a form of suppressed or concealed speech, a false consciousness that induces the other immortals to speak while he remains silent, "Dark revolving in silent activity" (pl. 3.18). Rather than beginning with God commanding light and light following, the Urizenic genesis begins with "The sound of a trumpet" (pl. 3.50), the last event in the Bible, a sure sign that Urizen has his ontology, epistemology, and priorities backwards. Only after the murkey apparition of "bleak desarts / Now fill'd with clouds, darkness & waters" (pl. 4.1–2), do the "Words articulate, bursting in thunders / That roll'd on the tops of his mountains" (pl. 4.3–4) appear.

Following nature in any of its dispensations is, for Blake, an unsatisfactory path to originality. Responding to Wordsworth's *Poems* (1815), he claims that "Natural Objects always did & now do Weaken deaden & Obliterate Imagination in Me" (p. 665). Blake understands nature as a murky detritus left over from suppressed or concealed first speech, relegated to the status of self-evident truth, axiom, what goes without saying, etc. Nevertheless, such an accumulation of ephemera can weaken or even extinguish the imagination because it forces the would-be exponent of imagination (and originality) to pause and acknowledge its false but collectively acknowledged presence before giving voice to that imagination (and originality). In *An Island in the Moon,* there is a telling exchange between Aradobo, who is of Blake's party, and the mathematician Obtuse Angle. Sensing that the God classicized and trivialized as "Little Phebus . . . / With his fat belly & his round chin" (p. 451, ch. 3) was originally the presence that said "let there be light," Aradobo exclaims, "Ah . . . I thought I had read of Phebus in the Bible." Obtuse Angle rebukes him, cautioning, "you should always think . . . before you speak" (p. 452). Thinking before one speaks fosters the false consciousness that takes suppressed or concealed prior speech as nature, and repeats that suppressed or concealed speech as it supposedly "imitates" what passes for nature. Speaking before one thinks is the biblical condition of speech, which grants language access to the infinite and recreates the world in unending and various succession, as in the "conversation" on which *Jerusalem* concludes. In the written medium, such language is clearly in the prophetic mode—what Blake has in mind when he has Isaiah, speaking at "dinner" in *The Marriage of Heaven and Hell,* say, "I cared not for consequences but wrote" (pl. 12).[30]

A final problem with following nature is the effect that such a pursuit has on figurative language. Language used properly, in Blake's view, is prophetic in the Hebraic sense of finding old ways (speech) to say new things (phenomena). Even God in Genesis follows this strategy, naming Adam after the earth he is made from and Eve after the man she is made from. "The votary of Science" relegates poetic language to the function of wit rather than vision, because the "new objects" of nature (phenomena) provide the figurative point or ornament necessary to decorate old things (speech). Thus following nature is a subversion of originality and expression, a betrayal of the authentic sequence. Although his account is not entirely friendly to his subject, Derrida's analysis of Husserl's views on language can easily be extended to apply as well to Blake. "Ex-pression is exteriorization. It imparts to a certain outside a sense which is first found in a certain inside. We suggested above that this outside and this inside were absolutely primordial: the outside is neither nature, nor the world, nor a real exterior relative to consciousness."[31]

Blake's program for originality is a program to establish the proper priority of speech over phenomena, which is found in the Bible, and which fosters originality. He uses Hebraic notions of originality to correct mistaken notions of originality arising from, or in response to, the English nativist tradition. The Hebraic tradition is of use in extirpating the classicizing tendency deeply latent in the English nativist tradition, as well as in identifying the classicizing tendency elsewhere. The extent of the problem is suggested by the preface to *The Everlasting Gospel.* Joseph of Arimathea, Blake's mythic link between the Hebraic tradition and the English nativist tradition, brings the prophetic line from Jerusalem to England. But Joseph, to his dismay, finds that the same Roman Empire he opposed in Jerusalem is already established in a position of apparent priority in England.

> I will tell you what Joseph of Arimathea
> Said to my Fairy was not it very queer
> Pliny & Trajan what are You here
> Come listen to Joseph of Arimathea

(p. 518, ll. 1–4)

The references to Pliny and Trajan are both historically accurate and an illustration of Blake's point. The invasion of England by Pliny the Elder (a naturalist), Pliny the Younger, (an orator and statesman), and Trajan (a soldier, then Emperor of Rome) brought political rhetoric, "nature," and imperial domination to England at the same time. Joseph of Arimathea can help undermine all three sorts of usurpation of priority, because he brings word of Christ's example of how to respond. In what amounts to an extended gloss of the argument, in *The Marriage of Heaven and Hell,* that "Jesus was all virtue, and acted from impulse: not from rules [i.e., Jesus spoke before he thought, rather than thinking before he spoke]" (pls. 23–24), Blake takes up Christ's alleged humility, chastity, and gentility, making it clear that Christ placed himself and his language first, before language privileging such fictions as nature or empire: "For he acts with honest triumphant Pride / And this is the cause that Jesus died" (p. 519, ll. 25–26).

The program for originality also lies behind the account in the letter of September 12, 1800, to Flaxman, where Blake alludes to early influences on his poetic development: " . . . Milton lovd me in childhood & shewd me his face / Ezra came with Isaiah the Prophet . . ." (p. 707). Ezra is charged by Cyrus, King of Persia, with overseeing the building of the Second Temple in Jerusalem, which continues through the reign of Darius and is completed in the reign of Artaxerxes. Notwithstanding the misgivings of John Dryden (and Walter Jackson Bate),[32] the story is fraught with hope as well as significance for Blake. This is no ordinary royal decree: God stirs the kingly spirit of Cyrus to make it (Ezra 1:1–2). And Cyrus, Darius, and Artaxerxes are not ordinary kings. All three opposed Greek military, cultural, and religious domination of their realm. Not only does Cyrus decree the Second Temple, his reign and those of Darius and Artaxerxes after him guarantee that the temple will not be rededicated to Phoebus Apollo or worse. Moreover, it is important to remember that the decree specifies the rebuilding of Solomon's Temple, in Jerusalem. "Such . . . rebuilding, of the ancient house of the Lord we have come to associate, properly, with Blake's prophecies," as Gleckner correctly notes.[33] But the rebuilding of Solomon's temple has added significance for Blake. From the time of Bacons' *Great Instauration*, rebuilding Solomon's Temple had been synonymous with reacquiring the pristine language of Adam and that language's ability to assert human domination over the created world. In the eighteenth century, Solomon's Temple became the central symbol of Freemasonry as well as the Brotherhood's figurative goal. While not entirely sympathetic to its rites or purposes, Blake was aware of Freemasonry's notion of a vocation as well as the movement's symbolism. These he adapted to his own needs.[34] The rebuilding of Solomon's Temple in Jerusalem signifies the righting of priorities, with speech once again in control of phenomena because it is placed before phenomena.

The priorities can only be righted in a holy locale—thus the significance of Jerusalem, with the implication that prophecy is the product of place, an autochthonous artifact. It is only in Jerusalem that the children of Israel can gather "Themselves up as one man" (Ezra 3:1), just as it is only in Jerusalem built in England's green and pleasant land that the Four Zoas can walk "To & fro in Eternity as One Man" (pl. 98.39). This is by way of suggesting that the importance of Isaiah—especially Isaiah 34–35—is to prophesy the advent of just such an autochthonous access of vision. To use Blake's reading of these chapters in *The Marriage of Heaven and Hell:* it is only when "on the bleached bones / Red clay" (pl. 2.12–13) such as Adam was created from brings forth that "the dominion of Edom [red earth], & the return of Adam into Paradise" (pl. 3) may be accomplished. The dominion of Edom is the dominion of Adam as well, and his return to Paradise entails taking control of language and placing it in the position of priority before phenomena that rebuilding Solomons' Temple entails.

Both Ezra and Isaiah, then, are prophecies about how the dominion of language over phenomena may be restored. The biblical accounts have some prophetic value for Blake, but he finds Milton a richer model. Had Blake never read anything else on the problem of originality, he would have found the problem and correct response suggested in Milton—especially in *Paradise Regained.*

The poem is not an account of a general temptation by Satan of Christ in the wilderness, but rather an account of a temptation that offers Christ classical eloquence and the worldly power that goes with it. At one point Satan claims that he offers not only eloquence and power but also originality. Christ replies with patient scorn on all three accounts, choosing nativist eloquence over classical, visionary power over worldly, and true originality over false. His reply concerns the status of "our native Language," a rather suggestive locution that refers within the context of the poem to one nativist language (Hebrew—Aramaic, to be precise about the dialect), but within the readerly context to another nativist language (the language it is rendered in—English).

> . . . if I were to delight my private hours
> With Music or with Poem, where so soon
> As in our native Language can I find
> That solace? All our Law and Story strew'd
> With Hymns, our Psalms with artful terms inscrib'd
> Our Hebrew Songs and Harps in *Babylon,*
> That pleas'd so well our Victors' ear, declare
> That rather *Greece* from us these Arts deriv'd;
> Ill imitated, while they loudest sing
> The vices of thir Deities, and thir own
> In Fable, Hymn, or Song, so personating [i.e.,
>   personifying]
> Thir Gods ridiculous, and themselves past shame.[35]

Christ's triumph over this temptation should not obscure the seductiveness of the temptation itself. It is a temptation against which the Milton that Blake depicts was not strong throughout his entire career. Although in *The Reason of Church Government* Milton can claim that inspired wisdom is not to be had "from the pen of some vulgar amorist, or the trencher fury of a riming parasite, nor to be obtained by the invocation of Dame Memory and her Siren daughters, but by devout prayer to that eternal Spirit who can enrich with all utterance and knowledge, and sends out his seraphim with the hallowed fire of his altar, to touch and purify the lips of whom he pleases" (671), that claim is not made good in his poetry until *Paradise Regained.* There, Milton petitions for the inspiration of the

> . . . Spirit who led'st this glorious Eremite [i.e., Christ]
> Into the Desert, his Victorious Field
> Against the Spiritual Foe. . . .
>
> (1.8–10)

If one thinks of the temptations and failures of nerve evident in Los, Blake's prophetic avatar, it becomes clear that Blake conceives his own poetic career as substantially like Milton's in this one respect: the work of establishing the Hebraic tradition in poetry and the poetic originality that tradition fosters is the work of a lifetime, in which the poet-prophet emerges from the civilized delusions of the classical tradition and plunges into the wilderness of the Hebraic tradition. There he struggles against classically induced delusions of power and temptations to return, until he is in-spired by the Holy Spirit, who at once fills him with the authentic impulse to utterance and purifies the means of utterance.

Blake's Seasons and the Program of Originality

As the first step in this struggle toward authentic utterance and poetic originality, *Poetical Sketches* is full of "irregularities and defects to be found in almost every page," though not of the sort that the smug persona would recognize. The irregularities are misappropriations of authentic inspiration by force of poetic convention and habit. And the defects are defects of poetical character in the face of the Satanic temptation to classicize. The seasonal group with which *Poetical Sketches* begins serves to illustrate the volume's central problem: how to establish the primacy of the Hebraic tradition and the originality it gives rise to in a poetical world dominated by the classical tradition, committed to its perpetuation, and fearful of—or at best indifferent to—the Hebraic alternative.[36]

"To Spring," the first of the seasonal poems, begins with an access of authentic, Hebraic inspiration. While commentators from Margaret Ruth Lowery onward have noted the connection between Blake's first stanza and *The Faerie Queene* 1.5.2.1–4,[37] those commentators have not noted how Blake's appropriation of Spenser reverses his classicizing tendency, thus moving an essentially nativist poem by Spenser back toward authentic originality. Where Spenser describes how "*Phoebus*, fresh, as bridegrome to his mate, / Came daucing forth, shaking his deawie haire," Blake describes a "thou, with dewy locks, who lookest down / Thro' the clear windows of the morning . . ." (p. 408, ll. 1–2). Given Blake's antipathy toward Greek mythology, the abuse heaped on "little Phebus" in *An Island in the Moon,* and the role of Phoebus as tempter and jailer in "Song" ("How sweet I roam'd from the field"), Blake could have deleted the reference on general principle. But there is more at work here.

The speaker who addresses a nameless "thou" finally, in the last word of the first stanza, confers the name "Spring" (p. 408, l. 4). In between, the speaker attributes physical presence ("dewy locks") and animate, sensible activity ("lookest down") to that object. Beginning without a name any more specific than *thou* suggests the Hebrew God, who first reveals himself to Moses bearing the name "I AM THAT I AM" (Exodus 3:14), then tells Moses, according to the Masoretic text of Exodus, that his name is "the ineffable name, read *Adonai,* which means, *the Lord* (6:2–3n.). The overall process of the first stanza seems remarkably close to one that Blake describes in *The Marriage of Heaven and Hell* when he tells how "the ancient Poets animated all sensible objects with Gods or Geniuses, calling them by their names and adorning them with the properties of woods, rivers, mountains, lakes, cities, nations, and whatever their enlarged & numerous senses could perceive" (pl. 11). The important thing about both Blake's stanza and his account is the sequence that each follows: a recognition of the fundamental "thou-ness," or otherness,[38] of the object of address; the humanization of that otherness by means of "animation," which causes sensible objects to become apprehensibly familiar objects; the naming of what has been "animated"; and the conferral of a local habitation ("woods, rivers, mountains, lakes . . .") to go with the name.

The sequence of the process is absolutely crucial to its successful completion. To begin by perceiving "Gods or Geniuses" rather than "sensible objects" is to be overwhelmed by unmediated numinous power. If "God becomes as we are, that we may be as he is," as Blake argues in *There Is No Natural Religion* [b], it is only through the inter-mediation of the sensible world: "He who sees the infinite *in all things* sees God" (p. 3; my emphasis). To begin with the names of "Gods or Geniuses" is to begin with a mythology, such as classical mythology. And to begin "with the properties of woods, rivers, mountains, lakes," etc., is to begin with *nature,* in the Wordsworthian acceptation of the term. An additional observation should be ventured regarding the religions that arise from beginning at the respective wrong steps of the sequence. Beginning at the second step results in the Mosaic mystery religion; beginning at the third step results in the religions of classical mythology, including the Norse; and beginning at the fourth step results in natural religion, with its Newtonian argument from design.

The matters of process and sequence are especially important, given the implications of Spring's arrival in England—the "western isle" (p. 408, l. 3). *If* Spring arrives in the England of the speaker (*To Spring* is, interestingly, the only one of the seasonal poems in which the season does not clearly arrive and is still being implored at the end of the poem), the result will be apocalyptic, and not in a trivial or a cataclysmic sense, but in the sense intended by Blake in *A Vision of the Last Judgment:* "The Last Judgment is not Fable or Allegory but Vision Fable or Allegory are a totally distinct & inferior kind of Po-etry. . . . (A Last Judgment is Necessary because Fools flourish. . . .) The Last Judgment is an Overwhelming of Bad Art & Science" (pp. 554, 561, 565). The overwhelming of bad art and the replacement of fable and allegory by vision are what lead Blake in the first place to remove the reference to Phoebus from his appropriation of Spenser. Similarly, the reference to Spring's "bright pavilions" (p. 408, l. 7) is an appropriation of Spenser with a difference, evoking and offering an implicit correction to *The Faerie Queene* 7.7.8.2., where Nature sits in her pavilion atop Arlo Hill to do justice,[39] a personification or allegorical figure rather than an authentic object of vision.

The case against Spenser is most clearly made in Blake's "An Imitation of Spen[s]er" which, far from showing Blake "engaged in a redaction of neo-Spenserianism," as Gleckner argues, is rather one of those imitations that shows the extent to which Blakean imitation is criticism.[40] Spenser, for Blake, is in several senses a classic case of what happens when one begins at the wrong step in the sequence and takes the allegory or fable as vision, confusing the actions of naming with the true first act of recognizing the infinite in otherness. To take one example from the poem's invocation of Mercury:

> If thou arrivest at the sandy shore,
> Where nought but envious hissing adders dwell,
> Thy golden rod, thrown on the dustry floor,
> Can charm to harmony with potent spell. . . .
>
> (p. 421, ll. 27–30)

The overt reference is to Mercury's caduceus, a staff of office comprised of entwined serpents. But the origins of that staff and the delusion of the Spenserian speaker in attributing it to Mercury are blatantly clear. To begin with, the reference, albeit garbled by delusion, is originally to Exodus, chapters 14 and 7. In chapter 14 Israel, pursued by the troops of Pharaoh, reaches the shore of the Red Sea, where God enjoins Moses not to throw down his rod, but to lift it. Moses does so and the Holy Spirit, working through the rod, does indeed "charm to harmony with potent spell." The waters part and the Israelites pass safely, while the pursuing Egyptians are drowned (14:15–30).

This same rod was originally Aaron's, until God commanded Moses to take it (7:15). Previously, Aaron had cast the rod down before Pharaoh, where it turned into a serpent to demonstrate the power that it and he represented. Pharaoh then commanded his wise men, sorcerers, and magicians to duplicate the feat, which they did creating the "envious hissing adders" of the deluded Spenserian allusion. But Aaron's rod showed the ability to "charm to harmony with potent spell." It swallowed up the other rods that had become serpents (7:8–12).

With no need to correct Spenserian delusions and other delusions, the inhabitants of the "western isle" of "To Spring" might well be ready for the Last Judgment and apocalyptic marriage they eagerly seek. "The hills tell each other, and the list'ning / Vallies hear" (p. 408, ll. 5–6), because when the fiery source that is Spring arrives, "Every valley shall be lifted up, and every mountain and hill be made low; the uneven ground shall become level, and the rough places a plain. And the glory of the LORD shall be revealed, and all flesh shall see it together . . ." (Isaiah 40:4–5). The approach of Spring echoes the male voice of the Song of Solomon: "the winter is past, the rain is over and gone. The flowers appear on the earth, the time of singing has come . . ." (2:11–12).

There are several Solomonic echoes in "To Spring."[41] Spring's "perfumed garments" (p. 408, l. 10) recall Solomons' figure, "the scent of your garments is like the scent of Lebanon" (4:11). The reference to a "love-sick land that mourns for thee" (p. 408, l. 12) directly echoes the female voice, "if you find my beloved . . . tell him I am sick with love" (5:8).[42] This last echo points to a central problem in the Song of Solomon and "To Spring" alike. The great consummation figured forth in Isaiah, the Song of Solomon, and "To Spring" may be ardently and devoutly awaited. But it cannot occur, in part because of a failure of nerve on the part of the Solomonic female voice—and, by extension, on the part of England.

Read typologically, the Song of Solomon is the Old Man's anticipation, in the Old Testament, of what is only finally to come to pass through the acts of the New Man, in the New Testament. The frustrated eroticism of Solomon and Tirzah is redressed by the wedding of Christ to his bride Jerusalem, the Church. Revelation figures forth this event and the Last Judgment it signifies in terms suggesting an awesome event. Spring is asked to place "a golden crown upon" England's "languished head, / Whose modest tresses were bound up for thee" (p. 408, ll. 15–16). The bound hair may be a traditional symbol "of chastity and continence that Blake probably found, appropriately, in Spenser's *Epithalamion* (62)," as Gleckner suggests.[43] But the original that Spenser apparently imitates in *Epithalamion* is found in Revelation. And it is hardly a steadfast, simple, or demure original. In chapter 9, John of Patmos tells of the locusts sent to harrow the earth for those not having "the seal of God upon their foreheads": "In appearance the locusts were like horses arrayed for battle; on their heads were what looked like crowns of gold; their faces were like human faces; their hair like women's hair, and their teeth like lions' teeth; they had scales like iron breastplates, and the noise of their wings was like the noise of many chariots with horses rushing into battle" (9:4, 7–9). The implication seems to be that to set the golden crown upon England's languished head is to turn her into an engine of the Apocalypse, like the locusts. Reasonably enough, the crown is never set, and the great consummation never occurs.

The depiction of a failed apocalypse in "To Spring" is typical of the early poetry, when Blake often used failed apocalypses as the start of a deluded fall into time and space. Obvious examples are the trumpet sounding in *The [First] Book of Urizen* and Newton blowing an enormous blast on the trumpet in *Europe.* A less obvious example is the introduction to *Songs of Innocence.* In these and other cases, the fall into time and space is in one sense fortunate. The uncertainty, mutability, and mortality of the fallen state are tempered by an art that is of some comfort to the fallen and provides hope for an ultimate transcendence of the fallen state.

But a failed apocalypse augurs ill for the sort of originality glimpsed at the end of *Jerusalem.* The endless, original visionary conversation there occurs when "The Four Living Creatures Chariots of Humanity Divine Incomprehensible / In beautiful Paradises expand . . ." (pl. 98.24–25). Paradise, both in Genesis and in Milton, is a condition of everlasting spring. To leave Paradise, as Adam and Eve do at the end of *Paradise Lost,* is to descend into the fallen human world and into the next season—summer—with its "*Libyan Air adust*" (12.635). It is also worth noting that the events that lead to conversation "in Visionary forms dramatic" can only occur after Blake proclaims the impending Apocalypse with the words "Time was Finished! The Breath Divine Breathed over Albion . . ." (pl. 94.18).

Albion "And England who is Britannia" (pl. 94.20) both "taste" this breath as the inhabitants of the "western isle" do not "taste" the Divine "morn and evening breath" (p. 408, ll. 3, 10–11) in *To Spring.* The taste is, like the taste the angel describes to John of Patmos when handing him the scroll, "bitter to your stomach, but sweet as honey in your mouth" (10:9). It causes a good deal of lamentation on the part of England, who is Britannia and Albion alike, but it is also the efficient cause of the great consummation that occurs. England can enter "Albions bosom rejoicing" (pl. 96.2) only after "The Breath Divine went forth over the morning hills . . ." (pl. 95.5). Albion enters the bosom of Jesus for the same reason. The bodily things of the stomach are accounted insignificant, if bitter, and left behind. The poetic things of the mouth are accounted significant as well as sweet, and are embraced in an unending exemplar of poetic originality, "Creating Space, Creating Time according to the wonders Divine / Of Human Imagination . . ." (pl. 98.31–32).

There is no apocalypse in "To Spring," and originality suffers accordingly. The three seasonal poems that follow are derivative poems—"copies" in the negative sense, rather than "imitations" in the positive sense. As suggested above, the poems that follow also chart a course of fallenness—both into time and space, and into increasing delusion regarding the human condition and humanity's relationship with its God. Taken as a group, the four seasonal poems also comment on the fate of originality in another way. With the exception of "To Autumn," the apparent anomaly of which is discussed below, the poems move from the gold of the "golden crown" in "To Spring" to the silver of the "Silver wire" in "To Summer" to the iron of the "adamantine doors" in "To Winter" (p. 408, l. 15; 409:14; 410:1). One classical idea that argues against originality is that of four ages—golden, silver, bronze and iron—through which the arts pass in process of decline. Blake senses decline in the arts of the day, as the comments in the preface to *Milton* make clear. But he does not believe that such decline is inevitable or irreversible. In fact, his joining of the concept of the four ages with the seasonal cycle suggests a position more nearly like that of Shelley in *A Defence of Poetry* than that of Peacock in "The Four Ages of Poetry," with the caveat that Shelley's cycles of imaginative power and decline move toward no end, while Blake's cycles do end in the Apocalypse.

Each of the seasonal poems after "To Spring" begins at a step subsequent to the first step in the sequence of poetic process suggested by Blake's remarks in *The Marriage of Heaven and Hell*. Because they do not emphasize each of the steps in the sequence equally, the poems are skewed or incomplete visions. Moreover, they begin from wrong initial premises—not absolutely wrong, but premises that can only follow from a suppressed initial premise. "To Spring" begins correctly with a recognition of the fundamental "thou-ness" or otherness of the object of address, but neither the speaker nor any of his companions is able to move toward the Apocalypse that such a recognition should set in motion. "To Summer" suppresses such a recognition in favor of an emphasis on the humanization of otherness by means of "animation," which causes sensible objects to become apprehensibly familiar objects. "To Autumn" in its turn suppresses "animation" in favor of an emphasis on naming what has been "animated." And "To Winter" in its turn suppresses the activity of naming in favor of conferring the local habitation that goes with the name. In each of these repetitions with a difference, the act of copying significant elements from preceding poems in the series increases the evidence of the classicizing tendency at work; it also distances each succeeding speaker increasingly from the recognition that the "thou-ness" or otherness of the object of address is what betokens the presence of "The Breath Divine," which is ready to issue forth and restore originality to the poet (or nation) that will accept it with all of its numinous and apocalyptic implications.

Although like "To Spring" it begins with formulaic apostrophes, "To Summer" is repetition with a difference. The emphasis on "animation" is suggested by the movement of an adjective clause into the place formerly occupied by a prepositional phrase preceding an adjective clause. Thus, "O thou, with dewy locks, who lookest down," becomes "O thou, who passest thro' our vallies . . ." (p. 408, l. 1; 409:1). The suggestion is underscored by what follows. Summer, passing through the valleys of England in its "strength," is asked to "curb thy fierce steeds, allay the heat / That flames from their large nostrils!" (p. 409, ll. 2–3). Summer is a powerful being, capable perhaps of the heroic sort of activity one finds in Homer. If not explicitly Homeric, Summer is nevertheless classicized. He is a chariot driver, whose voice is associated with that of a time when "noon upon his fervid car / Rode o'er the deep of heaven" (p. 409, ll. 8–9). Blake may be conflating Phoebus Apollo with his son Phaëton, confusing the two, or leaving the relationship deliberately vague; but it is clear that Blake associates "animation" with heroic action.[44]

The classicizing tendency is contagious, affecting the speaker who in the last stanza compares native English "youth" and "maidens" to their "southern [i.e., Greek and Roman]" counterparts, and finds the English "youth . . . bolder" and the English "maidens fairer in the sprightly dance" (p. 409, ll. 15–16). The assertion of superiority is tempered by the tenor of the comparison, which makes the classical *the* standard of comparison against which the value of what follows is measured. The comparison leads to a forsaking of authentic nativist inspiration and originality. The speaker's people "lack not songs, nor instruments of joy, / Nor echoes sweet, nor waters clear as heaven" (p. 409, ll. 17–18), suggesting that the basis for inspired originality is to be found in England itself. Indeed, the same accoutrements of originality are found at the end of *Jerusalem*, with its "Fountains of Living Waters flowing from the Humanity Divine" (pl. 96.37). But when the speaker of "To Summer" concludes by saying that his people do not lack "laurel wreaths against the sultry heat" (p. 409, l. 19), he takes back what he previously conceded. Laurel wreaths are worn by Greek and Roman poets, not Hebraic ones. The rationalization that such a wreath protects against the heat loses sight of the fact that the heat (and light) signal the presence of authentic inspiration. It is the same presence that the speaker of "Mad Song" turns away from when he cries, "light doth seize my brain / With frantic pain" (p. 416, ll. 23–24)—the same presence that frightens Blake in *Milton* when he recounts how "Los behind me stood; a terrible flaming Sun: just close / Behind my back . . ." (pl. 22.6–7). But unlike the speakers of "To Summer" and "Mad Song," Blake does not defend his selfhood in

Milton. He allows the access of light and heat, which turns out to be strengthening rather than overwhelming or painful, causing Blake to proclaim:

> I am that Shadowy Prophet who Six Thousand Years ago
> Fell from my station in the Eternal bosom. Six Thousand
>   Years
> Are finished. I return! both Time & Space obey my will

(pl. 22.15–17)

The classicizing tendency in "To Summer" is reinforced by biblical echoes signalling fall and betrayal. The classicized fiction of Apollo/Phaëton is a convenience for people who don't know exactly what it is that passes by when they hear it in their "mossy vallies," ensconced "Beneath . . . thickest shades . . ." (p. 409, ll. 10, 8). The echo is of Genesis, directly after Adam and Eve eat the forbidden Fruit and find that their eyes are opened: "they heard the sound of the LORD God walking in the garden in the cool of the day, and the man and his wife hid themselves from the presence of the LORD God among the trees of the garden" (3:8). In "To Summer," the speaker and his people are not only fallen and deluded; they also want the radiant presence called Summer to "cool it" and join them: "throw thy / Silk draperies off, and rush into the stream" (p. 409, ll. 11–12). Here the echo is of Ezekiel, who describes how God made Israel his chosen people and how Israel betrayed that trust. Ezekiel figures forth the election and betrayal in terms of a decking out for sacred marriage and a playing of the harlot. Ezekiel's God says, "I clothed you also with embroidered cloth and shod you with leather, I swathed you in fine linen and covered you with silk. . . . But you trusted in your beauty, and played the harlot because of your renown, and lavished your harlotries on any passer-by. You took some of your garments, and made for yourself gaily decked shrines, and on them played the harlot; the like has never been, nor ever shall be" (16:10, 15–16). The implication of the allusion seems clear: by succumbing to the classicizing tendency and worshipping at the "gaily decked shrines" of the classical tradition, England and English poetry have played the harlot on their own, shunning authentic divine presence and favor for false idols, choosing the rotten rags of memory by inspiration over the Robe of the Promise. Given England's betrayal, it would be more convenient for English poetry if its God went Grecian, stripped off his garments, and joined them in the Heraclitan stream.

"To Autumn" suppresses "animation" in favor of naming, a shift that is clear both from the change in formula—the apostrophe "O thou" gives way to "O Autumn" (p. 409, l. 1)—and from the speaker's injunction to "pass not, but sit / Beneath my shady roof, there thou may'st rest . . ." (p. 409, ll. 2–3). But there is no apparent heightening of the classicizing tendency, nor are there any of the Spenserian echoes found in the two preceding poems of the sequence. Instead, the echoes of English literature that are obvious are Miltonic. Commentators from Lowery onward have detected the last two lines of "Lycidas" in the last two lines of "To Autumn."[45] In addition to that echo, Autumn's speech, describing how "Blossoms hang round the brows of morning, and / Flourish down the bright cheek of modest eve" (p. 409, ll. 9–10), seems an echo of *Paradise Lost,* the precise provenance of which will be discussed below.

The shift from Spenserian to Miltonic echoings is significant. If the seasonal sequence also has to do with the four ages of poetry, then it would appear that the move from "To Summer" to "To Autumn" is a move from the poetry of the earlier Renaissance to the poetry of the later Renaissance, the former typified for Blake by Spenser's poetry, the latter by Milton's. What would otherwise have been the bronze age of the four is saved from that fate by Milton, who makes it golden instead.

But the rescue has a price. The "uncouth Swain" responsible for the landscape and poetic power of "Lycidas" rises in the last two lines of the poem and leaves the landscape behind, choosing instead to exercise that poetic power elsewhere in the future (186–93). And the blossoms that are hung around the brows of morning wither and die toward evening, when the only thing that flourishes on the not-so-bright cheek of the no-longer-modest Eve is a "distemper flushing." That is, the reference to *Paradise Lost* in the speech of Autumn is a reference to book 9. Adam, waiting for Eve to return from her work redressing the arrangement of the roses and myrtles, weaves something suitably autumnal,

> Of choicest Flowers a Garland to adorn
> Her Tresses, and her rural labours crown
> As Reapers oft are wont thir Harvest Queen.
>
> (9.840–42)

Eve returns, fresh from her encounter with the serpent and her fall. She tells of the encounter and its result "with Count'nance blithe . . .

/ But in her Cheek distemper flushing glow'd." Adam is "amaz'd, / Astonied . . . and Blank . . ." (9.886–93). His discomposure causes him to drop the garland, the flowers of which intimate the presence of death in the universe by shedding their petals. Moreover, Adam is speechless, a state that becomes all too common after the Fall, especially in the realm of poetry. The Miltonic achievement may have been great, but it verged on the end of poetic innocence and the advent of poetic silence in the history of English poetry.

Here as before, the biblical echoes corroborate the poem's other implications. The salient echo in "To Autumn" is of a poem in Deuteronomy that talks of Israel's falling away from its God. Specifically, the description of Autumn as "laden with fruit, and stained / With the blood of the grape" (p. 409, ll. 1–2) is a reminiscence of Deuteronomy's account of what God did for Jacob and his people: "He made him ride on the high places of the earth, and he ate the produce of the field; and he made him suck honey out of the rock, and oil out of the flinty rock. Curds from the herd, and milk from the flock, with fat of lambs and rams, herds of Bashan and goats, with the finest of the wheat—and the blood of the grape you drank" (32:13–14). But what sufficed for Jacob did not for Jeshurun who, cloyed with surfeit of divine favor, became bored and diverted himself with the all-too-predictable fall into idolatry. "But Jeshurun waxed fat, and kicked; you waxed fat, you grew thick, you became sleek; then he forsook God who made him, and scoffed at the Rock of his salvation. They stirred him to jealousy with strange gods; with abominable practices they provoked him to anger" (32:15–16). In relation to Milton, Blake's point is that God favored him with an access of authentic and divine inspiration, but he perverted or subverted that sign of favor; Milton's own strange gods and abominable practices called at least a temporary halt to authentic inspiration and originality in English poetry. The problem Blake identifies is obvious at the outset of book 9. Although he claims in his invocation that he is not committed to writing about wars, previously the sole subject of heroic poetry, Milton begins by telling his reader that the story of the Fall is at once sadder and more heroic than the account of Achilles dragging Hector's body three times around the walls of Troy (9.25–47, 13–16). By comparing his poetry to that of the classical tradition, Milton belittles his own original gift and insults its source, just as by worshipping false gods Jeshurun belittles his own good fortune and insults its divine source. What the Miltonic speaker of "To Autumn" slightly refers to as "The spirits of the air [who] live on the smells of fruit; and joy, [and

who] with pinions light, roves round / The gardens . . ." (p. 409, ll. 13–
15) is in fact The Divine Breath—the Holy Spirit itself. The mistake on
the speaker's part is foregrounded by the error in agreement: spirits
may *rove*, but only one spirit—the Holy Spirit in this case—*roves.*
The significance of the mistake is accentuated by the fact that only
one spirit *can* live on the smells in question. In book 9 of *Paradise
Lost*, the sunrise brings with it

> . . . morning Incense, when all things that breathe,
> From th' Earth's great Altar send up silent praise
> To the Creator, and his Nostrils fill
> With grateful Smell. . . .

> (9.194–97)

Despite the speaker's assertion, there is only one pinioned spirit, and
that one is the God of Jacob and Israel as described in Deuteronomy:
"Like an eagle that stirs up its nest, that flutters over its young,
spreading out its wings, catching them, bearing them on its pinions,
the LORD alone did lead him, and there was no foreign god with him"
(32:11–12).

The repetitions of the classicizing tendency give rise to delusion
and, ultimately, to solipsism. One of the implications of Blake's
pronouncement, in *There Is No Natural Religion* [b], that "the Poetic
or Prophetic character" is the means of transcending "the Philosophic
& Experimental," which is "unable to do other than repeat the same
dull round over again" (p. 3), is that such repetition can induce
"the Philosophic & Experimental" by deadening or driving out "the
Poetic or Prophetic character." The mind becomes its own place
through repetition, which deadens the ability to create new places
and heightens the palpability of the fiction of old places no longer
approachable by humans, be they the Paradise of *Paradise Lost* or
the gorgeous fictional landscape of "To the Muses." The analogue in
Deuteronomy to what Blake sees as Milton's ultimate failure to open
himself to an access of authentic originary inspiration is glimpsed
in God's reaction to Jeshurun's idolatry. Just as Miltons' classicizing
ultimately makes his mind its own place, Jeshurun's infatuation with
strange gods makes the mind its own place, because the false worship
denies access to divine inspiration and insults the bringer of such
inspiration. Of Jeshurun and his generation God says, "I will hide
my face from them, I will see what their end will be, for they are a
perverse generation, children in whom there is no faithfulness. They

have stirred me to jealousy with what is no god; they have provoked me with their idols" (32:20–21).

Blake's equivalent to Jeshurun's generation is the generation after Milton, the generation that is the subject of "To Winter." That God has hidden his face from this generation is apparent from the speaker's observation that Winter will rule "till heaven smiles, and the monster / Is driv'n yelling to his caves beneath mount Hecla" (p. 410, ll. 15–16). But from the beginning of the poem it is clear that "To Winter" enacts the fourth and final step in the sequence of poetic process, suppressing naming in favor of conferring the local habitation that goes with the name. Thus, after the formulaic apostrophe, "O Winter!" the emphasis shifts to a consciousness of Winter's "place"— its own, solipsistic place, replete with barred, "adamantine doors" (p. 410, l. 1). Keeping these doors barred helps to sustain the fictions of the philosophic and experimental that privilege Winter's solip- sistic repetitions and secure his "dark / Deep-founded habitation" (p. 410, ll. 2–3).

The North is the place of Winter's "habitation." The references to "cliffs," "storms," and "mount Hecla" (p. 410, ll. 13, 15, 16) suggest Iceland, the site of Mount Hecla and numerous steep volcanic cliffs, located in the stormy North Atlantic. Iceland is also the place of composition for the Norse Sagas and Eddas, written in the framework of Norse mythology, just as the *Iliad* and *Odyssey* are written in the framework of classical mythology. As Blake knew from read- ing Bryant and Mallet, Norse mythology was considered a debased and confused, if simplified, version of classical mythology. Thus the solipsistic place of Winter is one where the classicizing tendency has caused mythology to move yet one step further from the inspired, Hebraic original. The Arctic winter is as far from the warmth of the sun as it is possible to be—one could move no further from the sun that symbolizes the inspired access to authentic originality in the Hebraic tradition. In Ezekiel's account, God may have clothed Israel with embroidered cloth, fine linen, and silk. But in Winter's realm, "his hand / Unclothes the earth, and freezes up frail life" (p. 410, ll. 11–12).

Winter's realm is the place of Thomson, Gray, and Collins, and perhaps also the place of Macpherson and Chatterton. As Gleckner notes, Blake would have found winter, tyranny, and Mount Hecla already linked in the "Winter" section of Thomson's *The Seasons*.[46] By having Winter preside from a "seat upon the cliffs" inaccessible to "the mariner" (p. 410, l. 13) caught in a storm below, Blake does (*pace* Gleckner)[47] bring the westering of poetic genius to its terminus in this northern locale, since the role of Winter evokes the Milton familiar to Gray and Collins proclaim the decline that has come with the westering. In "The Progress of Poesy," Gray describes Milton as someone who, like Winter, looks down on the world. From the height of his sublimity, Milton flew "Upon the seraph-wings of ecstasy, / The secrets of the abyss to spy." Milton's place is explicitly what Winter's is implicitly—a throne: "The living throne, the sapphire-blaze, / Where angels tremble while they gaze." And, as Gray views it, Milton's place is unattainable by any that come to it after him, just as Winter's place is unattainable by the mariner. Gray's Milton "shall mount and keep his distant way / Beyond the limits of a vulgar fate. . . ."[48] For Collins, the trope of Milton looking down, like Blake's Winter, from a throne unattainable by any mortal that comes after and comes to that throne, is even more explicit than it is for Gray. In his "Ode on the Poetical Character," Collins places Milton's seat in Eden itself, "High on some cliff, to Heaven up-piled, / Of rude access, of prospect wild. . . ." Access is interdicted by "holy genii," and even if it were not, the implication is clear that Collins himself feels unable to attempt the Miltonic eminence, in order to equal Miltonic eminence. With the conviction that the bliss attendant upon divine inspiration was exclusively Milton's among his near-precursors, Collins confesses, "My trembling feet his guiding steps pursue; / In vain. . . ."[49]

The case for Winter as the place of Macpherson and Chatterton is more tenuous. Both poets reacted to the classicizing tendency by invoking a northern, nativist alternative, with the assumption that the best way to present this alternative, was to *forge* that nativist alternative, Macpherson in his Ossianic sagas and Chatterton in his fictive fifteenth-century ballads and "tragedies." To call Macpherson and Chatterton forgers is not to belittle their poetry, but to point to a pun deeply latent in the description of Winter's realm—it is, in the metallurgical sense of the term, a *forged* place, with its "adamantine doors," "iron car," storm-confining chains, and "ribbed steel" armor (p. 410, ll. 1, 4, 6, 7). Forgery, in the dual sense of fabricating metals and fabricating literature, is a necessary evil in the realm of Winter, which is also the realm into which Blake was born. Los's means for passing through "the Furnaces of affliction" (p. 256, pl. 96.35) is his own furnace, which he uses in the task of creating the system that helps him to identify all human forms. The system Los creates by means of his furnace, anvil, and hammer is in its own right a forgery, but it is his forgery, and recognizable by him as what it is and no more. Los proclaims, "I will not Reason & Compare: my business is to Create." And so he does, stamping "around the Anvil, beating blows of stern despair" (p. 153, pl. 10.20–21, 24).

The biblical echoes in "To Winter," far from reinforcing the despair of the poem's surface, are hopeful. Winter's uncreating darkness may mark the nadir of poetic originality and the furthest attenuation of the inspiration arising from the Hebraic tradition, but it also marks a limit, beyond which things must improve, whether by the repetition of the seasons or by some external means. Conditions anticipating the latter are built subtly into the poem. The description of Winter's "*dark / Deep*-founded habitation" echoes Genesis: "The earth was without form and void, and *darkness* was upon the face of the *deep;* and the spirit of God was moving over the face of the waters (1:2; my emphasis). The status quo will obtain in Blake's poem "till heaven smiles, and the monster / Is driv'n yelling to his caves beneath mount Hecla." The biblical analogue of heaven smiling is what happens to alleviate the darkness upon the face of the deep. "And God said, 'Let there be light'; and there was light. And God saw that the light was good . . ." (1:3–4).

The way that this action becomes heaven smiling is through Blake's understanding of how Hebraic metaphor operates here and throughout Genesis. Darkness in the uncreated universe is implicitly likened to darkness or unhappiness upon a face ("*face* of the deep . . . *face* of the waters"). The bringing of light begins the creation of that universe, reversing its condition of darkness or unhappiness to one of lightness or happiness, the common facial expression for which is a smile. Creation smiles; God sees that his work is good and smiles. For glosses one might recall Lowth's contention that in the Bible "a principal use of metaphors is to illustrate the subject by a tacit comparison," as well as the conclusion to *There Is No Natural Religion* [b] ("Therefore God becomes as we are, that we may be as he is" [p. 3]) and the question posed in "The Tyger" of *Songs of Experience*" ("Did he smile his work to see?" [p. 25, l. 19]).

Conclusion: The Middle Ground

The biblical echoes are seconded at a distance by the outcome of Thomson's *Winter*: "The Storms of WINTRY TIME will quickly pass, / And one unbounded SPRING encircle All."[50] But it must be emphasized that Thomson's vision occupies a sort of middle ground, opening on what comes after Winter and before "unbounded SPRING," or the paradisiacal return of the Last Judgment. This middle ground is very much the place of the rest of *Poetical Sketches* after "To Winter." Indeed, it is the middle ground that Blake's entire *ouevre* occupies until the end of *Jerusalem,* where "unbounded SPRING" is enacted rather than proclaimed:

> Circumscribing & Circumcising the
> excrementitious
> Husk & Covering into Vacuum evaporating revealing the
> lineaments of Man
> Driving outward the Body of Death in an Eternal Death
> & Resurrection
> Awaking it to Life among the Flowers of Beulah. . . .
>
> (pl. 98.18–21)

The two poems following "To Winter" underscore the notion that the remainder of the volume rests on such middle ground. Both poems are situated between night and day, a recurrent motif throughout *Poetical Sketches.* The speaker of "To the Evening Star" enjoins Venus to approach "Now, while the sun rests on the mountains" (p. 410, l. 2). But the notion that the sun rests calls its movement, let alone the direction, into question. The evening star can also be the morning star. Like "To Spring," "To the Evening Star" is a record of the speaker's desires, not of their fulfillment. Such is also the case in "To Morning," apparently addressed to the morning star, who is enjoined to "Awake the dawn that sleeps in heaven" (p. 41, l. 3).

The confusion of the middle ground is in some measure a Miltonic legacy, which tempers the brilliant light of prophetic inspiration with the shadows of the classicizing tendency to create the twilight that poetry must inhabit until Milton overcomes his confusion, allowing his posterity in its turn to overcome confusion. Blake seizes upon the quality of twilight grey in "Song" ("When early morn walks forth in sober grey") and "Contemplation" (" 'Tis contemplation, daughter of the grey Morning!" [p. 416, l. 1; p. 442]), fully cognizant of Milton's contrary uses of the trope in "Lycidas" and book 4 of *Paradise Lost.* In "Lycidas," "the still morn went out with Sandals gray" signals the conclusion of Lycidas's apotheosis (187). In *Paradise Lost* evening approaches, "and Twilight gray / Had in her sober Livery all things clad . . ." (4.598–99).

The final movement beyond the poetic twilight cannot begin until Blake's Milton has struggled with and subdued his perverse tendencies at the "streams, of Arnon / Even to Mahanaim . . . (p. 112, pl. 19.6–7). This allusion to Jacob wrestling with the "man," who delivers a coerced blessing, points to the substance of the blessing itself; "Your name shall no more be called Jacob, but Israel, for you have striven with God and with men, and have prevailed." Jacob calls the place Peniel, saying, "For I have seen God face to face, and yet my life is preserved" (Genesis 32:24–30). It is not until this point in *Milton*, some twenty-one years after *Poetical Sketches*, that the fall described in "To Autumn" and "To Winter" is reversed and authentic Hebraic originality is restored as a possibility.

As Gleckner observes, *Poetical Sketches* "is the genesis of poetry at once conventional and radically expansive in its imaginative manipulations of conventionality."[51] The goal of these manipulations is to reattain the originality that precedes conventionally by invoking "the Sublime of the Bible," as Blake terms it in the preface to *Milton*. Such originality is the work of a lifetime, whether the lifetime be that of Moses, Isaiah, Jesus, or Milton. From the very outset, Blake made such originality the work of his lifetime too.

Notes

Much of the research for, and some of the actual writing of, this essay were done under the auspices of an NEH Summer Seminar for College Teachers, directed by Professor Joseph Anthony Wittreich, Jr., and held at the Huntington Library during the summer of 1983. I am extremely grateful to Professor Wittreich for his kind and astute guidance, and to the other members of the seminar for their support and suggestions.

1. John Thomas Smith, *Nollekens and His Times,* 2 vols. (London: Henry Colburn, 1828), 2:454. See also Alexander Gilchrist, *Life of William Blake,* 2nd ed., ed. Ruthven Todd (1880. Reprint. London: J. M. Dent, 1942), 241–55; Arthur Symons, *William Blake* (1907. Reprint. London: Jonathan Cape, 1928), 216–20; Northrop Frye, *Fearful Symmetry* (1949. Reprint. Princeton: Princeton Univ. Press, 1969), 4–13.

2. See Michael Phillips, "William Blake and the 'Unincreasable Club': The Printing of *Poetical Sketches,*" *Bulletin of the New York Public Library* 80 (1976): 6–18, esp. 13.

3. Robert F. Gleckner, *Blake's Prelude: "Poetical Sketches"* (Baltimore: The Johns Hopkins Univ. Press, 1982), 153, concludes that Blake did not write the Advertisement but does not propose any candidate in his place.

4. For a discussion of the consensus esthetic of the late eighteenth century and Blake's opposition to it, see Morris Eaves, *William Blake's Theory of Art* (Princeton: Princeton Univ. Press, 1982), 92–96, 124–27.

5. Gleckner, 138, notes that Blake "didn't need Thomas Tyrwhitt's appendix to his 1778 edition of Chatterton's *Miscellanies* to convince him that Rowley was a fiction, however magnificently so. More to the point, though, was Blake's reasonably quick sense of the inadequacies of Chatterton's (and Macpherson's) capacities to their visionary conceptions. Just as the use of oil by painters 'became a fetter to genius,' so biblical-prophetic vision was, finally, hidden behind a mannered facade. . . ."

6. For an integration of the verbal and the visual treatments of the "door" into one of Blake's illuminated works, see David E. Latané, Jr., "The Door into *Jerusalem*," *Romanticism Past and Present* 7.2 (1983): 17–26.

7. Harold Bloom, *Poetry and Repression: Revisionism from Blake to Stevens* (New Haven: Yale Univ. Press, 1976), 46–47, notes that "Blake, even more than Nietzsche, is a master of creative parody. . . ."

8. Northrop Frye, *Anatomy of Criticism: Four Essays* (1957. Reprint. Princeton: Princeton Univ. Press, 1971), 308–12, defines the "anatomy," or Menippean satire, in terms that are fortuitous for a reading of *Poetical Sketches* as well as for *the Marriage of Heaven and Hell*, the more usual exemplar of Blakean "anatomy." For example, "The Menippean satire deals less with people as such than with mental attitudes" (309). This subject focus is characteristic of *Poetical Sketches*, as is "The short form of Menippean satire . . . usually a dialogue or colloquy, in which the dramatic interest is in a conflict of ideas rather than of character" (310).

9. *The Complete Poetry and Prose of William Blake*, ed. David V. Erdman, comm. Harold Bloom, rev. ed. (Garden City, N.Y.: Anchor-Doubleday, 1982), 846. All quotations from Blake will be to this edition, and will appear in the text of the essay by page and line or plate and line numbers.

10. See M. H. Abrams, *The Mirror and the Lamp: Romantic Theory and the Critical Tradition* (1953. Reprint. New York: Norton, 1958), 8–14, 21–26.

11. Eaves, 64.

12. Eaves, 78.

13. Jerome J. McGann, *The Romantic Ideology: A Critical Investigation* (Chicago: Univ. of Chicago Press, 1983), 71. Eaves implicitly agrees "to de-historicize Romantic Poetry by refusing to accept its special, self-determined limits."

14. See Harold Fisch, *Jerusalem and Albion: The Hebraic Factor in Seventeenth-Century Literature* (London: Routledge & Kegan Paul, 1964), chs. 2–4, 24–62.

15. William Warburton, *The Divine Legation of Moses Demonstrated*, 2nd ed., 2 vols. (London: Fletcher Gyles, 1738–41), 2:150.

16. Robert Lowth, *Lectures on the Sacred Poetry of the Hebrews,* tr. G. Gregory, 2nd ed. (1787. Reprint. Boston: Buckingham, 1815), 78. Although the first English translation of Lowth's *Lectures* did not appear until the first edition of Joseph Johnson in 1787, the Latin original was in print from 1753 onward. Blake could have known Lowth's work directly, if he had sufficient Latin to read the original, or he could have known the work second-hand, through someone with a classical education, such as Mathew or others of that *salon*.

17. Gleckner, 31.

18. Warburton 2:7 150–51. An interesting, recent extension of Warburton's insight is provided by Clifford Siskin. "Personification and Community: Literary Change in the Mid and Late Eighteenth Century," *Eighteenth-Century Studies* 15.4 (1982): 371–401, esp. 379. Implicit in Warburton's comments is the notion that knowledge of the arcana that arise from the process of personification is an essential prerequisite for full participation in the life of the *polis*. Such knowledge is the basis of a distinction between the *aristoi* and the *hoi-polloi*. Siskin, 39, finds the same notion to be operative in Augustan England. "The Mob . . . can be shut out. Thus personification is an essential tool in creating the Augustan configuration of communities. . . ." Blake questions such a notion of priestcraft and oratorical manipulation, as does Jacob Bryant, *A New System, or an Analysis of Ancient Mythology*, 3 pts. in 5 vols. (London: T. Payne, 1774–76). Bryant terms Greek mythology, which rests on the basis of personifications such as those recounted by Warburton, "a vast assemblage of obscure traditions. . . . A great deal of this intelligence has been derived to us from the Poets; by which means it has been rendered still more extravagant and strange" (l:xvii). Blake engraved plates for

Bryant's book. Lowth, 90–91, comments on the natural community of the Hebrews, a function of their isolation from other cultures because of their religion and their livelihood as shepherds. If, as Cowper says in *The Task* (1785), God made the country and man made the town, there is an interesting distinction to be observed between the natural and God-created Hebrew community and the artificial and man-created Greek community.

19. See Jacques Derrida, *L'Écriture et la différence* (Paris: Editions du Seuil, 1967), 314. "Always already" is the accepted translation of Derrida's *toujours déjà*.

20. See Lowth, 280.

21. William Duff, *An Essay on Original Genius and Its Various Modes of Exertion in Philosophy and the Fine Arts, Particularly in Poetry*, ed. John L. Mahoney (1767. Reprint. Gainesville, Flor.: Scholars' Facsimiles and Reprints, 1964), 143, 277.

22. James Beattie, *Essays on Poetry and Music, as They Affect the Mind; on Laughter and Ludicrous Composition; on the Usefulness of Classical Learning*, 3rd ed., corr. (London: E. and C. Dilly; Edinburgh: W. Creech, 1779), 234, 247, 242–43.

23. James Beattie, *Of Memory and Imagination, in Dissertations Moral and Critical* (London: W. Strahan, T. Cadell, and W. Creech, 1783), 157, 159.

24. John Aikin, *An Essay on the Application of Natural History to Poetry* (London: J. Johnson, 1777), 1, 7–9.

25. *Edward Young's Conjectures on Original Composition*, ed. Edith J. Morley (1759. Reprint. London: Longmans, Green & Co., 1918), 11. This passage is also the source of Young's injunction to "imitate not the *Composition*, but the *Man*," a principle that Blake adopts after purifying it of any association with Homer.

26. See Edmund Husserl, *The Crisis of European Sciences and Transcendental Phenomenology*, tr. David Carr (Evanston: Northwestern Univ. Press, 1970), 48–59.

27. See Jacob Bronowski, *Science and Human Values*, rev. ed. (1965. Reprint. New York: Harper and Row [Perennial Library], 1972), 38–40.

28. I have discussed this *aperçu* of Blake's in "Blake and Newton: Argument as Art, Argument as Science" *Studies in Eighteenth-Century Culture* 10 (1980): 205–26. Gödel's demonstration appears in *On Formally Undecidable Propositions* (1931. Reprint. New York: Basic Books, 1962).

29. The illocutionary-perlocutionary distinction arises with J. L. Austin, *How to Do Things with Words* (Oxford: Oxford Univ. Press, 1954). I draw my discussion from John R. Searle, *Speech Acts: An Essay in the Philosophy of Language* (Cambridge: Cambridge Univ. Press, 1969), 22–26, 45–46.

30. Michael Ferber, *The Social Vision of William Blake* (Princeton: Princeton Univ. Press, 1985), 167, makes much the same point: "As one grows in spiritual power one wastes no more time on the past. The past is the realm of the dead, and our serious spiritual business must go forward without reverence or nostalgia. Blake calls the entire fallen world "Eternal Death" in part because it is determined by the dead events of the past and their traces in our memories.

31. Jacques Derrida, *Speech and Phenomena, and Other Essays on Husserl's Theory of Signs*, tr. David B. Allison (Evanston: Northwestern Univ. Press, 1973), 32.

32. See John Dryden, *To My Dear Friend Mr. Congreve, on His Comedy Call'd The Double-Dealer*, in *The Poems of John Dryden*, 2 vols., ed. James Kinsley (Oxford: Clarendon, 1958), 2:852. See also Walter Jackson Bate, *The Burden of the Past and the English Poet* (Cambridge, Mass.: Belknap, 1970), 3, 15–18.

33. Gleckner, 2.

34. See my "Blake, Freemasonry, and the Builder's Task," *Mosaic* 17.3 (Summer 1984): 35–57.

35. John Milton, *Paradise Regained* 4.331–42, in *John Milton: Complete Poems and Major Prose*, ed. Merritt Y. Hughes (New York: Odyssey, 1957), 523. All subsequent quotations from Milton will be to this edition, and will appear in the text of the essay.

36. Ferber, 180–81, discusses the relationship between spatialization and the reification of time as an exercise in political authority based in history. The discussion leads him to a provocative comparison of Hebraic and Greek ideas of history: "Historical time, for the Hebrew, was not an even-flowing medium containing more or fewer events, but a function of events themselves, their "occurrence rather than their stand of measure. . . . Yahweh revealed himself by deeds, not by ideas, and these deeds are absorbed into the people of Israel the way the actions of our life, and not our numerical age, define our sense of who we are. Qualitative or psychological time is more important than 'objective' (really spatial) time."

37. See Margaret Ruth Lowery, *Windows of the Morning: A Critical Study of William Blake's "Poetical Sketches," 1783*, Yale Studies in English, no. 93 (New Haven: Yale Univ. Press, 1940), 100. The salient text from Spenser is found in Edmund Spenser, *The Faerie Queene*, ed. Thomas P. Roche, Jr., with C. Patrick O'Donnell, Jr. (New Haven: Yale Univ. Press, 1978), 92.

38. See Martin Buber, *I and Thou*, tr. Ronald Gregor Smith (New York: Charles Scribner & Sons, 1937), 408. See also Philip Wheelwright, *Metaphor and Reality* (Bloomington: Indiana Univ. Press, 1968), 150: "in praying a worshipper speaks as if to a living presence in direct address, and by speaking to it he tends to conceive it in a certain way, as a semi-personal being who can hear and respond." Siskin, 379, calls metaphor "the trope of desire."

39. *The Faerie Queene*, 1042.

40. See Gleckner, 148.

41. See Michael J. Tolley, "Blake's Songs of Spring," in *William Blake: Essays in Honour of Sir Geoffrey Keynes*, ed. Morton D. Paley and Michael Phillips (Oxford: Clarendon, 1973), 96–115, esp. 99.

42. There is an earlier reference to lovesickness in 2:5. That verse, coupled with the following one, may provide a source for Blake's rendering of the female's "languish'd head" in "To Spring." The female voice of the Song of Solomon exclaims, "Sustain me with raisins, refresh me with apples; for I am sick of love. O that his left hand were under my head, and that his right hand embraced me!" (2:5–6).

Another possible source for these ostensibly solomonic echoes is Milton, who is clearly one of the earliest influences on Blake's poetry—by Blake's own admission. At the conclusion of the fourth section of *Animadversions upon the Remonstrant's Defence against Smectymnuus* (1641) (*The Complete Prose Works of John Milton*, 8 vols., ed. Don M. Wolfe, et al., [New Haven: Yale Univ. Press, 1953-], 1:706–707) Milton implores Christ in a manner highly reminiscent of the manner in which Blake's speaker implores Spring:

> [F]or who shall prejudice thy all-governing will? seeing the power of thy grace is not put away with the primitive times, as fond and faithless men imagine, but thy Kingdome is now at hand, and thou standing at the dorre. Come forth out of thy Royall Chambers, O Prince of all the Kings of the earth, put on the visible roabes of thy imperiall Majesty, take up the unlimited Scepter which thy Almighty Father hath bequeath'd thee; for now the voice of thy Bride calls thee, and all creatures sigh to bee renew'd.

43. Gleckner, 64.

44. Gleckner, 66, notes the Spenserian echoes, with their allusions to the Apollonian myth.

45. See Lowery, 85; Harold Bloom, *Blake's Apocalypse: A Study in Poetic Argument* (1963. Reprint. Ithaca: Cornell Univ. Press, 1971), 15–16. Gleckner, 67, is not persuaded.

46. Gleckner, 73, 175n. The salient lines of *Winter* are 886–87, 897.

47. Gleckner (73, 175n) disagrees with the position taken by Geoffrey H. Hartman in "Blake and the 'Progress of Posey,'" in *William Blake: Essays for S. Foster Damon,* ed. Alvin H. Rosenfeld (Providence: Brown Univ. Press, 1969), 57–68. However, I do not agree with Gleckner that "Hartman's view of Winter as 'the Genius of the North' (Ossian, et al.) . . . confounds the normal westering of the poetic spirit with a North-South movement." Given the southern locale in which Hebraic poetry originates, and given poetry's subsequent movement westward and northward—from Judea to Greece and Rome to England—the northward movement is integral with the westward movement from the start.

48. *The Progress of Poesy: A Pindaric Ode,* 95–123, in *The Complete Poems of Thomas Gray,* ed. H. W. Starr and J. R. Hendrickson (Oxford: Clarendon, 1966), 16–17.

49. *Ode on the Poetical Character* 3.55–76, in *The Poems of Gray and Collins,* 4th ed., ed. Austin Lane Poole (London: Oxford Univ. Press, 1948), 256–57.

50. *Winter,* 1068–69, from *The Seasons,* in *The Poetical Works of James Thomson,* ed. J. Logie Robertson (1908. Reprint. New York: Oxford Univ. Press, 1961), 289.

51. Gleckner, 157.

Troping the Seasons: Blake's Helio-Poetics and the "Golden Load"

Thomas A. Vogler

Nature never set forth the earth in so rich
tapistry as divers poets have done. . . .
Her world is brasen, the Poets only deliver a
golden. (Sidney)

How many bards gild the lapses of time!
(Keats)

He prophets most who bilks the best. (Joyce)

I am that Shadowy Prophet. . . . (Blake)

At the threshold of William Blake's poetic career we find a small, much-mined volume of poems called *Poetical Sketches* (1783). His only work published in conventional letterpress, it begins with a little poem of beginnings, "To Spring," followed by three other poems addressed in turn to the other seasons. On the face of it these poems would seem to be eminently simple and comprehensible as representations of a human voice, changing and developing in an on-going relationship with an external Nature, yet like the rest of the volume they are unreadable—save in the most banal sense—unless we locate them in a context of discourse mapped by codes of literary practices. Considered as the clearly imitative and derivative work of a late-eighteenth-century adolescent, bringing them under the reins of interpretive control seems at first to pose few problems.[1] But as Blake's reputation for originality and creative genius has grown in the last few decades, the situation has become more problematic. How can the moment of origin for an "original" genius occur in a belated scene of copying or imitation? A re-reading of origins is clearly called for, and interpreters of Blake have answered the call.

Several lines of approach offer themselves to Blake scholars who confront the *Poetical Sketches.* One of the most popular of these has been dismissed by Robert Gleckner as the "anticipative fallacy" (*Prelude* 2), an apt phrase for those like the early Harold Bloom, who maintains that "at an astonishingly early age, Blake has grasped in sure potential all the fundamentals of his great program and theme" (*Apocalypse* 17). Even Gleckner cannot resist anticipation's power when he comes to Blake's season poems, where his goal is "to demonstrate the continuity of conception [Blake] inaugurated in these early poems" (*Prelude* 74), which for him embody a theme "clearly anticipative of Blake's states of Innocence and Experience . . . [the theme] anticipates Los the creator and Urizen, the destructive, tyrannical 'god of this world.'" (*Prelude* 63–64). Stuart Peterfreund shares this view, claiming that these poems signal "from the very outset" what Blake made "the work of his lifetime," *viz.*: "to reattain the originality that precedes conventionality" (701).

Most critics do not limit themselves to looking forward, but Janus-like look backward also to Blake's "sources." By prowling through the Bible, works of Spenser and Shakespeare, various Elizabethan songs, Milton, Thomson, Young, Colllins, Gray, Beattie and the Wartons, Chatterton and the Ossianic prose poems, one can collect an impressive flood of words, phrases and images that reappear in the *Poetical Sketches.* But this harvest of "sources" and "borrowings" then begins to suggest a Blake who sounds more and more like his precursors—not an origin but an echo. Fortunately, through the miracle of interpretive ingenuity, there are ways to show that the more he sounds like them, the most different he is from them. For example, Geoffrey Hartman can read the last two lines of "To Winter" ("till heaven smiles, and the monster / Is driv'n yelling to his caves beneath mount Hecla") as deliberately conventional, so that they become in his oxymoronic formulation "an inspired period cliché" (204). And Gleckner finds Blake "amid the remnants of conventional, even hackneyed, phraseology and diction" engaged in "ostensible apishness" which nevertheless manages somehow to transform "the verbal and imagistic traditions he inherited" into "vision inspired and articulated by true art" (*Prelude* 68, 12). Peterfreund, while disagreeing with Gleckner on a number of localized issues, is in basic agreement with a mode of reading that argues for Blake's "authentic originality" (686) by tracing his borrowings and echoes. It would seem that Blake has anticipated Borges' Pierre Menard, whose "*visible* work" is unexceptionable and conventional, but whose "other work . . . perhaps the most significant of our time" is a "subterranean" project "to produce a few pages which would coincide—word for word and line for line—with those of Miguel de Cervantes. . . . Cervantes' text and Menard's are verbally identical, but the second is almost infinitely richer. (More ambiguous, his detractors will say, but ambiguity is richness)" (38–42). The technique of the "deliberate anachronism" allows him to trope his precursor; it is a technique that "fills the most placid works with adventure" and "has enriched . . . the halting and rudimentary art of reading" (44) that concerns us here, as would-be miners of textual riches.

Blake's text appears in a context where copying and allusion, or "imitation," was not only an expected first stage in any artistic career, but an essential part of the poetic enterprise as an accepted style or mode of composition.[2] For Blake to offer us "echoes and themes from the Bible, the classics, and even the high odic tradition of the eighteenth century" is not simply "poetic diction in search of its truth" (Hartman 194) but poetry in search of a *context,* finding one in an echo chamber where it is impossible to echo the Bible directly without also echoing a style or mode of echoing in which the original source of sound has long been lost. The task of the reader is similarly difficult, if s/he wants to hear the voice of a controlling and self-contained individual poet escaping all the forces that undermine and challenge his individuality. How can we grant Blake a distance from the conventions he seems to invoke, granting him that ORIGIN-ality that means being present at the time and place of a *new* beginning? There is obviously more at stake here than a reading of a few individual poems if we are seeking the birth of an "original" poetic career, one which signals the coming of the new era of Romanticism. To seek this understanding is to attempt to find in a poetic gesture the rebirth of language itself, an act comparable to the originary event that might have generated the first human utterance; and since individual words can do their work only in a field of discursivity, we must locate Blake's work in a completely new context rather than as a moment in a series that is governed by prior organization and differentiation. We must do this in spite of the fact that the discourse of Romanticism was not yet in place (though it is for us, hence we may well bring it with us *to* Blake), and in spite of the fact that the external form or surface of Blake's work presents itself to us in a form which Hartman can call a "splendid pastiche" (194). Splendid or not, a "pastiche" is a work that imitates the style of prior works, a mode of organization where originality is neither valued nor possible. Finally, what if a text represents itself to us as an echo of a series of echoes of an originary voice, each echo invoking the master-trope of irony, to distance itself from the naive presumption of saying something new?

There is an uncanny and unacknowledged similarity between the logic of this strategy and that of many enthusiasts for the "postmodern"in the 1980s. I am thinking here, for example, of the frequently cited discussion of Fredric Jameson that posits "the well-nigh universal practice today of what may be called pastiche" as the "mesmerizing new aesthetic mode" of postmodernism ("Cultural Logic" 64, 68). For Jameson "pastiche" is intended as an aesthetic of quotations pushed to the limits in a limbo of stylistic diversity and heterogeneity without any universal norm or original to react against. In a statement that sounds as fitting for the 1780s as for the 1980s, he claims: "All that is left is to imitate dead styles, to speak through the masks and with the voices of the styles in the imaginary museum. But this means that contemporary or post-modernist art is going to be about art itself in a new kind of way; even more, it means that one of its essential messages will involve the necessary failure of art and the aesthetic, the failure of the new, the imprisonment of the past" ("Consumer Society" 115–16). Letting go of the fantasy of an "originality that precedes conventionality" (Peterfreund 701), the poststructuralist critic replaces origins and essences with the universality of conventional codes in which the superior works of art will be those that acknowledge their semiotic nature, reflecting on an "exposing" the very system that allows them to function.[3] Even though a critic like Hal Foster can employ the term "pastiche" in a politically pejorative sense, as elitist in its allusions and manipulative in its clichés (representing a co-opted avant-garde that pacifies the consumer), he too sees all postmodern art as art that is about signs. For him that art is "radical" or "critical" which functions as a critique of the codes and signs it deploys, calling our attention to the cultural and political practices that it resists by conspicuous imitation and citation.

The problem here, as with the eighteenth-century practice, is how to tell those works that are "resisting" the system from those that are comfortably operating within its pluralistic accommodations— those that *force* their readers and viewers to perceive them as culturally constructed objects and to recognize the ideological interests that regulate semiosis. This is even more difficult if we agree with Derrida that all language acts are by definition conventional, dependent on "iterability" and "citationality"—"identifiable in a way as 'citation'" because they function only by conforming "to an iterable model" (*Margins* 320).

> This is the possibility on which I wish to insist: the possibility of extraction and of citational grafting which belongs

to the structure of every mark, spoken or written, and
which constitutes every mark as writing even before and
outside every horizon of semiolinguistic communication;
as writing, that is, as a possibility of functioning cut off,
at a certain point, from its 'original' meaning and from
its belonging to a saturable and constraining context. . . .
This citationality, duplication, or duplicity, this iterability
of the mark is not an accident or an anomaly, but is that
(normal/abnormal) without which a mark could no longer
even have a so-called 'normal' functioning. What would a
mark be that one could not cite?

(*Margins* 320–21).

Given this "possibility," Derrida insists, it is also possible that "every
sign . . . can be cited . . . thereby it can break with every given context,
and engender infinitely new contexts in an absolutely nonsaturable
fashion" (*Margins* 320). But it will therefore also be the case that any
sign will *already* be an iteration, available for a "postmodern" reading,
since "repetition, were it to change neither thing nor sign, carries
with it an unlimited power of perversion and subversion" (*Writing
and Difference* 296). Thus even the most traditional and conventional
text (if conventionality can still have degrees) can therefore be read
as a citational performance with the critical potential usually reserved
for special artists and their texts.

Morris Eaves's reading of Blake's "theory" argues for a "radical"
Blakean transformation, where he "may in some respects seem to
echo Reynolds and Opie," but in fact is "not recycling classicism but
performing a critical experiment in encoding radical romantic ideas
in an Enlightenment vocabulary."

It is fair to say that Blake parodies Enlightenment criticism
in such instances but essential to see also that the parody
is in another way true. The method involves nothing more
unusual . . . than retaining the manner of the object of
parody while altering the matter, or, more specifically,
silently shifting the grounds on which decorum rests.
Reynolds' concessions to truth for the sake of oversetting
truth are grounded in Enlightenment mimesis, Blake's
truth in romantic expression.

(158)

For Eaves the same terms can function as "mimesis" or "expression" through a shift of "grounds" which doesn't involve the *surface* of the text, which functions only as a mask. Except for its insistence on "Blake's truth," Eaves's reading here is clearly within the postmodern paradigm. We might well ask how "parody" (which is dependent on its object) can either signal or effect a shift of grounds, unless it is pushed to the Brechtian point of alienated and alienating mimesis, where dramatic gesture both represents and produces the hollow absence at the core of conventional behavior. Similar problems are found if we invoke the trope of irony, a rhetorical mask which signals a metalinguistic code which is either the most distant from the essence of an autonomous expressive subject (the *eiron* is not responsible for what he says) or the closest to it (his *personal* meaning is not determined by the conventional meanings of the words he uses). In the ironic mode only the speaker knows what he really means, and sometimes perhaps even he does not know. What we have in these approaches is a system of similarities and difference, where even the most extreme similarity is seen as superficial, while the difference claimed is radical. In the precursor text the poetic surface hides error, while in Blake it reveals truth—even if the truth it reveals is only the self-reflexive truth of its own echoic superficiality. In one case any simplicity of the surface reveals radical simplicity, but in another it proves radical complexity, a difference between " 'copies' in the negative sense" and " 'imitations' in the positive sense" (Peterfreund 691). Writing of "To the Muses," Gleckner notes "the fundamental Augustan conventionality of the diction," yet claims that "it owes virtually nothing to any poetic model and achieves a bold complexity belied by its limpid surface" (29). Even the conventional tropes of eighteenth-century verse can be transformed if we agree with Bloom, who claims that "Thomson's personifications are clear and simple," but Blake's "become actual mythmaking" (*Apocalypse* 1).

Were I to develop it here, my own interpretation of the season poems might in some ways provide a similar instance, since it would doubtless sound *like* various aspects of other readings. I do agree with the general view that these poems are early and vigorous instances of what Blake would later call "Mental Fight." But I do not find in them "the mental warfare that resurrects the crucified truth" or a "Blake" who "demands that we fly with him on his plumed wide wings to the realms of truth" (Gleckner *Prelude* 11, 13–14). To put it another way, Blake does not give us *his* "golden load" of song and truth, but rather follows in an epitomizing manner the seasonal and tropological system for producing "truth" that prevailed in the eighteenth century. One of the problems of fully appreciating parody is that we cannot understand it unless we have some minimal sense of the original. A parody *(paroidia)* is a song written alongside another song, as though in the margins or between the lines of a prior book. The qualities we associate with style or 'voice' are important for its recognition, and Blake gives a great deal of attention to qualities of voice throughout the *Sketches*. His attention is not merely to isolated nuances or repetitions of prior voices in the form of verbal echoes, but to the power and potential of those voices as they are inscribed in and practiced within a systematized code of poetic discourse—including those rhetorical techniques or strategies (such as apostrophe, use of the pentameter) that operate to create the representational effect of a "speaking voice." In the *Sketches* Blake may be read as trying on a variety of voices, not in the superficial manner that one can try on a suit of clothing, but in the manner of his advice to God: "If you have formd a Circle to go into / Go into it yourself & see how you would do" (*E* 516).

Such trials do not in every case have to be critical or ironic, even if they are self-conscious and tentative. In "L'Allegro" Milton pretends to test the Allegro mode partly to see how it would do ("These delights, if thou canst give, / Mirth with thee, I mean to live"), but also to find grounds to bid it go "hence," to trope on it in order to *turn* from it to the pleasures of the melancholy prophetic mode in "Il Penseroso." Like all poets after Milton, Blake tries both modes, but in doing so—in a poem like "Memory, hither come"—he shows that he understands how the two modes have been structured by Milton and his followers into a system, a poetic progression from the "merry notes" of the music of day to "places fit for woe; / Walking along the darken'd valley, / With silent Melancholy." Blake's "Mad Song" shows signs of discomfort with this systematic progression, representing the singer's awareness that even though the system is constituted by his own song ("My notes . . . strike the ear of night, / Make weep the eyes of day; / They make mad the roaring winds, / And with tempests, play") he can imagine no way out of a system which links his potential for song with a cyclical diurnal progression. The speaker here is caught in a tropic machine that forces him continually to "turn" his back to the illusory "comforts" of the east, the daily return of the sun and the annual return of spring and eros, in order to remain in a metaphoric night of his own making.

> I turn my back to the east,
> From whence comforts have increas'd;
> For light doth seize my brain
> With frantic pain.

The conventional seasonal invocation begins with an apostrophic address *to* the "east," with the poet figuratively turning his back to an implied audience. There is then a 'rhetorical' madness in Blake's song, where the fictive singer, while trying to turn against the system, can only turn within it. Light, whether the false light of the physical sun, or the metaphorical "light" of philosophical insight, seizes his *brain* in its epistemological grasp. The speaker here is much more like a lyrical photophobic Edward Young than the Elizabethans with whom he is so often compared. The song "How sweet I roam'd" is quite different in tone and effect, but deserves comparison on a number of points. Chief among them is that recurring shock of recognition each time we read the poem and realize that *this* poem is the "song" that is sung *in* the "golden cage," with its "golden pleasures" and its "golden wing" incapable of free poetic flight. In it we can simultaneously hear Blake singing the song, indulging in its golden pleasure, and taking the role of the Phoebus who

> loves to sit and hear me sing
> Then, laughing, sports and plays with me;
> Then stretches out my golden wing,
> And mocks my loss of liberty.

There is a complex system of poetic power at work here, in which the seductive force of a poetic mode is inextricably intertwined with the powerlessness of that mode. The poem is not merely "about" a process of entrapment, it is a formal embodiment and demonstration of entrapment in action.

The seasons poems give us a three-fold use of the word "golden" with the third instance concluding the third season, as Autumn departs leaving behind his "golden load" or harvest of song:

TO SPRING

> O deck her forth with thy fair fingers; pour
> Thy soft kisses on her bosom; and put
> Thy golden crown upon her languish'd head,
> Whose modest tresses were bound up for thee!

TO SUMMER

O thou, who passest thro' our vallies in
Thy strength, curb thy fierce steeds, allay the heat
That flames from their large nostrils! thou, O Summer,
Oft pitched'st here thy golden tent, and oft
Beneath our oaks has slept, while we beheld
With joy, thy ruddy limbs and flourishing hair.

TO AUTUMN

O Autumn, laden with fruit, and stained
With the blood of the grape, pass not, but sit
Beneath my shady roof. . . .
Sing now the lusty song of fruits and flowers.
"The narrow bud opens her beauties to
"The sun, and love runs in her thrilling veins;
"Blossoms hang round the brows of morning, and
"Flourish down the bright cheek of modest eve,
"Till clust'ring Summer breaks forth into singing,
"And feather'd clouds strew flowers round her head.
"The spirits of the air live on the smells
"Of fruit; and joy, with pinions light, roves round
"The gardens, or sits singing in the trees."
Thus sang the jolly Autumn as he sat,
Then rose, girded himself, and o'er the bleak
Hills fled from our sight; but left his golden load.

Clearly we have here some version of a "progress of poesy" that we
must understand in order to read the poem. The Spring-Summer-Fall
progression has tempted many critics to perceive a poetic alchemy in
which Blake transforms his lode of conventional material into what
Bloom calls "This 'golden load' " of lyricisim that "the departing
poet bequeaths us." Whereas "How sweet I roam'd" is for Bloom
an account of "the deceptions of nature as the responsible agent of
transition" (19), he detects in "To Autumn" "a mature harvest bard
who sings a song of fruition" (16). For Peterfreund the movement is in
the opposite direction. After starting "correctly" in "To Spring," "with
an access of authentic, Hebraic inspiration" (691, 686), the series
charts "a course of fallenness" as "the poems move from the gold of
the 'golden crown' in "To Spring" . . . to the iron of the 'adamantine
doors' in "To Winter," (691).

Gleckner's assay of Blake's golden load determines, as so many readings do, that the Spring-Summer-Autumn series is superior visionary poetry, complete in itself, representing "the imaginative achievement of oneness, fullness, and joy" (*Prelude* 69) in "a vision of what eternally exists really and unchangeably" (*Prelude* 68). At the end "Autumn flees, but only from corporeal vision" (*Prelude* 68), in a move that escapes the seasonal cycle which for Blake represents "error." Blake is thus deconstructing the "prevailing seasonal paradigm" (*Prelude* 70) and "the conventional framework of the cycle" that asserts "the comforts of a conventional rebirth of Spring to console our sense of loss in Winter . . . the very mythological construct and tradition Blake is at some pains to subvert. Time is not *the* Time" (*Prelude* 71, 73). In thus raising the question of Blake's relationship to discursive structures, and in particular to "seasonal and diurnal paradigms," Gleckner is moving toward an important context. But without reference to those seasonal and diurnal paradigms as they are embodied in such eighteenth-century works as Thomson's *Seasons*, Young's *Night Thoughts,* and Cowper's *The Task*, Gleckner is unable to perceive either the similarities or the differences that might profitably guide our attention. For example, Thomson wrote and published his "Winter" first, and held it constantly in mind through decades of composition and revision as the end-point of his complete poem on the seasons. Whatever Blake may be "subverting" in his season poems, it cannot be the "winter" that Gleckner attributes to Thomson, because Thomson's "Winter" emphatically does not assert "the comforts of a conventional rebirth of Spring" (*Prelude* 73). Rather, as Ralph Cohen shows in his discussion of a series of revisions (28), Thomson was from the beginning trying to say exactly what Gleckner attributes to Blake. In missing the point, Gleckner re-enacts the seasonal paradigm itself, ironically (for us) attributing that re-enactment to Blake, confirming thereby its continuing rhetorical and paradigmatic power. Peterfreund, although he disagrees with Gleckner's gratulant reading of the series, shares with him this complete misreading of the organizing structure of Thomson's sequence.

A more careful reading of Blake's precursors shows that the season of Winter was important for them precisely because it was the season *within* the seasons that forced a rupture of the otherwise endless cycle of the physical ratio. Winter provided the opportunity to experience the rupture of the moral sublime, in the form of a felt experience of the incommensurability between the empirical and the spiritual or rational, an experience that was occasioned by external sense yet forced a recognition of the need to transcend the limitations of external sense. Poets of the eighteenth century had already made a turn that Gleckner and others have missed. By combining the epistemology of Locke with the discoveries of Newton in the *Opticks,* the colors of Nature were perceived as "colors of rhetoric," brought closer to the realm of human language, requiring a new reading and opening the way to a new writing. The seasons could thus be read as tropes, "turns" in a rhetorical progression and a tropological curriculum in which the *absence* of color (wintry whiteness for Thomson and Cowper, the blackness of night for Young) was the final trope of insight. Thus Thomson's claim that his song called "Spring" is *painted* by Spring means that it is colored by the same "bright enchantment" that deceives those who do not have the "sage-instructed eye" which can separate the "ethereal" colors of the rainbow from the "white mingling maze" that cannot be directly perceived by the human eye or expressed in human language.[4]

The apostrophic trope that opens most poems addressed to seasons has the appearance of an authentic event, an act of power and participation. As a "turn" (*apostrophe,* turning away) from the reader to Nature, the poetic trope mimics the seasons as turns in the year, consequences of the turns in the circuit of the sun. The poet's "language *turns,* so to speak, as the earth turns" (Derrida, *Grammatology* 216). In apostrophizing Spring, Blake's opening poem turns to Spring ("our longing eyes are turned / Up to thy bright pavillions") to ask Spring to "turn / Thine angel eyes upon our western isle." For the first three seasons, natural event seems to correspond with and respond to poetic event, responsive to the pathos of human desire, until we reach Winter where "He hears me not" and, the speaker declares, "I dare not lift mine eyes"—unable to perform the turning gesture which inaugurated the re-turn of Spring. Or did it? The turn in Winter is a turn in the circuit of communication which emphasizes a *break* in that circuit, and it raises the possibility that the turning eyes and voice in the apostrophic discourse were united only in a contingent and illusory union.

Blake's season poems need to be read in the context of a self-conscious use of figurative language in the interests of a verbal self-negation that marks so much of the poetry of his precursors. This self negation leads them to locate their vantage-point in Winter, on the metatropological level of irony: Though the poems continue to use what Hayden White calls the "naive tropes" of metaphor and metonymy, by using them self-consciously, they can evoke a difference that is expressed as the non-expressible, represented as the non-representable. The "natural" seasonal turn to winter thus becomes a rhetorical turn to the trope of irony and difference, a turn away from the naive tropes of resemblance and contiguity that produce an illusory metaphoric golden load as the fruit of the union of Logos and Eros. This turn anticipates Eliot's world-weary equivalent of Blake's "Mad Song" in a *Waste Land* that experiences April as "the cruelest month" and tries to turn its back to the East, as well as the ironically reductive humor of Burns's ode to spring in *The Merry Muses of Caledonia:*

> Latona's Sun looks liquorish on
> Dame Nature's Grand impetus
> Till his pego rise, then westward flies
> To roger Madame Thetis

If we return not to Gleckner's reading of Blake's seasons, we can see more clearly some of the problems in his claim that Blake produced a "vision" that "is complete with the end of 'To Autumn' in a totality inherent in and symbolized by Autumn's 'golden load.'" The negative truth that Gleckner attributes to that vision is Blake's discovery of the error of a contrary vision based on the paradigm of the natural cycle. This "truth" requires a final turn "To Winter," and our reading of it as "a spectrous parody, in proper sequence, of Spring-Summer-Autumn" (70). Such a reading, while claiming to define a Blake different from his seasonal precursors, unwittingly locates him in a prior discourse of Truth already inscribed in a rhetorical system especially designed to produce that Truth, so that interpreters can recognize its familiar iterability at the same time they insist that it comes forth with the novelty and freshness of a new spring. In this system the same Truth needs the same error, time after time, and cannot exist without it. The cycle of Truth ("coming and going . . . united") is inseparable from the cycle of Error. The Truth that language can express *in* sensory images is the inability of language tied to sensory images to express the Truth.

Readers can find this message in Blake's poems *not* because they are different from the tropological curriculum of other season poems, but because they are in fact so much like them in general outline and technique. Blake is not merely echoing words and phrases, or "borrowing" whatever he finds attractive or useful; he is fully engaged with a rhetorical machine designed for producing the effect of Truth, a machine that parallels and doubles the cyclical turn of the seasons even as it presumes to produce a difference from that cycle. No doubt Blake was trying on the seasonal paradigm, going into and repeating its progression to see how he would do, and to see how *it* would do. I imagine him therefore in a much more problematic and interesting situation, feeling strongly the tug of what Vico called "sensory topics," the libidinal tug of the East, and of the sun continually rising as "the unique, irreplaceable, natural referent, around which everything must turn, toward which everything must turn" (Derrida, *Margins* 251). But I imagine Blake also feeling the counter-tug, of the sun as the paradigm of metaphor, the sensory sun which may exist in poetic discourse only as metaphor, that heliotropism which is both a movement toward the sun and the turning movement of the natural sun that *sets* each day as surely as it rises. Blake ambivalently contemplates this ambiguous "golden load," left behind by his troping precursors and by the ever-westering sun. Then he too flees from our sight, leaving a rhetorical "golden load" for our assay.

Made in the Shade

Sol tibi signa dabit. solem quis dicere falsum audeat? (VERGIL)

Begin, ephebe, by perceiving the idea
Of this invention, this invented world,
The inconceivable idea of the sun. (STEVENS)

OUI, l'Ombre ici déjà est en pouvoir. (PONGE)

One of the most widely shared views of the eighteenth century was that civilization and the arts flourish best, and could only have started, in a temperate zone.[5] In an imagined golden age before the fall, when the ecliptic and equatorial circles coincided, this special relationship with the sun would have been perpetually maintained in certain favored equinoctial areas where sowing and harvest could follow their own rhythm. With the tilting of the earth's axis the ecliptic became oblique, and the alternations of the seasons began.

[W]hile the Earth was in its first and natural Posture, in a more easy and regular disposition to the Sun, that had also another respective Train of Consequences, whereof

> one of the first, and that which we are most concern'd
> in at present, was, that it made a perpetual, Æquinox
> or Spring to all the World, all the Parts of the Year had
> one and the same Tenor, Face and Temper; there was no
> Winter or Summer, Seed-Time or Harvest, but a continual
> Temperature of the Air and Verdure of the Earth. And
> this fully answers the first and fundamental Character
> of the Golden Age and of Paradise; and what Antiquity,
> whether Heathen or Christian, hath spoken concerning
> that perpetual Serenity and constant Spring that reign'd
> there, which in the one was accounted Fabulous, and in
> the other Hyper-bolical, we see to have been really and
> philosophically true.
>
> (Burnet I:243–44)

As an endless cycle of difference, the changing of the seasons constitutes an indexical sign (in Peirce's sense) of that primal change
from and loss of the golden age of anti-tropic stability. Whether
Christian or pagan, a seasonal poetics must find a way to locate itself
in these seasonal changes, and in a relationship with the sun, in order
to flourish and bear fruit. Thus Vergil's first *Eclogue,* in the pastoral
convention that provides the aegis for all seasonal poems, defines the
poetic place and posture as that occupied by Tityrus (*lentus in umbra,*
"relaxed in the shade"), whose special location allows uninterrupted
fertility for his crops and flocks, and the corresponding leisure for
poetic production. In this he differs markedly from Meliboeus, whose
lack of protection means he must drive his goats on an unending path,
a slave to the seasonal sun, ranging the world from the torrid deserts
of Africa to the frigid climes of England (*At nos hinc alii sitientis
ibimus Afros,* / . . . *et penitus toto divisos orbe Britannos*). Commentary
has speculated since Servius on the human identity of the absent
protector/benefactor who provides Tityrus with his creative *libertas,*
but I would like to suggest as a metaphorical alternative that the absent
benefactor is the sun, whose *absence* (as natural force and object) is
necessary to provide an artistic place of *libertas* for the free reign of
the poet's tropes.

We can see Blake's text defining a similar relationship in "To
Summer," just before the onset of the "fruitful" song of Autumn:

> Beneath out thickest shades we oft have heard
> Thy voice, when noon upon his fervid car

Rode o'er the deep of heaven; beside our springs
Sit down. . . .
Our bards are fam'd who strike the silver wire:
Our youth[s] are bolder than the southern swains:
Our maidens fairer in the sprightly dance:
We lack not songs, nor instruments of joy,
Nor echoes sweet, nor waters clear as heaven,
Nor laurel wreaths against the sultry heat.

The sun leaves Virgo near the end of August to enter Libra, where the autumnal equinox coincides with the "time" of Blake's "Autumn." Blake's "shades" here are autumnal, as the song of jolly Autumn evokes the full vegetable spectrum from spring to harvest. It is a special kind of shade conducive to poetry, the special shade of the laurel wreath, the shade of pastoral poetry that provides a situation close to but protected from nature and the sun; it is not a transitory diurnal shade, or a seasonal equinox, but a literary topos (i.e., "place") which presumes to escape the contingencies of a fallen natural world and reconstitute the qualities of the golden age before the fall. By Blake's time, as indicated in Gray's "The Progress of Poesy" (1768), the "track" of pastoral had followed the sun westward, leaving "Parnassus for the Latian plains," but also moving northward to "climes beyond the solar road" so that Shakespeare could be born "far from the sun and summer-gale." By locating Blake's inaugural poems in the context of pastoral poetic tropes we can best see his point of entry into the practice of poetry, and see his work as paradigmatic for poetry and its interpretation. Pastoral has a special place among the genres as a set of organizing and enabling conventions, and a hallowed function as the organizing genre for the progression of the poetic career. As such, part of its function is to be ostensibly left behind by the poet, while its organizing effects, though hidden, continue to determine the fate of poetry. "What is the pastoral convention, then, if not the eternal separation between the mind that distinguishes, negates, legislates, and the originary simplicity of the natural? . . . There is no doubt that the pastoral theme is, in fact, the only poetic theme, that it is poetry itself" (de Man, *Blindness* 239).[6]

Pastoral was inaugurated in England with Spenser's *Shepheardes Calender* (1579), confirming the Vergilian "progression" and making pastoral the inevitable beginning point for a poetic career. In this tradition "our new poet" (as E. K. calls him), even while "inaugurating the great age of Elizabethan poetry" (Alpers 83) and self-consciously inaugurating his own poetic career, finds his starting-point to be situated in an old place—the topos protected by the pastoral *umbra* and especially prepared by Theocritus and Vergil for his beginning efforts.[7] Although sheltered, it is a place in a dynamic system which turns, moving the poet forward, so that the beginning gesture in the genre receives the promise of self-transcendence: "to invoke it is already to assume the insufficiency of the tradition in the very act of rehearsing its tropes" (Fish 6). "That is, the desire of the poet to rise above the pastoral is itself a pastoral convention, and when the speaker . . . gives voice to that desire he succeeds only in demonstrating the extent to which his thoughts and actions are already inscribed in the tradition from which he would be separate. . . . [H]e is only playing out the role assigned him in a drama not of his making" (Fish 10). Pastoral is thus continuously troping toward something it is not, something absent, something greater on the ascending scale of generic progression; and it is much easier to get into this pastoral machine than to get out of it, as the singer in Blake's "golden cage" ("How sweet I roam'd") found out too late.

Wordsworth's whole poetic career can be read as an exemplary attempt to move from a redeemed pastoral lyric to the higher flight of epic.[8] One of the most revealing moments of that prolonged effort can be found in the opening lines of the first book of *The Excursion:*

> 'Twas summer, and the sun had mounted high:
> Southward the landscape indistinctly glared
> Through a pale stream; but all the northern downs,
> In clearest air ascending, showed far off
> A surface dappled o'er with shadows flung
> From brooding clouds; shadows that lay in spots
> Determined and unmoved, with steady beams
> Of bright and pleasant sunshine interposed;
> To him most pleasant who on soft cool moss
> Extends his careless limbs along the front
> Of some huge cave, whose rocky ceiling casts
> A twilight of its own an ample shade,
> Where the wren warbles, while the dreaming man,
> Half conscious of the soothing melody,
> With side-long eye looks out upon the scene,
> By power of that impending cover, thrown
> To finer distance.

As the would-be poet toils Meliboeus-like through the vision-oblit-
erating glare of the bright sun, his eager anticipation is expressed not
for the actual "Friend" he seeks, but for a place of vision, the pastoral
topos where the combination of poetic posture and "power of that
impending covert" will allow him the desired perspective.

> Mine was at that hour
> Far other lot, yet with good hope that soon
> Under a shade as grateful I should find
> Rest, and be welcomed there to livelier joy.
> Across a bare wide common I was toiling
> With languid steps that by the slippery turf
> Were baffled; nor could my weak arm disperse
> The host of insects gathering round my face,
> And ever with me as I paced along.
> Upon that open moorland stood a grove,
> The wished-for port to which my course was bound.
> Thither I came, and there, amid the gloom
> Spread by a brotherhood of lofty elms,
> Appeared a roofless Hut; four naked walls
> That stared upon each other!—I looked round,
> And to my wish and to my hope espied
> The Friend I sought; a Man of reverend age,
> But stout and hale, for travel unimpaired.
> There was he seen upon the cottage-bench,
> Recumbent in the shade . . .

The place having been defined in advance by the imaginary "dreamer,"
it will be physically occupied by the figure of the Wanderer, whose
lengthy genealogy ("So was he framed; and such his course of life")
provides yet another deferred approach to the re-framing and re-
posing of this redundantly recumbent idealized figure of power and
knowledge: "Upon that cottage-bench reposed his limbs, / Screened
from the sun, Supine the Wanderer lay, / His eyes as if in drowsiness
half shut, / The shadows of the breezy elms above / Dappling his
face" (596). From this sheltered perspective the Poet will learn to go
beyond "the impotence of grief," to see into "the forms of things" so
that they convey "an image of tranquillity."

In the world of pastoral poetry Winter is typically represented
as a time when human speech is impossible (Blake: "He withers all in
silence"), the silence before speech blossoms in spring and to which

it returns in the cycle. In between there is a "temperate zone" of poetic utterance, the pastoral zone that defines—in de Man's phrase—"the only poetic theme . . . poetry itself." The poet's entry into poetic "discourse," at the beginning of a poetic "career," can be compared with an infant's (*infans*, incapable of speech) entry into language, since in the development of a child there is a moment when it enters language by becoming aware of certain places which it can occupy as a speaking subject—places that function as identity-producing points of insertion into language. Both are instances of the individual's assumption of a place prepared in advance by a complex of discursive formations; and in both cases what appears to be a new beginning reveals that the subject always already finds itself and its discourses in place.[9] As tales of origin, both take the same form of a "diachronic fable of a synchronic functioning" (MacCabe 87).

If the possible subject of poetic enunciation is already inscribed in a synchronic pastoral machine that constantly provides the already-available position characteristic of any discursive formation, then that position can be seen to have a special relationship to the sun, a prototypical relationship characteristic of that between all signifiers and their "real" signifieds, which are mental constructs rather than the natural objects with which they have only a rhetorical relationship. Our experience of the natural sun embodies this relationship of presence/absence with unavoidable universality, so that the natural relation has become exemplary for poetic troping.[10] We are affected by the sun without seeing it directly, and our mediated perception (in the "shade" of language) is *figured* by the literal impossibility of looking directly at the sun without becoming blind. "But such a light as that of the sun, immediately exerted on the eye, as it overpowers the sense, is a very great idea. . . . Extreme light, by overcoming the organs of sight, obliterates all objects, so as in its effects exactly to resemble darkness" (Edmund Burke 80). Lucretius's warning that the sun will blind you if you gaze at it (*Sol etiam caecat, contra si tendere pergas*) can be safely ignored only in allegory: "Last of all, he would be able to look at the Sun and contemplate its nature, not as it appears when reflected in water or any alien medium, but as it is in itself in its own domain" (Plato 230). Plato's metaphor for ultimate philosophical insight here does not contradict the fact that "unmediated expression is a philosophical impossibility" (de Man, *Blindness* 9) but embodies that fact in its language-mediated troping on the equation between natural blindness and philosophical insight. In *Phaedo* Socrates illustrates the need for a mediating distance in thought by invoking the precautions necessary for watching a solar eclipse. In order not to be blinded, the sun even in eclipse must be watched in its reflection in water as *eikona* or image rather than its direct sensory manifestation. Similarly, not to be blinded by things, we must consider them by means of their images as they are assimilated to the *logoi* of discursive forms in which we must look for the truth of beings. In each case the "source" of *logos* is both hidden and revealed by the *logos* as resource: "*Logos* is thus a *resource.* One must *turn* to it, and not merely when the solar source is *present* and risks burning the eyes if stared at; one has also to turn away toward *logos* when the sun seems to withdraw during its eclipse" (Derrida, *Disseminations* 84). The unmediated representation of the sun is an artistic impossibility too, as Jay Appleton has shown in *The Experience of Landscape.* There he makes the familiar point that while the sun can illuminate a landscape, it cannot participate in it as a component without difficulty, because "the eye cannot contemplate it except at the risk of great discomfort and even physical damage" (109). To represent the sun the artist must make it manageable by reflecting it from the surfaces of other objects like clouds and trees, or interrupt its passage by placing something between the sun and its observer. Since it is "not only by far the most powerful source of light but . . . also a symbol of distance on a supraterrestrial scale," the possibility of "prospect" emerges as an artistic way to achieve what Appleton sees as a psychological function of landscape. The observer's point of view is thus located in a shaded foreground—Claude's *coulisse*—where we can see but not be seen, and "prospect and refuge can be at least partially achieved simultaneously" (110).

The epistemological model of this mediated relationship was worked out by a number of thinkers in the seventeenth century, and Descartes' third meditation is one of the clearest and most accessible examples of a common formulation. The distinction he makes between "adventitious ideas" that appear "foreign to me and coming from without," ideas that are "innate," and those that are "made or invented by me" (196–97) leads him to the sun as exemplary instance:

> For example, I find present to me two completely diverse ideas of the Sun; the one in which the Sun appears to me as extremely small is, it would seem, derived from the senses, and to be counted as belonging to the class of *adventitious ideas*; the other, in which the Sun is taken by me to be

many times larger than the whole Earth, has been arrived at by way of astronomical reasonings, that is to say, elicited from certain notions *innate in me,* or *formed by me in some other manner.* Certainly, these two ideas of the Sun cannot both resemble the same Sun; and reason constrains me to believe that the one which seems to have emanated from it in a direct manner is the more unlike.

(198–99, italics added)[11]

Since the "made sun" (one of Descartes' *factae vel factitiae*) has "more objective reality" than the natural sun, it can be carried over mataphorically to figure the "innate" idea of the sun which hides its rhetorical origins in the image of the "inexhaustible light" of a God who dazzles the powers of the human mind as the natural sun dazzles its powers of sensory perception.[12]

Hobbes echoes the dynamic aspect of this "constructed" sun by finding the model for its making already in the mediated structure of sensory experience. For him our sense of outward forms comes neither directly from external objects nor from the "divers motions" exerted by those objects on the senses. Instead it is the "resistance or counterpressure, or endeavour of the heart, to deliver itself" of the pressure of those motions (85). What we call "sense . . . in all cases, is nothing else but original fancy, and our image making faculty ["Imagination"] is what "is called *Sight*; and seemeth not to be mere Imagination, but the Body itself without us" (85, 657). Imagination is a faculty of mediation (like an *umbra*) which functions in the *absence* of the objects of sense perception: "and the motion made by this pressure, continuing after the object is removed, is that we call *Imagination* and *Memory*" (658). For Hobbes our "image" of the sun, like our "idea" of it, is known only through the inward motions of the heart, an inward imagination that produces light in spite of the 'blindness' of natural perception. Imagination, or "decaying sense" (88) can reappropriate as metaphor the solar phenomenon of the eclipse as an external image of internal phenomena: "The decay of Sense in men waking, is not the decay of the motion made in sense; but an obscuring of it, in such manner, as the light of the Sun obscureth the light of the Starres; which starres do no less exercise their vertue by which they are visible, in the day, than in the night" (88).

These two models, the ontological and the epistemological, exhibit the conceptual basis for the endless set pieces on the sun that shine out with special brilliance in seventeenth- and eighteenth-century poetry. Cut off from sensory perceptions, safe in the rhetorical shade of a nocturnal *umbra* ("from objects free, from passion cool . . . these tutelary shades / Are man's asylum"), poets like Young could revel in a "Darkness [that] strikes thought inward . . . drives back the soul / To settle on herself, our point supreme!" (*Night* V, 120–30). From this withdrawn vantage point the domain of language turns heliotropically toward the "dominions" of the sun:

> Full ample the dominions of the sun!
> Full glorious to behold! How far, how wide,
> The matchless monarch, from his flaming throne,
> Lavish of lustre, throws his beams about him,
> Farther and faster than a thought can fly,
> And feeds his planets with eternal fires!
>
> (*Night* IX, 1617–22)[13]

The dazzling radiance of the absent sun becomes an implicit figure for the poet, also "lavish of lustre," who throws out his tropes like rays of light emitted from the sun. In both cases the effect of presence and familiarity hides by its brightness and vividness the absence that makes it possible:

> Behold the light emitted from the Sun,
> What more familiar, and what more unknown?
> While by its spreading Radiance it reveals
> All Nature's Face, it still itself conceals.
>
> (Blackmore ii/386–89)

If we can leap now, from Descartes in his little room and Edward Young at his midnight desk, to Proust in his cork-lined study, we find him writing an exemplary passage in *Swann's Way* that both hides and reveals his scene of writing. Having resisted his grandmother's suggestion that he go outside to play, Marcel assumes the *lentus in umbra* posture, "lying stretched out on my bed with a book in my hand" in a room sheltered from "the afternoon sun behind its almost closed shutters."[14] The only light in the room is a "gleam of daylight," which is captured in the image of "golden wings" to remain "motionless . . . like a butterfly poised upon a flower" (89).

> It was hardly light enough for me to read, and my sense
> of the day's brightness and splendour was derived solely

from the blows struck down below . . . upon some dusty packing-cases . . . and also from the flies who performed for my benefit, in their tiny chorus, as it were the chamber music of summer, evoking it quite differently from a snatch of human music which *heard by chance* in high summer, will remind you of it later, whereas the music of the flies is *bound to the season by a more compelling tie*—born of the sunny days, and not to be reborn but with them, *containing something of their essential nature,* it not merely calls up their image in our memory, but guarantees their return, *their actual, circumjacent, immediately accessible presence.*

This dim coolness of my room was to the broad daylight of the street what the shadow is to the sunbeam, that is to say equally luminous, and presented to my imagination the entire panorama of summer, which my senses, if I had been out walking, could have tasted and enjoyed only piecemeal.

(88–89, italics added).

De Man gives this passage what he calls "a rhetorically conscious reading" *(Allegories* 15) by following the movement of its tropes as they express two different ways of evoking the natural experience of summer—the difference between chance/contiguity (metonymy) and necessity/analogy (metaphor). For my purposes here the names of the tropes are not as important as the underlying distinction that continues the crucial Romantic opposition between symbol and allegory. For Coleridge the symbol is a motivated sign; "it always partakes of the Reality which it renders intelligible; and while it enunciates the whole, abides itself as a living part in that Unity, of which it is the representative," while allegorical signs are "but empty echoes which the fancy arbitrarily associates with the apparitions of matter" (30).[15] For Proust the indirect sunlight and the music of the flies seem at first to offer the "compelling tie" of the motivated sign or symbol, free from the fortuitous chance of sensory experience which can yield only fragments. The passage can be seen as self-referential in its implicit claims to have transcended the contingent natural world through the kind of mastery by which a lepidopterist captures a specimen and mounts it on a board. But de Man exposes the dependence of this dominion (of essential figures of substitution) on contingent figures of substitution, so that the "return" of "resurrection" of the flies in the text is a "rhetorical mystification" in which "metaphor becomes a blind metonymy" (102).

De Man's concern here with the battle between the tropes can create its own mystification, but it can also help us to see that the real battle being staged is between "nature" and "art." In this encounter *both* metaphor and metonymy are crucial weapons, but each has a drawback which makes it inadequate to create the illusion of permanently present value by itself. Metaphor, with its reliance on resemblance and analogy, can create the effect of a relationship unchanged by the absence of one of its terms; but the other side of this effectiveness is that its terms must always be separate and distinct—I can assert "x is y" metaphorically only when x is *not* y (otherwise I would be making a literal statement, not a figurative one). So if I write "Love is golden," only certain parts of the "gold" are carried over in the metaphoric transfer because—as Midas found out—love and gold can be different. As signifiers both words are present in my discourse, their signifieds absent; yet I claim a link or relationship that obtains between "love" and "gold" even if there is neither love nor gold in the world. If I write "the air is golden" (even though at the moment I write it is in fact raining), my implicit claim is that the sun is shining or glimmering through the air; the air will be golden only as long as the contingent relationships (sun, air and clouds, my position, and so on) remain the same. But these are notoriously transitory.

As the metaphor finds a permanent link dependent on separation, metonymy finds a contingent link, a moment of proximity that cannot remain in a world of comings and goings. With this distinction in mind, we can now see more clearly the strategy of Proust's text, which is to achieve the *combined* effect of metaphor and metonymy, thereby convincing us that Marcel *really was* in that room as described. Of course that fleeting moment ("like a butterfly poised upon a flower") is gone; but its departure testifies to its authenticity, since it must have been there to in order to fade. It can be "resurrected" in the "present" text being written by "Marcel" ("I would be lying stretched") and the resurrection confirms for us that Marcel *was* there in the shade "with a book" that he was writing about "a book" that he was reading *in the same shade.* But the real 'Marcel' for us is Proust, whom we must read and 'resurrect' in *our* shade.

The important opposition here is not simply between metaphor and metonymy, for both are, in spite of their differences, merely tropes. The difference is between "the chamber music *of* summer" and the "human music" that was only "heard by chance" in the summer—which can therefore only remind one of summer by an accidental association. For Coleridge this was the distinction between the Imagination (which worked like nature in achieving its organic unities) and the Fancy, which was arbitrary and mechanical. We can see in it also the contrast between the plenitude of nature, with its motivated signs and the emptiness of human writing, the arbitrariness of human signifiers. It is precisely this distinction that allows writing to triumph over nature by losing to nature, since the Nature that triumphs over art is itself an effect produced by an art that hides its artfulness. Proust's text must suggest the evocative quality of the flies' "tiny chorus," which in turn is evocative of summer because the song is "is born of the sunny days, and not to be reborn but with them, containing something of their essential nature." The text's change at this point to the present tense emphasizes the paradoxical identity of the two modes of song that are being contrasted; what was is, and will always be, because of the "necessary link" between the flies' "little concert" and beautiful days. The repetitive drone of the pronoun through this long Proustian sentence (*"elle ne l'evoque . . . elle est unie . . . elle n'en réveille pas seulement l'image dans notre mémoire, elle en certifie le retour, la présence effective, ambiante, immédiatement accessible"*) and the emphatic shift to the present tense wager the enactment of a redemptive identity between the music of the flies and the evocative power of the text. The effect here is matched perfectly with Wordsworth's present-tense play of entomological music in *The Excursion*: "At this still season of repose and peace, / This hour when all things which are not at rest / Are cheerful; while this multitude of flies / With tuneful hum is filling all the air" (598). Proust's punning trope "chamber music of summer" (*"la musique de chambre de l'été"*) hints that the music, like the flies, can exist for us only as textual effects, chamber music produced and consumed in the pastoral *umbra* of a darkened room (*"dans ma chambre. . . . Cette obscure fraîcheur de ma chambre"*). For we too are figured in the triumph of the text, produced as readers who like Marcel turn our backs on nature for the text which has captured and unified its essence. Joyce's Bloom, in the shadowy golden mirroring world of the Ormond hotel, listening to the illusionist siren-song, comes up with a distinctly anti-illusionist version of the same trope: "Chamber music, Could make a kind of pun on that. It is a kind of music I often thought when she. Acoustics that is. Tinkling. Empty vessels make most noise" (282).

At this point it is tempting to linger over Proust's text, or to listen also to the "chamber music" of Keats's "small gnats" that provide their similar fragile metonymic link ("borne aloft / Or sinking as the light wind lives or dies" "To Autumn"), or to Yeats's "sensual music" in "Sailing to Byzantium":

> That is no country for old men. The young
> In one another's arms, birds in the trees,
> —Those dying generations—at their song,
> The salmon-falls, the mackerel-crowded seas,
> Fish, flesh, or fowl, commend all summer long
> Whatever is begotten, born and dies.
> Caught in that sensual music all neglect
> Monuments of unageing intellect.

Yeats changed his indexical opening from "This . . ." to "That . . . ," reflecting the way in which the voyage "to Byzantium" is always over before the poem beings. A "that" can only be produced by a "this," in a mutual but structurally differentiating production. In order to escape from being "Caught in that sensual music" and to get "out of nature" the poet aspires to a higher "artifice of eternity." In the meantime *that* "sensual music" has been caught in the golden cage of *this* poem's form, the 'chamber music' of its ottava rima stanzas (*stanza* = "room").

Once the effect of the opposition between nature and art (symbol and allegory, metonymy and metaphor, inside and outside, and so on) has been established *within* a text, then the text (or its 'textuality') will always win. The strategy of Gray's "Ode on the Spring" provides a humorous example. In the first 'stanza' the poet calls on spring to "wake the purple year" to new life, so that the poet can retire beneath an "oak's thick branches."

> Beside some water's rushy brink
> With me the Muse shall sit, and think
> (At ease reclined in rustic state)
> How vain the ardour of the crowd,
> How low, how little are the proud,
> How indigent the great!

Nature would seem to have produced a special vantage-point from which position, paradoxically elevated though "reclined," the poet can look down on the many, the proud, the great. As the images of shade and coolness in the first stanza echo Milton's "shady Grove" "where the Muses haunt" (III.29, 28) they evoke in turn the mediating shade and metonymic presence of the sun. In the second stanza the inevitable flies appear as "insect youth," floating "amid the liquid noon" and reflecting sunlight in their "gaily-gilded trim." In the third stanza the poet conspicuously appropriates the flies for reflection in "Contemplation's sober eye" and as a metaphor for the "race of man." The "race" image is ironic, for all progressive motion is circumscribed in the "airy dance" of lives that "end where they began," whether "brushed by the hand of rough Mischance, / Or chilled by age." At this point we might well be struck by the circularity of a poetic progression looking for its origin and finding it first in the shade (whence the poet called on the sun and spring to come and *make* the shade), and then in the 'dead' cliché of the flies' dance of death, causing the poem itself to end where it began, in the dust of dead metaphors. But this closed circuit of bookish rebirth is ruptured in the fourth stanza when the flies ("the sportive kind") turn the tables on Contemplation's sober eye, labeling the poet "A solitary fly!" who violates the "race" of nature, by beginning where he should end, with death:

> On hasty wings thy youth is flown;
> Thy sun is set, thy spring is gone—
> We frolic, while 'tis May.

The chain of substitutions here seems to lead to the desired effect of a structured truth-progression that moves toward victory for an authentic originary voice of Nature. That voice says "we frolic" *now* "while 'tis May," providing a send-up of the pedantic poet caught in the intertextual circuit or pastiche of his clichés. We can see, however, that the flies have not broken the circuitous web through their opposition between "we" and "thou," but have simply taken their pre-inscribed place in the rhetorical machine of Gray's poem. Seeming to win, they instead lose to the poet who has 'won' by staging his own defeat. The endless regression of preinscribed commonplaces is ruptured by a 'return' to the synchronic 'return' of nature, reborn every year as fresh as ever, redeeming dead metaphors as well as the dead land. The implied redemption of poetic language is made explicit by Rosamund Tuve in her assertion that "the commonplaces of seasons poetry are . . . not traceable to any 'influence' except life under the same stars" (58). But that vision of life and art unified under and by the stars is only an effect produced within language, a (very common-) place within discourse ready long before Tuve occupied it, offering a self-serving commonplace *about* commonplaces that can be repeated indefinitely ("Moreover, as Rosamund Tuve *properly* has warned us . . ." Gleckner *Prelude* 57; and again in *Blake and Spenser*, p. 5).

If we return now to Blake's texts (especially "To Summer" and "To Autumn") we can see that he has exploited the same devices in the same ways to the same effects, although the ambiguity of his structure makes it equally possible to read several quite different messages. Art is superior to nature; nature is superior to art. *Blake's* art unifies nature and art, is superior to nature, is superior to conventional art. The complete annual circuit of the sun is evoked, from absence in Spring ("our longing eyes are turned / Up") to absence ("I dare not lift mine eyes") in winter. The effect of presence is produced in summer ("we oft have heard thy voice") through the mediating figure of echoes and reflected light:

> We lack not songs, nor instruments of joy,
> Nor echoes sweet, nor waters clear as heaven,
> Nor laurel wreaths against the sultry heat.

Peterfreund illustrates how well this effect works as he endorses "the fact that the heat (and light) signal the presence of authentic inspiration. . . . [T]he same presence that the speaker of 'Mad Song' turns away from . . . the same presence that frightens Blake in *Milton* when he recounts how 'Los behind me stood, a terrible flaming Sun: just close / Behind my back'" (693). Peterfreund's eagerness "to be overwhelmed by unmediated numinous power" (687) passes over the careful structuring of this passage from *Milton* (and its visual counterpart in the non-verbal plate) in its mediated representation, as well as the fact that "Los" ("that Shadowy Prophet") is not "Sol," but its mirror-inversion, its reflection—as Plato would say—in the poetic *logos*. Blake's "terrible flaming sun" may be "close" (as in "cLOSe"), but it's "behind." If we want to gauge its actual closeness, its "presence," we would do well to remember Kenneth Burke's warning: "If anybody ever turns up with a poem that has the real sun in it, you'd better be about ninety-three million miles away" (9). Ponge, dealing with the sun "*à la Radio*," reminds us of what Blake knew equally well:

> THE BRIGHTEST of all objects in the world is—consequently—NOT—is not an object; it is a hole, the metaphysical abyss: the formal and indispensable condition of

everything in the world. The condition of all other objects. The condition of sight itself.

And now that part of which is atrocious. Really in poor taste! That leaves us really unsatisfied. . . . [I]t reveals itself in such a way that it forbids you to look at it, that is forces your eyes back into your head!

Really, what a tyrant! . . .

YES and NO!

It is a tyrant and an artist, a fireworks specialist, an actor!"

(99, 101).[16]

It is thus in a double sense the *condition* of art and of the rhetorical practices that produce the *effect* of what Peterfreund calls "the radiant presence called Summer" (693).

This effect of presence is intensified in "To Autumn" by a move to the imperative present ("Sing now the lusty song of fruits and flowers") followed by quotation marks suggesting that we have the actual *words* sung by Autumn, in the form of "a song of praise for what the land does under Autumn's auspices" (Gleckner, *Prelude* 67). But the effect of the quotation marks also confuses the identity of the singer. Autumn does not produce words but fruits; if words are the 'fruits' of Autumn they are so by metaphor only, so that we can take these as the words of the poet (or "a mature harvest Bard" for Bloom, *Apocalypse* 15) indulging in an implicit prosopopoeia. The confusion is further compounded by the effect of another song within this song within a song, as the response to "Sing *now*" is a turn elsewhere, back (or forward?) to spring when "The narrow bud opens her beauties to / The sun . . . Till clust'ring Summer breaks forth into singing." The authentic and authenticating "jolly voice" (as "song *of* fruits," song that grows like fruit, is about fruit, and is fruit) doubles the poet's own song of seasonal/solar progression from Spring to Summer. It starts not with full-blown flowers, but with "blossoms" that "hang." And the present tense, like the blossoms themselves, turns out to be past, anticipating the climax of Autumn's song in the "singing" of "clust'ring Summer" which is also past; and then the Autumn's song (where was it?) gives way to the past of "He sang," and to the absence that turns out to have governed the whole progression, which, while seeming to move forward, has only produced a series of copies of itself within itself, a *mise-en-abyme* of representation without origin or referent. The song *of* Autumn is a song *of* Spring and *of* Summer, a song that sings that Summer (now feminized!) sings, that joy "sits singing in the trees." Is its song "their" song? What is/was their song? If the song that presumably belongs to Autumn, sung *by* Autumn in a poem formally addressed *to* Autumn, can only repeat the singing that the prior seasons sang, then how is this golden load of song (or fruit) properly (i.e., as property) *his*? or in any sense "original?"

These questions do not appear in discussions of Blake because the poems are skillfully designed to focus our attention elsewhere and produce a different effect of organic progression and unity. It is in this "clust'ring" effect of union (a cluster is a group of things or persons 'growing together' into a 'clot') that the combined play of metaphor and metonymy can best hide itself as rhetoric, so that we 'hear' the song of Autumn as we 'heard' Marcel's flies. That the effect can be overpowering is evidenced by Gleckner's rhapsody in the verb-mood of Truth, the indicative:

> Love now *is* united with the land: earth and season *are* one. Blake accents this union. . . . [T]he song of the season and the songs of the land *are* the same songs. Autumn indeed *is* definable now only in terms of its union with the earth: it *is* 'laden with fruit'; it *is* 'clust'ring Summer'; it *is*, in succession, poetry, dance, fruits and flowers, buds and beauties, the sun, love and the blood pulsing through human veins, blossoms, morning and eve . . . song, spirits of the air, joy, gardens, trees. [Blake's Autumn is no allegorical] Spenserian reaper holding 'in his hand a sickle.' Instead he *is* his fruits.
>
> (*Prelude* 67–68, emphasis added)

It is "Blake's vision" that reveals all this to us, a vision based on "ideas, concepts, not percepts" but which has the "solidity of symbol and the sensory verbal qualities" (68). This Autumn that "*is* his fruits" flees for Gleckner, but "only from corporeal vision" (68), so that "Blake's vision" can be "ontologically verified by his [Autumn's? Blake's?] disappearance from sight" (69), anticipating the status of Tom Dacre's hair in "The Chimney Sweeper": "Hush Tom never mind it, for when your head's bare, / You know that the soot cannot spoil your white hair" (*E* 10). "Autumn may be 'fled from our sight,' but his 'golden load' is clearly the wholeness of the seasons as Blake's vision has just revealed that to us" (67). As in Proust, we are told to believe that he/it must have been there in order to have disappeared. This scenario of vanishing wealth is as old as Proverbs: "Wilt thou set thine eyes upon that which is not? For riches certainly make themselves wings; they fly away as an eagle toward heaven" (23.5). If Gleckner's Blake "demands that we fly with him on his plumed wide wings to the realms of truth" (*Prelude* 13–14), then what is to be made of the "golden load" that is left behind?

Nor all that glisters gold

Puisque tel est le pouvoir du langage,
Battrons-nous donc soleil comme princes monnaie,
Pour en timbre le haut de cette page? (PONGE)

The poem functions like gold. (POUND)

Money is a kind of poetry. (STEVENS)

I would have some body put the Muses under a kind of contribution to furnish out whatever they have in them that bears any relation to Coins. (ADDISON)

More questions: How has "Blake's vision" revealed that "golden load" to us? What are we as readers left with in the form or figure of a "golden load?" Have we too become like "The spirits of the air [that] live on the smells / Of fruit"? If there is the *smell* of fruit, there must ("through his [Blake's] fusion of cause and effect, tenor and vehicle, literal and figurative" [*Prelude* 68]) *be* fruit *there* somewhere. But the fruit has always already gone, leaving behind only the metonymy of smell, and even metonymies can only "smell" figuratively. So what can we make of the ambiguous "golden load" that seems to shimmer before us, offering itself as a reward for reading the poem as Melville's "gold doubloon" offered itself to the first one to 'see' the white whale? At the end of a day, on the threshold of its departure, the light of the sun is caught briefly by clouds and motes in the air which "reflect" it most just before the darkness of its absence.[17] This is the most transitory of phenomena, and since the sun is always coming and going it is our contingent relationship—or vantage point—that constitutes the threshold of arrival or departure. To trope on the image of shimmering air is to trope on the contingencies of transitory relations, to lose the golden load even in the act of imaging it.

Something of the permanent effect of metaphor is necessary if the "load" is not to slip through our fingers, but it must by a "symbolic" metaphor, one that in Coleridge's terms "always partakes of the Reality which it renders intelligible" rather than "empty echoes that the fancy arbitrarily associates with the apparitions of matter" (what Melville's Ishmael would call a "hideous and intolerable allegory"). The task for the poet's words is an alchemical one, to trope on tropes themselves, as "a material of vulgar origin," turning them from a debased analogon of "real" gold into the thing itself.[18]

But real gold is already so implicated in tropological circuits that for the poet it can only function as the metaphor *of* metaphor. It is in fact gold's remarkable availability to be taken *as something else* that allows it to circulate as the measure of that 'real value' which is always elsewhere. As Marx points out, the precious metals are useless in the direct process of production and easily dispensed with as articles of consumption or means of existence (130). Their value inheres instead in how they appear: "*Sie erscheinen gewissermassen als gediegenes Licht, das aus der Unterwelt hervorgegraben wird, indem, das Silber alle Lichstrahlen in ihrer ursprünglichen Mischung, das Gold nur die höchste Potenz der Farbe, das Rot, zurückwirft*" (130) / "They appear, in a way, as spontaneous light brought out from the underground world, since silver reflects all rays of light in their original combination, and gold only the color of highest intensity, viz. red light" [Stone 211]). Traditionally gold stands for the absent sun, its 'shining' ability to reflect red light giving it the effect of a literalized metaphor of the sun, or of an actual deposit produced and left behind by it. Pope describes how the "shining mischief" of gold is not the generative sun, but a son who presumes to take its place

> . . . Nature, as in duty bound,
> Deep hid the shining mischief under ground:
> But when by man's audacious labour won,
> Flam'd forth this rival to, its Sire, the Sun
>
> (Epistle to Burlington 9–12)

Since the sun is the putative source of all 'natural' production, the *appearance* of gold produces the effect of an essential value. "Nature no more produces money than it does bankers or discount rates." But since the capitalist system of production requires the "crystallization" of wealth as a fetish in the form of a single article (*den Reichtum als Fetisch in der Form eines einzelnen Dings kristallisieren muss*), gold and silver *appear* as its appropriate "incarnation" (*Inkarnation*). Even while denying its naturalness, Marx here invokes the metaphor of the myth of natural solar production (*kristallisieren, Inkarnation*) for that "silver or gold money crystal" which is "not only the product of the process of circulation, but in fact is its only final product." Thus "the universal product of the social process or the social process itself as a product is a peculiar natural product, a metal hidden in the bowels of the earth and extracted therefrom" (131).[19]

The 'peculiarity' of gold as a 'natural product' is its combination of durability, malleability and relative indestructibility, together with its *Schein*, all of which allow it to "appear, in a way, as spontaneous light." "Spontaneous" is only one of many ways to translate the adjective in Marx's "*gediegenes Licht*," but all of them emphasize genuine value (*gediegen* = "solid, massy, unmixed, pure, genuine, true, superior"). The relationship of gold to that value is its "shining in a certain way" (*Sie erscheinen gewissermassen*), so that it has a *Schein*, an "appearance" (the meaning can range from "light" to an I.O.U. or paper money). Thus insofar as the power *to appear* (i.e., to reflect or represent) is understood to be an essential part of the gold itself, we might say that gold offers itself oxymoronically as a *gediegenes Schein*, a source of value and the appearance of value combined, as if the gold reflects itself or is its own reflection.

Marx suggests yet another way in which gold "becomes idealized within the process of circulation" (116). For gold properly to circulate as money, it must be stamped with an inscription that indicates its value, and the fact that the inscription is on the coin gives it an indisputable authenticity. But in spite of its special natural properties, the process of circulation which *realizes* gold's ability to function as a medium of exchange also *idealizes* its essence:

> The circulation of money is a movement through the outside world. . . . In the course of its friction against all kinds of hands, pouches, pockets, purses, money-belts, bags, chests and strong-boxes, the coin rubs off, loses one gold atom here and another one there and thus, as it wears off in its wanderings over the world, it loses more and more of its intrinsic substance. By being used it gets used up. . . . It is clear, says an anonymous writer, that in the very nature of things, coins must depreciate one by one as a result of ordinary and unavoidable friction."
>
> (88)

This leads the coin almost instantly to a situation in which it "represents more metal than it actually contains" so that the longer it circulates the greater the discrepancy between its form (as inscribed coin) and its substance, until finally "the body of the coin becomes but a shadow" (89). This inevitable decay—so often compares, as Derrida points out in "White Mythology," with the *usure* of language and metaphor—assures that the gold coins will become "transformed by the very process of circulation into more or less of a mere sign or symbol" (91).

"But no thing can be its own symbol" (91), and gold will be "brought to rest" to form a "hoard" or *Schatz* (105), to be substituted for in the process of circulation by "subsidiary mediums" (*subsidiären Zirkulationsmittel*) which can "serve as symbols of gold coin not because they are symbols made of silver or copper, not because they have certain value, but only in so far as they have no value." We thus have a series of substitutions (from exchange value of commodities to gold money, sublimated by circulation into its own symbol, first in the form of worn coin, then in the form of subsidiary metal currency) which ends "finally in the form of a worthless token, paper, mere *sign of value*" (94). Pope in the *Epistle to Burlington*:

> Blest paper-credit! last and best supply!
> That lends Corruption lighter wings to fly!
> Gold imp'd by thee, can compass hardest things,
> Can pocket States, can fetch or carry Kings;
> A single leaf shall waft an Army o'er,
> Or ship off Senates to a distant Shore.
>
> (69–74)

Marx shares Pope's political emphasis as he goes on to show how the state, which at first only impressed its stamp on gold, "seems now to turn paper into gold by the magic of its stamp" (98). Thus paper money, worthless in itself, can circulate as a signifier of difference, mediating between the relative worth of commodities based on the consumers' faith in the presence elsewhere of the absent signified whose value is governed by labor value or the system of 'natural productivity' governed by the sun. The importance of 'faith' in this system of exchange is brought home by Marx's approving paraphrase of Bishop Berkeley, who asked, "if the denomination of the coin remains, after the metal has gone the way of all flesh, cannot the circulation of commerce still be maintained?" (*Werke*, 97: *Wenn die*

Denomination der Münze beibehalten wird, nachdem ihr Metall den Weg alles Fleisches gegangen, würde nicht dennoch die Zirkulation des Handels fortbestehn?). Berkeley's point is that the presence—even elsewhere—of something that is absent from "the circulation of commerce" is unnecessary, since it functions precisely as an absence. With this comment we find ourselves located in a system like that claimed by Gleckner for the seasons poems at the end of "To Autumn"—a structured system of exchange that needs both absence and faith and that functions precisely as the structure of writing:

> When a man writes, he is in a structure that needs his absence as its necessary condition (writing is defined as that which can necessarily be read in the writer's absence), and entails his pluralization. Writers ignore this troubling necessity and desire to record the living act of a sole self— an auto-biography. Whatever the argument of a document, the marks and staging of this resistance are its 'scene of writing.' When a person reads, the scene of writing is usually ignored and the argument is taken as the product of self with a proper name. Writers and readers are thus accomplices in the ignoring of the scene of writing. The accounts of texts are informed by this complicity.
>
> (Spivak 19)

Whether we call it "complicity" or "faith," this newest fable of writing is the rediscovery in our time of a link between absence and writing that is probably as old as the invention of writing as a practice that depends on and exploits absence.[20]

Hence the importance of "Blake's" in my title, and in Gleckner's repeated phrase: "Blake's vision." After the sterility of a debased, rhetorically wintry age, Blake's voice seems to call out and by its power transform the wintry "climate" of English poetry into the spring of Romanticism. The imputed power of his authentic word not only names being as a presence, it *calls itself into being* as the authentic utterance of a subject, William Blake, who says (i.e., writes) "Sing *now*" and whose voice becomes one with nature, present to us as the natural emanation of a transcendental principle higher even than nature, an epiphany of a permanent presence ordinarily hidden from 'vision,' which can be revealed through the poetic word.[21] The poet in this system takes the place of the dazzling absent sun/god, who can both sanction and be *credited* with everything discovered in his verse. Blake's vision is the "golden load" of a treasure he has produced alchemically from the debased coin of previous poetic discourse, and that is his property—proper to him—as the effective agent of transformation. It is a treasure hoard which he has taken out of the value-destroying "circulation" of language or prior discourse, a poetic treasure removed even from the circuit of the natural sun and the seasons and kept elsewhere to prevent decay:

> Re-engraved Time after Time
> Ever in their youthful prime
> My Designs [shall still *del.*] unchanged remain
> Time may rage but rage in vain
> For above Times troubled Fountains
> On the Great Atlantic Mountains,
> In my Golden House on high
> There they Shine Eternally.
>
> (*E* 480–81)

This is one of Blake's many versions of the system of circulation, and one which contains an interesting *change* precisely at the point of asserting the permanence of an absent treasure, suggesting perhaps that what the work of art is, is not what it is supposed to be. Instead of presence, we have yet another golden metaphor of presence. Presence itself is preserved by remaining absent. What circulates below the "Golden House on high" are only messengers, Blake's 'messages' that circulate like paper money, their value dependent on faith in the author as autonomous subject and source of value, dependent on the AUTHOR-ity of his intentions.

Hazard Adams provides an exemplary instance of the process of circulation in the Blakean literary economy. In 1982 he predicted "a spate of . . . works in the poststructuralist language" to be devoted to Blake, but felt confident that Blake scholarship would eventually return to the right track:

> In the end, though, there is a message or there are messages in Blake, and Blake scholarship and criticism ought to be involved in making these messages available to a needy world. Its end is teaching Blake. Blake's messages are mainly ones of enthusiasm and good news, and there is no reason for our sense of our various tasks with Blake not to be enthusiastic, too.
>
> (402–3)

In this circular view Blake's messages are authoritative because they come from Blake who is their source. Blake's "golden load" is then redundantly Blake himself as original author. Adams's "enthusiasm" is a telling word here, since it literally means being possessed by a god (*en + theos*) who is in us. In our "enthusiasm" we become Blakes who are Blake's, subjects of the author who manifests himself to us as Zeus to Danae, in a shimmering shower of gold. Ruskin offers us a less ravishing version of the same gold standard and "our various tasks" as critics in a work he appropriately called *The Political Economy of Art*, where he develops at length an image of the artist as a kind of golden natural resource that can only be found, not made:

> You have always to find your artist, not to make him: you can't manufacture him any more than you can manufacture gold. You can find him, and refine him: you dig him out as he lies nugget-fashion in the mountain stream; you bring him home; and you fashion him into current coin or household plate, but not one grain of him you originally produce.
>
> (*Works*, 16: 29–30)

Although the "message" in Ruskin's scripture here is anti-alchemical, this technique is the familiar rhetorical alchemy we have been following. This economy of the poetic production is made explicit by the "editor-translator" Macpherson who "found" his golden poet Ossian in the Scottish highlands, and whose rhetoric of faithfulness to the absent original is an essential part of the machinery that guarantees the existence of its poetic lode:

> That they [i.e., his "translations"] have been well received by the Public, appears from an extensive sale; that they shall continue to be well received, he may venture to prophecy without that gift of that inspiration, to which poets lay claim. Through the medium of version upon version, they retain, in foreign languages, their native character of simplicity and energy. Genuine poetry, like gold, loses little, when properly transfused; but when a composition cannot bear the test of a literal version, it is a counterfeit which ought not to pass current.
>
> (Preface xlviii)

The existence of the genuine golden poems is the guarantee of the value of Macpherson's prose "translations." They are a functional example of Marx's "hoard" or *Schatz*, which must be substituted for by the "subsidiary medium" of translations in the process of circulation—and of Bishop Berkeley's observation that the circulation of commerce can still be maintained even after the gold has gone the way of all flesh.

Like the sun itself, the author's intentions are not available to our unmediated perception; we see only the *Schein* of a golden load as the signifier of those intentions. The relationship is one for which Locke takes gold as his prime example, where the appearance of gold in its secondary qualities must "depend" on (i.e., "hang from") its "substance" (that which "stands under"). For Locke, the gap between the essence of a substance and its *Schein* means that we can never know true gold. "For let it be ever so true, that all gold, i.e. all that has the real essence of gold, is fixed, what serves this for, whilst we know not, in this sense, *what is or is not gold*? For if we know not the real essence of gold, it is impossible we should know what parcel of matter has that essence, and so whether *it* be true gold or no" (2: 97).

Added to the uncertainty of the relation between the appearance and the essence of gold is the inevitable slippage between the signifier "gold" and its signified, for "the precise signification of the names of substances will be found not only not to be well established, but also very hard to be so" (2, 114). "That which I mean is this, That these being all but properties, depending on its real constitution, and nothing but powers, either active or passive, in reference to other bodies, no one has authority to determine the signification of the word gold (as referred to such a body existing in nature) more to one collection of ideas to be found in that body than to another: whereby the signification of that name must unavoidably be very uncertain" (2, 116). Marx provided an alternative to this lack of authority when he observed that as the state, in fixing its mint price, gave "a certain name to a piece of gold," so the state "can turn paper into gold by the magic of its stamp" (98). For those involved in the economy of poetry and literary interpretation this function of the state is performed by the literary establishment through its various departments or 'interpretive communities,' which seem to be the agencies that establish the exchange value of the poet's "endlesse moniment" reared against the way of all flesh.[22]

De Man has identified as a typical response to the poetic "moniment" that practice which he calls 'monumentalizing,' in which "the

dead are made to have a face and a voice which tells the allegory
of their demise and allows us to apostrophize them in our turn.
No degree of knowledge can ever stop this madness, for it is the
madness of words." If *knowledge* cannot stop the madness *of* language
itself, what are we to do? "What would be naive is to *believe* that
this strategy . . . can be a source of value and has to be celebrated
or denounced accordingly" ("Shelley" 73, italics added). Either to
celebrate or denounce "accordingly" would be to play the same naive
game 'of the heart' (*accordare,* from *cor*) which seeks to bring into
agreement the play of language and the real world. The high rhetorical
tone of de Man's demand that we must give up the pursuit of literature
as a *source* of *value*, and that we must also renounce the temptation to
denounce, is thus yet another example of that madness of language.
For him to *announce* is rhetorically to *denounce*, to become a "messenger" (both words come from *nuntius*, "messenger," and originally
meant the same thing) of a different truth, a truth—or inevitably
(*toujours déjà*)—of the no-Truth of *différance*. A "renounce" is also
the failure to follow suit in a card game. We might say that de Man has
taken up Descartes' invitation to *jouer aux cartes*, trumping Descartes'
ontological suit with that of a 'trickster god' of language who makes
and rules (madly) all discourse—the only game in town while we
wait for another trump, the last trump that signals the harvest of
death. Until the end, he pursued his project to show that the claims
of metaphor and symbol, the most privileged of Romantic tropes, can
always on close reading be decomposed into chains of metonymic or
causal-associative formations. The attempts of Romantic metaphor to
"carry over" a metaphoric golden load that bridges the gap between
the dualisms of subject/object, man/nature, inward/outward, can do
so only by hiding its own rhetorical path, passing off as self-sufficient
metaphor or symbol a golden load that can always be seen to be a kind
of allegory whose 'message' is artificially contrived and sustained.

Relentlessly, de Man called our attention to the paper money of
allegory, that "other word" which is all we can ever *read.* Paradoxically,
such efforts can seem to value the efforts of Romanticism precisely
because they so clearly fail to make good their promise, producing
instead language that approaches an inevitable limit in self-conscious
reflection on its own nature and genesis. In doing so, de Man had
to resist even the temptation "to conclude that our own literary
modernity has reestablished contact with a 'true' Enlightenment that
remained hidden from us by a nineteenth-century Romantic and
realist epistemology that asserted a reliable rhetoric of the subject

or of representation," since all such "syntagmatic narratives" are themselves "part of the same system as paradigmatic tropes . . . a correlative of rhetoric and not the reverse" ("Epistemology" 29–30). An "epistemological discipline" can always discover the same gap between faith and knowledge, pointing us towards Paul's truism that "faith is the substance of things hoped for, the evidence of things not seen" (Hebrews 11.1).[23]

It's a bird! It's a plane!! It's a BLAKE!!!

Gleckner ends his discussion of Blake's "seasons suite" with a summation of the message that, "if we do not dare to lift up our eyes, we shall, of course, not see" (*Prelude* 75). But ironically, as I have tried to demonstrate, in spite of his frequent insistence on "the most fundamental and radical difference between Blake and Thomson" (*Prelude* 62) and "the satellite poems of others that it [i.e., Thomson's *Seasons*] spawned" (*Blake and Spenser* 5), Gleckner is himself repeating precisely the message of Thomson's *Seasons,* with its endless appeal to "the Philosophic Eye" or "the sage-instructed Eye" that transcends the limits of "the vulgar stare," sharing its privileged truths with those

> Attun'd to happy Unison of Soul;
> To whose exalting Eye a fairer World,
> Of which the Vulgar never had a Glimpse,
> Displays its Charms; whose Minds are richly fraught
> With Philosophic Stores, superior Light.
>
> (123–24)

Another example of Gleckner's claims for Blake shows even more clearly the tendency to echo the echoes that Blake was echoing even while claiming Blake's ability to break free and "redeem" the "eternal verities . . . from the error of their previous or conventionally accepted expression" (*Blake and Spenser* 2). If we follow Gleckner's Blake's demand "that we fly with him on his plumed wings to the realms of truth" (*Prelude* 13–14) we will find the airways so crowded that we need an air traffic controller to find a path. Gleckner's Blake's "plumed wings" themselves come from Blake's Spenser imitation by way of the flapping wings that filled the eighteenth-century air, in which even the "ample pinion" of Pindar, the "Theban Eagle" were still "sailing with supreme dominion / Through the azure deep of air" in Gray's "Progress of Poetry." Spenser's "idle hopes" were fluttering about up there on their "golden plumes," mounting "above the native might / Of heavie earth, up to the heavens hight" (*Hymne of Love* 178), perhaps to be joined by the "pierlesse Poesye" in its "famous flight" or by Colin who, "were he now with love so ill bedight, / Would mount as high and sing as soote as swanne" (*October* 79, 88, 90). Gray knew how crowded it was up there, how much room Milton required ("no room is here for Writers left, / But to detect their ignorance or Theft" as Andrew Marvell put it) for his soaring above th'Aonian Mount with "no middle flight." So he shot Milton down by sending him up as "he, that rode sublime / Upon the seraph-wings of Ecstasy, / The secrets of the abyss to spy." That is, he does to Milton what Milton had done to his own Satan; for Satan's boast ("I alone first undertook / To wing the desolate Abyss, and spy / This new created World") is borrowed by Milton from Lucretius (who is praising Epicurus with it) in order to confound utterly any claims for originality in a web of derivative echoes produced by poets making endless "copies" for which—like Plato's conception of the 'simulacrum'—no original exists. Thus when Gray launches himself (and his poem) into these crowded skyways he can only hope to "keep his distant way" by charting his flight "Beneath the Good how far—but far above the Great." If we follow him there, "Beyond the limits of a vulgar fate," we find that space too already occupied. Gray clearly alludes to the final Ode of Horace's second book, as the Latin Bard (self-styled *vates*) makes himself into a bird before our eyes in a serio-comic grotesque metamorphosis. This put-down of prideful predecessors (in the Miltonic moral mode) then segues to an echo of the second poem of the virtuous pagan's Book III. Gray's apparent claim for a *new* form of inspiration (i.e., not based on images of nature, but on the "Muse's ray" and imagination "unborrowed from the sun") is thus "borrowed" from this ode of Horace, along with the contrast between the egotistic self-agrandizement of Book II, XX and the moral flight of *Virtus* in Book III, spurning the *coetus vulgaris* that Gray calls "the limits of a vulgar fate."[24]

Another telling repetition is worth our concluding attention, if we realize that Gleckner's formulation ("lift up our eyes") puts him—and his Blake—in the position of Shakespeare's Edgar, urging the blind Gloucester ("Look up a-height . . . do but look up" *King Lear* 4:5.58–59) to look at something that isn't *there*. All of the "good" characters in *Lear* are always looking "up" to the stars or gods, like so many Blake critics, to help them understand that which they are turning their eyes away from. But Edgar knows that he needs also to employ some tricks of persuasion if he is to bring Hazard Adams's messages of "enthusiasm and good news" to "a needy world," as Cordelia knows that an army of invading troops will improve her chances of restoring harmony to "England's green & pleasant Land." We might recall at this point that Blake's Milton does not "look up," but chooses to "go down to the sepulcher to see if morning breaks" (*E* 108) and that Thel (whose name suggests "desire" or "wish") cannot bear the vision of "her own grave plot" with its insistent questions, at the end of a poem whose motto is, "Does the Eagle know what is in the pit? / Or wilt thou go ask the Mole . . . ?" (*E* 3).

A better model than Shakespeare's Edgar for assaying the putative "golden load" of any poem or poetics can be found in his Touchstone. Literally a "touchstone" is a black stone used to test the purity of gold, but figuratively it may work with poetry:

> AUDREY: I do not know what poetical is. Is it
> honest in deed and word? Is it a true thing?
> TOUCHSTONE: No, truly; for the truest poetry
> is the most feigning, and lovers are given to
> poetry, and what they swear in poetry may
> be said, as lovers, they do feign.

Whether we like it or not, the result for poetry may always be "as you like it," with faith—and desire—our only "touchstone" for determining the value of the golden load. The pun on "feign" (to fake and to desire or fain) points to the link between lovers and poets and readers that enables them to persuade themselves that they have found the object of their desire, whether it be an "ill-favoured thing" or a "golden load." Art and interpretation are rhetoric; and rhetoric is the art of persuasion.

> Isaiah answer'd. I saw no God. nor heard any, in a finite
> organical perception; but my senses dicover'd the infinite
> in every thing, and as I was then perswaded. & remain
> confirm'd; that the voice of honest indignation is the voice
> of God. I cared not for consequences but wrote.
>
> Then I asked: does a firm perswasion that a thing is so,
> make it so?
>
> He replied. All poets believe that it does, & in ages of
> Imagination this firm perswasion removed mountains; but
> many are not capable of a firm perswasion of any thing.
>
> (*The Marriage of Heaven and Hell*, 38–39)

Notes

As always, I wish to acknowledge an unrepayable debt of gratitude to a stimulating and ongoing exchange of ideas and manuscripts with Nelson Hilton, Paul Mann and the Santa Cruz Blake Study Group. Although in what follows I take issue with them on some points, I have benefitted much from the work of Robert Gleckner and Stuart Peterfreund.

1. Blake was 26 when the volume was published; the "Advertisement" says they were written between the ages of 12 and 20.

2. When he collected his *Poems* in 1768, Gray acknowledged a large number of "imitations," all of them clearly acceptable according to traditional standards, and some of them so obscure as to suggest ostentation. He claimed in a letter to Edward Bedingfield that he "could shew them a hundred more instances, which they never will discover themselves" (*Correspondence* II.477). Some critics, like Edward Young in his *Conjectures on Original Composition* (1759), were beginning to protest that the best way to "imitate" the originality of the renowned ancients was not to copy them. But others, like William Duff (*Essay on Original Genius*, 1767), argued that no form of true originality was still possible for the modern poet, imitation being therefore a necessary part of the poetic process. Malcom Laing's painstaking enthusiasm for the poetry of Ossian led him, in his 1805 edition, to claim that he had traced "every simile" and "almost every poetic image" to their classical sources.

3. The "newness" so often claimed for the postmodern pastiche is surprising, since the combinations of parody, pastiche, direct quotation and allusion in early twentieth-century art (e.g., Joyce, Eliot, Pound) is familiar enough to constitute something of a modernist orthodoxy. New names (like the *detournement* and *derive* of the Situationists) and new techniques (like the rephotography of the "appropriationists") do not in themselves provide a theoretical advance or produce a rupture with the past.

4. I discuss these issues at greater length in "The Tropology of Silence in Eighteenth-Century English Blank Verse." In "Intertextual Signifiers and the Blake of That Already" I offer some views on "influence" and intertextuality in Blake and his precursors.

5. The geographical/tropological sense of a temperate zone in Europe had already by the time of Rousseau become "a most banal opposition" (Derrida *Grammatology* 216). Always accompanied by some dimension of libidinal "temperance," this aspect became dominant by the end of the century. Thus Mary Wollstonecraft could observe that "the mass of mankind" are "the slaves of their appetites" (133) and speculate that "if from their birth men and women be placed in a torrid zone, with the meridian sun of pleasure darting directly upon them, how can they sufficiently brace their minds . . . ?" (116). "Happy the nations of the moral north!" (1.64.1) echoed Byron, far from "that indecent sun" (1.63.2), "Where all is virtue, and the winter season / Sends sin, without a rag on, shivering forth" (1.64.2–3). Freud emphasizes the necessity of mastering both internal and external "heat" in his famous micturation myth (37).

6. Annabel Patterson's study of the reception of Vergil's pastorals uses them as the focus for an integrated account of European cultural history. Although she has little to say about Blake—except for an interesting discussion of the Thornton Vergil—she does provide an excellent context for better understanding the pastoral significance of Blake's season poems.

7. The range of later modes of entry extends from the relatively straightforward approach of Pope, who "imitates expressly those which now stand first of the three chief Poets in this kind, Spenser, Vergil, Theocritus" (note to first edition, p. 15 Oxford) through the ironic self-mocking futility of Gray in his first major poem in English, writing "At ease reclined in rustic state" ("Ode on the Spring" [1741]), to the heroic ambition of Wordsworth, receiving "assurance of some work / Of glory" while stretched out at ease in his "green shady place," or Coleridge in his umbrageous "little lime-tree bower" with "The shadow of the leaf and stem above / Dappling its sunshine." Goethe's Werther,

who knows exactly how to play the role of poet, finds his place where "the high sun strikes the impenetrable foliage of my forest, and but a few rays steal into the inner sanctuary, I lie in the tall grass by the tickling brook and notice a thousand familiar things."

8. See my *Preludes to Vision* (especially 1–18, 60–116) for a more extended discussion of this point.

9. "Discourse" comes from the Latin verb *discurrere*, to run about, by way of the French *discourir*. The poet's "career" ("a course of continued progress," from *carraria*, road for vehicles) finds its path already laid out.

10. "The sun is the sensory object par excellence. It is the paradigm of the sensory *and* of metaphor: it regularly turns (itself) and hides (itself). As the metaphoric trope always implies a sensory kernel, or rather something like the sensory, which can always not be present in act and in person, and since the sun in this respect is the sensory signifier of the sensory par excellence, that is, the sensory model of the sensory . . . then the turning of the sun always will have been the trajectory of metaphor" (Derrida, "White Mythology," in *Margins*). Ricoeur Dismisses Derrida's discussion as "fantastic extrapolation" (289).

11. This conclusion was to become a commonplace of the eighteenth century. For John Dennis, the natural sun was "a round flat shining Body, of about two foot diameter" but the Cartesian sun, "made or invented" in 'meditation' is "a vast and glorious Body, and the top of all the visible Creation, and the brightest material Image of the Divinity." Blake rewrites the distinction as that between "a round Disk of fire somewhat like a Guinea" and "an Innumerable company of the Heavenly host crying Holy Holy Holy is the Lord God Almighty I question not my Corporeal or Vegetative Eye any more than I would Question a Window [cf. "the clear windows of the morning" in "To Spring"] concerning a Sight I look thro it & not with it" (*E* 565–66).

12. Blakean apocalypticists should note that Descartes has here already achieved in meditation an "uncovering" of the Truth hidden behind the natural sun. Is this the Truth Blake's inverted sun Zoa Los/Sol is reaching for in *The Four Zoas*?

> Los his vegetable hands
> Outstretched his right hand branching out in fibrous strength
> Seizd the Sun. His left hand like dark roots coverd the Moon
> And tore them down cracking the heavens across from immense to immense
> Then fell the fires of Eternity with loud & shrill
> Sound of Loud Trumpet
>
> (*E* 386)

13. Young's "matchless monarch" here is the same producer of "matchless Works" (including Britannia's "unmatch'd" Guardian-Oaks) described at such enthusiastic length by Thomson (69, 126). Hence the "Want Matches" chant in *An Island in the Moon* and the idea of "something very pritty & funny . . . about Matches" (*E* 458).

14. My English versions of Proust are from the Moncrieff and Kilmartin translation. French references are to the Pleiade edition.

15. Coleridge is often credited as the source of this distinction. Todorov's chapter of "The Romantic Crisis" traces it back to Karl Philipp Moritz, though he admits "a certain arbitrariness in this decision" (148).

16. LE PLUS BRILLIANT des objects du monde n'est—de ce fait—NON—n'est pas un objet; c'est un trou, c'est l'abîme métaphysique: la condition formelle at indispensable de tout au mode. La condition de tous les autres objets. La condition même du regard.
    Et voici ce qui en lui est atroce. Vraiment, du dernier mauvais goût! Vraiment, qui nous laisse loin de compte. . . . [E]lle s'y montre de telle façon qu'elle interdit qu'on la regarde, qu'elle repousse le regard, vous le renfonce à l'intérieur du corps!

> Vraiment, quel tyran! . . .
> OUI et NON!
> C'est un tyran et un artiste, un artificier, un acteur!

17. "*or* colors the bedtime hour of all sunsets. . . . At the end of the sun's course, afternoon, gold repeats and (re)doubles, after midnight, the horror and the aurora" (Derrida, *Dissemination* 263).

18. Paul Valéry defines poetry as "*an effort by one man* to create an artificial and ideal order by means of a material of vulgar origin" (192). This is the "*alchemie du verbe*" of Rimbaud which later inspired Breton and his group.

19. Marx uses these figures repeatedly in the *Kritik*. "In its virgin metallic state it holds *locked up* all the material wealth which lies unfolded in the world of commodities. . . . [I]t is the direct *incarnation* of universal labor in its form, and the *aggregate* of all concrete labor in its substance" (103).

20. In Herodotus' *Histories* we find the story of Deioces the Mede, a king famous for establishing one of the world's first bureaucracies, and for combining invisibility and absence with writing. First he built his seven-walled city (Ecbatana) in concentric circles, with the innermost wall of gold, for his inner sanctum where he lived and ruled; then he introduced written communication as his medium of ruling, in order to assure his invisibility. "And when all was built, it was Deioces first who established the rule that no one should come into the presence of the king, but all should be dealt with by the means of messengers; that the king be seen by no man" (1.99). Similar stories are told of Kublai Khan.

21. Gleckner's Afterword to this volume quotes this passage at length, calling it "Vogler's formulation," while claiming it has "a kind of uncanny resemblance to my point, which is far less pointedly and elegantly made." The uncanny resemblance is intentional, since I was offering a parodic exaggeration of *his* "point." What seems uncanny to me is that Gleckner thereby provides another example of the very inability I have been attributing to him, a failure to detect rhetorical effects, this time doing with *my* text what he does with *Blake's* poems. "What Vogler calls my 'rhapsody in the verb-mood of Truth, the indicative,' . . . can't hold a candle to that—with all *its* indicatives hurrying after the seeming tentativeness of 'seems' in the preliminary sentence." Precisely: it "seems [i.e., to Gleckner] to call out . . . [t]he imputed [i.e., by Gleckner] power of his authentic word." When Gleckner writes "*His* [i.e., mine], however, just may be too grand for that volume to support," he is doing me the favor of confirming *my* point about *his* reading. Perhaps my tone in this particular passage was too subtle? I don't think so, given the repeated and explicit emphasis of my entire essay.

22. For Pound, to locate the source of value in the interpretive community would amount to that practice of usury which is "contra naturam" (*Kultchur* 281), or false value created *ex nihilo* with nothing to back it up, no congruency between sign and referent. But his argument for genuine money (and authentic poetry or art) as a "representation of something else" (*Prose* 443) simply raises the same problem of the relationship correspondence or difference) between the metaphor's tenor and vehicle. It must thus evoke precisely that which will always be absent from the metaphor or word, inscribed in a system of *differance*: "It is nature, the actual existence of goods, or the possibility of producing them, that really determines the 'economic' capacity of the state [or poem]. . . . Economic habits arise from the nature of things (animal, mineral, vegetable)" (*Prose* 312, 257). In such a system both money and language operate by effacing their own materiality, disappearing (as signifier) when they mediate (as a signified *difference*) between the relative values of commodities. See Andrew Parker for a more detailed discussion of Pound's economic models.

23. "Substance" here translates Paul's *hypostasis* ("that which stands under"). The meaning seems to be either that things without reality in themselves are made real (given "substance") by faith, or that there are realities for which we have no material evidence, whose real existence we can only know through faith.

24. See Nisbet and Hubbard for notes and comments on Horace that bring out the relationship with Milton and Gray as well as Pindar and the full range of classical echoes and allusions. James Michie's translation of Ode XX, Book II, catches its humor better than most: "Mine are no weak, or borrowed wings: they'll bear / Me, bard made bird, / through the compliant air, / Earthbound no longer, leaving far behind / The cities and the envy of mankind. . . . Already the rough skin is forming on / My ankles; metamorphosis into swan / Moves up my body; downy plumage springs / On arms and elbows; shoulderblades sprout wings. / And now I rise, singing, a portent more / Talked of than Icarus was. . . . No dirges, please. Mine being no real death, / Tears would be ugly, sighs a waste of breath. / Restrain your noisy sorrow, then, and save / Yourselves the needless rituals of the gave." *Non usita nec tenui ferar / Penna biformis per liquidum aethera / Vates, neque in terris morabor / Longius invidiaque maior / Urbis relinquam. . . . Iam iam resident cruribus asperae / Pelles et album mutor in alitem / Superne, nascunturque leves / Par digitos umerosque plumae. // Iam Daedaleo notior Icaro / Visam gementis litora Bospori / Syrtisque Gaetulas canorus / Ales Hyperboreosque campos. . . . Absint inani funere neniae / Luctusque turpes et querimoniae; / Compesce clamorem ac sepulcri / Mitte supervacuos honores* (Horace 55–56). Clive Hart has risen to this thematic occasion by tracing images of flight (as tropes for transcendental movement) in the Judeo-Christian tradition from Greek vases and Pompeiian and Roman fragments through medieval manuscripts up to Tintoretto.

Works Cited

Adams, Hazard. "Post-Essick Prophecy," in *Studies in Romanticism* 21:3 (Fall 1982); 400–403.

Appleton, Jay. *The Experience of Landscape.* New York: Wiley, 1975.

Blackmore, Richard. *Creation. A Philosophical Poem.* London, 1712.

Blake, William. *The Complete Poetry and Prose of William Blake.* Ed. David V. Erdman, newly revised edition. Berkeley and Los Angeles: University of California Press, 1982.

Bloom, Harold. *Blake's Apocalypse.* Garden City, New York: Doubleday & Company, 1963.

Borges, Jorge Luis. *Labyrinths: Selected Stories & OtherWritings.* Ed. Donald A. Yates and James E. Irby. New York: New Directions, 1964.

Burke, Edmund. *A Philosophical Enquiry Into the Origin of Our Ideas of the Sublime and Beautiful.* 2nd. ed. 1959. Scolar Press facsimile. Menston: The Scolar Press Limited, 1970.

Burke, Kenneth. *The Rhetoric of Religion: Studies in Logology.* Berkeley and Los Angeles: University of California Press, 1970.

Burnet, Thomas. *The Sacred Theory of the Earth: Containing an Account of its Original Creation, And of all the General Changes which it hath undergone, or is to undergo, until the Consummation of all Things.* 2 vols. London: Printed for T. Osborn et al., 1759.

Byron, George Gordon (Lord). *Don Juan.* Boston: Houghton Mifflin, 1958.

Cohen, Ralph. *The Art of Discrimination: Thomson's* The Seasons *and the Language of Criticism.* Berkeley: University of California Press, 1964.

Coleridge, Samuel Taylor. *The Statesman's Manual.* In *Lay Sermons,* vol. 6 of *The Collection Works of Samuel Taylor Coleridge.* Ed. R. J. White. London: Routledge and K. Paul, 1972.

De Man, Paul. *Allegories of Reading.* New Haven and London: Yale University Press, 1979.

———. *Blindness and Insight: Essays in the Rhetoric of Contemporary Criticism.* 2d ed., rev. Minneapolis: University of Minnesota Press, 1983.

———. "The Epistemology of Metaphor." *Critical Inquiry* 5.1 (Autumn 1978): 13–30.

———. "Shelley Disfugured." In Bloom et al., *Deconstruction and Criticism.* New York: Seabury, 1979: 39–74.

Dennis, John. "The Grounds of Criticism in Poetry," in *The Critical Works of John Dennis.* Ed. E. N. Hooker. Baltimore: Johns Hopkins University Press, 1939.

Derrida, Jacques. *Margins of Philosophy.* Trans. Alan Bass. Chicago: University of Chicago Press, 1982.

———. *Of Grammatology.* Trans. Gayatri Chakravorty Spivak. Baltimore and London: The Johns Hopkins University Press, 1976.

———. *Dissemination.* Trans. Barbara Johnson. Chicago: University of Chicago Press, 1981.

Descartes, René. *Philosophical Writings.* Norman Kemp Smith. New York: Random House, 1958.

———. *Meditations touchant la premiere philosophie.* In *Oeuvres de Descartes* vol. IX. Paris: Librairie Philosophique J. Vrin, 1964.

Eaves, Morris. *William Blake's Theory of Art.* Princeton, New Jersey: Princeton University Press, 1982.

Fish, Stanley E. "*Lycidas*: A Poem Finally Anonymous." *GLYPH* 8 (Baltimore and London: The Johns Hopkins University Press, 1981): 1–18.

Foster, Hal. *Recodings: Art, Spectacle, Cultural Politics.* Port Townsend: Bay Press, 1987.

Freud, Sigmund. *Civilization and its Discontents* Trans. James Strachey. New York: W. W. Norton, 1961.

Gleckner, Robert. *Blake's Prelude: Poetical Sketches.* Baltimore and London: The Johns Hopkins University Press, 1982.

———. *Blake and Spenser.* Baltimore and London: The Johns Hopkins University Press, 1985.

Gray, Thomas. *The Complete English Poems of Thomas Gray.* London: Heinemann, 1973.

Hart, Clive. *Images of Flight.* Berkeley: University of California Press, 1988.

Hartman, Geoffrey. "Blake and the 'Progress of Poesy,'" in *Beyond Formalism.* New Haven and London: Yale University Press, 1970, 193–205.

Herodotus. *Herodotus* trans. A. D. Godley, 4 vols. London: Loeb, 1931–38.

Hobbes, Thomas. *Leviathan* Ed. C. B. Macpherson. Harmondsworth and London, 1968.

Horace. *Odes and Epodes.* Ed. Paul Shorey, rev. Paul Shorey and G. J. Laing. Chicago, New York, Boston: Benj. H. Sanborn & Co., 1919.

———. *The Odes of Horace.* Trans. James Michie. Indianapolis, New York, Kansas City: The Bobbs-Merrill Company, Inc., 1963.

Jameson, Fredric. "Postmodernism and Consumer Society." Hal Foster, ed., *The Anti-Aesthetic.* Port Townsend: Bay Press, 1983, 111–125.

———. "Postmodernism, or the Cultural Logic of Late Capitalism." *New Left Review* 146 (July-August 1984) 53–92.

Joyce, James. *Ulysses.* New York: Random House, 1961.

Laing, Malcolm, ed. *The Poems of Ossian.* Edinburgh: Constable and Co., 1805.

Locke, John. *An Essay Concerning Human Understanding.* 2 vols. New York: Dover Publications, 1959.

MacCabe, Colin. *Tracking the Signifier.* Minneapolis: University of Minnesota Press, 1985.

Macpherson, James. *Poems of Ossian*, 2 vols. London: Lackington, Allen, and Co., 1806.

Marx, Karl. *Zur Kritik der Politischen Ökonomie.* In *Karl Marx, Friedrich Engels, Werke. Band* 13. Berlin: Dietz Verlag, 1964.

Nisbet, R. G. M. and Margaret Hubbard. *A Commentary on Horace: Odes, Book II.* Oxford: Clarendon Press, 1978.

Parker, Andrew. "Ezra Pound and the 'Economy' of Anti-Semitism." *Boundary* 2 XI. 1 & 2 (Fall/Winter 1982/83): 103–128.

Patterson, Annabel. *Pastoral and Ideology: Virgil to Valéry.* Berkeley, Los Angeles: University of California Press, 1987.

Peterfreund, Stuart. "The Problem of Originality and Blake's *Poetical Sketches.*" ELH 52.3 (Fall 1985): 673–706.

Plato. *The Republic of Plato.* Trans. Francis M. Cornford. New York & London: Oxford University Press, 1965.

Ponge, Francis. "Le soleil lu à la radio," (from *Le Soleil placé en abîme*). *The Power of Language*: *Texts and Translations.* Trans. Serge Gavronsky. Berkeley, Los Angeles, London: University of California Press, 1979.

Pope, Alexander. *The Poems of Alexander Pope,* ed. John Butt. New Haven: Yale University Press, 1963.

Pound, Ezra. *Guide to Kultchur.* New York: New Directions, 1970.

———. *Selected Prose.* Ed. William Cookson. New York: New Directions, 1973.

Proust, Marcel. *A la recherche du temps perdu.* Paris: Éditions Gallimard (Pléiade), 1954.

———. *Remembrance of Things Past.* Trans. C. K. Scott Moncrieff and Terence Kilmartin, 3 vols. New York: Random House, 1981.

Ricoeur, Paul. *The Rule of Metaphor.* Trans. Robert Czerny, Kathleen McLaughlin and John Costello. Toronto: University of Toronto Press, 1979.

Ruskin, John. *The Works of John Ruskin.* 39 vols. Ed. E. T. Cook and A. Wedderburn, London: G. Allen, 1903–12.

Spivak, Gayatri Chakravorty. "Love Me, Love My Ombre, Elle." *Diacritics* Winter 1984, 19–36.

Stone, N.I. (Trans.) *A Contribution to the Critique of Political Economy by Karl Marx.* Chicago: Charles H. Kerr, 1904.

Thomson, James. *The Seasons.* Ed. James Sambrook. Oxford: Clarendon Press, 1981.

Todorov, Tzvetan. *Theories of the Symbol.* Trans. Catherine Porter. Ithaca, New York: Cornell University Press, 1982.

Tuve, Rosamund. *Seasons and Months: Studies in a Tradition of Middle English Poetry.* Paris: J. Gamber, 1933.

Valéry, Paul. "Pure Poetry." *The Art of Poetry.* Trans. Denise Folliot. New York: Vintage Books, 1961.

Vergil. *The Eclogues and Georgics of Vergil.* Trans. C. Day Lewis; includes Latin text. Garden City, New York: Doubleday & Company, 1964.

Vogler, Thomas A. "Eighteenth-Century Logology and the Book of Job." *Religion and Literature* 20.3 (Autumn 1988): 25–47.

———. "Intertextual Signifiers and the Blake of That Already." *Romanticism Past and Present* 9:1 (1985): 1–33.

———. *Preludes to Vision: The Epic Venture in Blake, Wordsworth, Keats and Hart Crane.* Berkeley: University of California Press, 1971.

———. "The Tropology of Silence in Eighteenth-Century English Blank Verse." *The Eighteenth Century: Theory and Interpretation* 26:3 (Fall 1985): 211–237.

White, Hayden. *Metahistory: The Historical Imagination in Nineteenth-century Europe.* Baltimore: The Johns Hopkins University Press, 1973.

Winckelmann, Johann Joachim. *Reflections on the Imitation of Greek Works in Painting and*

Sculpture (with German text). Trans. Elfriede Heyer and Roger C. Norton. La Salle, Illinois: Open Court, 1987.

Wollstonecraft, Mary. *A Vindication of the Rights of Woman*. Photo-facsimile reprint of 1792 ed. (Boston). New York & London: Garland Publishing, Inc., 1974.

Wordsworth, William. *The Prelude* (1805). Ed. Ernest De Selincourt. London: Oxford University Press, 1960 (Revised impression).

————. *The Poetical Works of William Wordsworth*. Ed. E. De Selincourt and Helen Darbishire. Oxford: Clarendon, 1949.

Yeats, William Butler. *W. B. Yeats: The Poems*. Ed. Richard J. Finneran. New York: Macmillan Publishing Company, 1983.

Young, Edward. *The Poetical Works of Edward Young*. 2 vols. Westport, Connecticut: Greenwood Press, 1970. Originally published by Bell and Daldy, London.

"Crouding After Night": Troping and the Sublime in *Poetical Sketches*

Vincent A. De Luca

And now the raging armies rush'd
  Like warring mighty seas;
The heav'ns are shook with roaring war,
  The dust ascends the skies!
            ("Gwin, King of Norway," 69–72)

Joys upon our branches sit,
Chirping loud and singing sweet;
Like gentle streams beneath our feet
Innocence and virtue meet.
            ("Song [Love and harmony]," 5–8)

Lo! now the direful monster, whose skin clings
To his strong bones, strides o'er the groaning
rocks
            ("To Winter," 9–10)

To begin with a commonplace, in *Poetical Sketches* Blake displays
an extraordinary fondness for tropes. The streams of similitudes in
a poem like "Gwin, King of Norway," the extended baroque conceit
in the Song "Love and harmony combine," the apotheosizing personifications of "To Winter" and "To the Evening Star," the curious
fusions of metaphoric and metonymic elements in "To Spring" and
"To Summer"[1]—devices such as these abound in the series and at some
points cluster so densely that for the reader the discrete properties and
boundaries of phenomena are virtually effaced. As is often remarked,
in *Poetical Sketches* nature is consistently humanized and humanity
likened to the sublime forms of nature. Through similitudes and
personification, each thing typically becomes either more than its
proper self or interchangeable with something else. One can easily
see how such a style of profuse troping would appeal deeply to a
young poet with idealistic and visionary aspirations, offering as it
does opportunities for mythopoeia and for unifications of nature,
man, and spirit.

In this essay I seek to connect Blake's early style with his aspiration to become a poet in the sublime mode and to show some of the built-in attractions and dangers of this aspiration. To begin with, the figurative style, according to various eighteenth-century commentators, is a potent agency of the sublime. Because of its associations with biblical style, it receives its endorsement virtually from the Holy Spirit, and thus comes charged with a sense of spiritual plenitude and intensity. The Hebrew poets, Robert Lowth tells us in his *Sacred Poetry of the Hebrews,* "have assiduously attended to the sublimity of their compositions by the abundance and splendour of their figures; . . . For in those poems at least, in which something of uncommon grandeur and sublimity is aimed at, there predominates a perpetual, I had almost said a continued use of the metaphor, sometimes daringly introduced, sometimes rushing in with imminent hazard of propriety."[2] When aiming for the sublime, then, the Spirit dictates a profusion of tropes, figures in rapid flux, and an indecorous, even dangerous, transgression of "propriety" or discrete bounds. An example of the continuous troping that Lowth has in mind is offered by his contemporary Edmund Burke as an illustration of the "Magnificence" displayed by the sublime style. Burke quotes the description of the High Priest Simon in Ecclesiasticus 50:

> How was he honoured in the midst of the people, in his coming out of the sanctuary! He was as the morning star in the midst of a cloud, and as the moon at the full: as the sun shining upon the temple of the Most High, and as the rainbow giving light to the bright clouds: and as the flower of roses on the spring of the year; as lillies by the rivers of waters and as the frankincense tree in summer; as fire and incense in the censer; and as a vessel of gold set with precious stones; as a fair olive tree budding forth fruit, and as a cypress which groweth up to the clouds.[3]

In this passage we can hear faintly but unmistakably the idiom of *Poetical Sketches,* conveyed in the imagery of natural fertility, of spring and summer, sun and morning star. The beauty and appeal of such a passage rest partly in the ever-changing succession of images and partly in the character of the images themselves, all of them evoking states of change and transitory form—images of hours and seasons, of moving, dissolving, or veiled light, of rivers and fire, of flowering and growing things. At the same time all these metamorphic, quicksilver forms remain attributes of one centripetal presence, the Servant of God who stands "in the midst." Sweet transience and metamorphosis are united to stable presence, forming a oneness that resembles what Robert Gleckner, speaking of the seasons poems of *Poetical Sketches,* has called an "atemporal state of eternal becoming."[4]

In the place of God or his surrogate standing in the sanctuary of the temple, however, the trope-mad poets of the eighteenth century, like Collins in "The Ode to Evening" or Blake in the first six poems of the *Sketches,* raise as their divinities the transient states of natural cycles. There is no stable, unchanging center of presence to hold in equilibrium the multiplicity of divinity's transient modifications. Hence the trope becomes an equivocal ally in the quest of these poets to promote a naturalized visionary sublime. For one thing, a conspicuous penchant for troping may easily suggest a view of reality as consisting simply of endless transformations, becomings, and potentialities. In the verbal surface metaphors efface the original images of the things they represent and yet retain traces of those originals. When Blake calls his Evening Star a "fair-hair'd angel," he nonetheless continues to locate this ethereal being in its former station in the western twilight. We read "angel" but remember "star," as if the personification substituted itself for something that once occupied the same space, shared the same identity, but was altogether different in form. I have deliberately used the terminology of past and present ("was once," "is now") in the last two sentences to suggest that in troping there is always an image of temporal substitution, of a form *becoming* another subsequent form.[5] Troping is a representation of metamorphosis enacted on the level of style, and conversely, things that change their form in time are natural tropes. Tropes after all are "turns," whether we are referring to the turns of figurative language or to those bi-annual turns of the sun which tell the change of seasons and which are marked on globes with the name of Tropics. Now *Poetical Sketches* opens with a flourish of turning seasons, followed by what Gleckner calls "marginal moments of dawn and evening."[6] In these six poems of temporal turning Blake lavishes the most intense and concentrated effects of his figurative style in *Poetical Sketches.* He tropes most profusely that which Nature has already troped before him. This perspective on the poems yields a paradoxical and somewhat unsettling impression: that the myth-making, apotheosizing, universally assimilating ambience effected by their style is somehow saturated in time, is like time.

In his discussion of this first group of poems in the *Sketches,* Gleckner sets the two diurnal poems "To the Evening Star" and "To Morning," with their "thrust . . . toward continuousness or sequentiality,"[7] against the seasons poems, which he reads as embodying a kind of visionary *nunc stans* transcending cyclic time. Yet late in the *Sketches* Blake himself advertises the sequentiality of the seasons; in the prose poem "Contemplation," his eponymous allegorical heroine declares: "Like a triumph, season *follows* seasons while the airy music fills the world with joyful sounds" (*E* 443 italics mine). Seasons are after all no less transitory than mornings and evenings; not only does each season yield to its successor, but in itself it is continuously in transition from moment to moment. In the poems on the seasons Blake may personify them as four quasi-eternal beings, but there is no *nunc stans* in the language of these poems, and if we were to connect them end to end as if they were one continuous piece, the single line of transformative motion that flows through them would become evident. If we ignore the boundaries between the poems and focus on the succession of active verbs attached to the seasonal subjects, we discern an ever-changing force that (in this order) *approaches, issues forth, comes, passes, pitches tent, sits down, throws off, rushes, pauses not, rises, flees, builds, rides, strides, withers, unclothes, freezes,* and *is driven.* These swift transformations and restless movements reappear in exaggerated form elsewhere in the volume: in the frenzied chase of the speaker in the "Mad Song" to stay within the ever receding liminal interface of day and night; in the overwhelming flood that concludes "Gwin, King of Norway"; in the manic impulses to rush into the chaos of battle displayed in "Edward III" and some of the later patriotic pieces.

These motifs of "becoming," of hurry, and of transformations from state to state are, like the troping style itself, entirely suited to the aesthetic of the eighteenth-century sublime, for this aesthetic postulates sudden transformations of the mind, episodes in which we are rushed away from our proper selves. "Hence arises the great power of the sublime," Burke says, "that far from being produced by them, it anticipates [i.e., intercepts] our reasonings, and hurries us on by an irresistible force."[8] The stimuli that provoke the mind to such highly fluxile instabilities are often themselves unstable objects, objects whose discrete bounds have been effaced. Burke tells us that "hardly anything can strike the mind with its greatness . . . whilst we are able to perceive its bounds,"[9] and in poetry the trope plays a conspicuous role in effacing these bounding outlines. To illustrate his point Burke cites one of the powerful descriptions of Satan in *Paradise Lost*, Book I:

> he above the rest
> In shape and gesture proudly eminent
> Stood like a Tow'r; his form had yet not lost
> All her original brightness, nor appear'd
> Less than Arch-Angel ruin'd, and th'excess
> Of Glory obscur'd: As when the Sun new ris'n
> Looks through the Horizontal misty Air
> Shorn of his Beams, or from behind the Moon
> In dim Eclipse disastrous twilight sheds
> On half the Nations, and with fear of change
> Perplexes Monarchs.
>
> (*PL* I.589–99)

Of this passage Burke comments, "Here is a very noble picture; and in what does this poetical picture consist? in images of a tower, an archangel, the sun rising through mists, or in eclipse, the ruin of monarchs, and the revolution of kingdoms. The mind is hurried out of itself, by a croud of great and confused images; which affect because they are crouded and confused. . . . The images raised by poetry are always of this obscure kind."[10] In the sublime Miltonic passage discussed here, Satan the archangel is triply troped into ruin. First the images representing him, the sun in eclipse, the monarch perplexed, and so on, are themselves "confusions," intermixtures of a passing glory and a coming gloom. Second, each time Satan is troped with an image drawn from the natural, artificial or political world, the diachronically substitutive features of troping come into play, mediating a "then" of archangelic brightness in eternity and a "now" of dark materiality bound to the changes of time. Third—and here Burke places his particular stress—each dark trope displaces its predecessor trope, but too quickly for the former lineaments to be effaced in the memory, so that all the images heap together or "ruin" together (like the stones of the tower toppling) in a cumulative disfigurement or obscurity. Overcome by a crowding avalanche of images, the mind is swept away into its own darkness, as Satan is into his.

The superimposition of images, then, according to Burke, is a subtractive rather than an additive process. Each new trope removes light and clarity from the amassing whole until we are left with a final dark. The tropic style is always in danger of becoming en-tropic, an enactment and celebration of slippage, loss, and depletion, the grim corollaries of a vision of things that places transformation and instability at its center. What tropes do to the signifying functions of language, time does to the seasons of our lives and to nature as a whole; spring and morn only seem to return, for time is a form of troping that goes in one direction only, toward that final moment of entropy that "unclothes the earth and freezes up frail life" ("To Winter," 11), returning all things to the womb of night. The kind of poetry that Burke favors merely speeds up the process. The "croud of great and confused images" presses upon us, rushing us away before our time to that final obscurity. This dreaded and yet delicious foretaste of doom, which for Burke constitutes the sublime, might aptly be called "crouding after night."

This returns us, of course, to *Poetical Sketches* and to the element of melancholy that is strongly evident in the series. Blake tells us that he "read Burkes Treatise when very Young" (*E* 660), and felt "Contempt & Abhorrence" for its views. But it is one thing to abhor a powerful antithetical voice and another thing to escape its influence, especially if one is "very young"—adolescent, one presumes—and about to embark on one's first attempt at the poetry of the sublime. Let us turn for evidence of this influence to what I take to be the crucial poem in the series, the "Mad Song":

> Lo! to the vault
>   Of paved heaven,
> With sorrow fraught
>   My notes are driven:
> They strike the ear of night,
>   Make weep the eyes of day;
> They make mad the roaring winds,
>   And with tempests play.
>
> Like a fiend in a cloud
>   With howling woe,
> After night I do croud,
>   And with night will go;
> I turn my back to the east,
> From whence comforts have increas'd
> For light doth seize my brain
> With frantic pain.

(9–24)

When the speaker declares, "After night I do croud, / And with night will go," are we perhaps intended to see him as an impressario of the Burkean sublime? There is something "willed," as L. C. Knights has said,[11] and self-gratifying about his embrace of the dark and something grandiose in his estimation of his poetic powers. No poor weak Tom-o'-Bedlam he, despite his generic origins; rather, "Like a fiend in a cloud" (17), he resembles the storm-king Winter described earlier in the series, playing with tempests and inducing a contagious madness in the roaring winds. To characterize the Madman as a poet of the dark sublime prompts one to consider the degree of Blake's self-identification with this figure.[12] While allowing for the presence of some obvious, self-consciously theatrical role-playing, we should not be too quick to read the mature Blake's views back into the attitudes of the youth, as those critics do who consign the Madman's enterprise to the realm of satire and cautionary tales.[13] Or, if there is satire present in the poem, we should consider how much Blake is himself implicated in the problem that he addresses. Certainly the last stanza of the poem briefly reenacts the movement of *Poetical Sketches* as a whole. Situated at the center of the volume, the thirteenth of the twenty-six poems in the collection, the "Mad Song" shows Blake turning his back to the east, where the series began (in "To Spring," with its lovely periphrasis of "east" in the second line) and choosing to go with the epic chants of warfare and death that will soon come to dominate the volume in its latter half. The pivot of *Poetical Sketches* and the paradigm of its progress, the "Mad Song" acts as a kind of "signature-poem," binding the author more closely to his Madman's program of crowding after night.

If corroboration is needed for Blake's share in this program, one has only to observe that fully sixteen of the twenty-six poems in *Poetical Sketches* end either literally in a scene of night or in analogous states such as death, darkness, constriction, cold, entropy, or blindness. The first of these night-rushing poems is "To Winter," only perfunctorily relieved by what Gleckner has called its "deliberately conventional "ending,[14] followed by "To the Evening Star," with its literal onset of dangerous night, and "Fair Elenor" groaning "her last." The series of eight songs that follow gives us such finalities as the following: "my loss of liberty" ("How sweet I roam'd"); "down I'll lie, as cold as clay / True love doth pass away" ("My silks and fine array"); "I'll go / To places fit for woe . . . along the darken'd valley / With silent Melancholy" ("Memory, hither come"); the "Mad Song" *in toto;* "sleep beneath night's shade" ("Fresh from the dewy hill");

and I'd "die in peace, and be forgot" ("When early morn walks forth").
The paralyzed strings, forc'd sounds, and few notes at the end of "To
the Muses" continue the entropic trend; the tide of tyrants' blood that
overwhelms the lands of peace in "Gwin" historicizes it (see 109–116);
and the echoes of historical disorder and blood lust continue in the
"Prologue to Edward IV" and the fatalistic battle-death preparations
of "A War Song to Englishmen." Of the concluding prose-poems,
the death-bed lamentations of "The Couch of Death," strike the
most lugubrious note in the whole volume, while "Contemplation"
ends with "Sorrow on a tombstone"; although "Samson" appears to
conclude on a prophetic, Messianic note, we cannot forget that the
poem breaks off just as Samson is about to tell Dalila his secret;
blindness lies ahead.

Left out of this reckoning are certain works that end on an
equivocal note: "Edward III" enlarges precisely the same dramatic
situation as "A War Song to Englishmen" while maintaining a hope-
infused perspective, and although the final song of the Minstrel is
millennial, the final word of spoken dialogue is "death." In a similar
fashion, "Autumn" leaves a "golden store" but also "bleak hills." In
the "Imitation of Spenser" Minerva, who loves to walk in "solemn
gloom" (48), may or may not be moved by the "weary wanderer" and
"th'afflicted man." Finally, to shift from these particular instances to
the general shape of the volume as a sequence, we observe that the
thematic movement of the sequence mirrors and magnifies the pre-
dominant movements of its individual parts. The lambent visionary
pastorals cluster almost entirely in the first half, before the "Mad
Song," while death and the dark clashes of jagged powers take over in
the second.[15] The miniature series on the seasons that opens *Poetical
Sketches* appropriately moves from Spring to Winter[16] and thus serves
as a kind of prospectus to the whole.

If the seasons poems form a prospectus and the "Mad Song" a
condensed mid-point synopsis of the light-dark movement that we
have been concerned with, the neglected prose-poem "Contemplation" late in the volume provides a clearly delineated retrospective
summary of Blake's ambiguous posture as a poet in *Poetical Sketches*.[17]
The poem is a debate between two contrary visions of nature, time,
and human experience, in which the allegorical figure of Contemplation maintains the positive perspective:

" . . . delights blossom around; numberless beauties blow;
the green grass springs in joy, and the nimble air kisses

the leaves; the brook stretches its arms along the velvet
meadow, its silver inhabitants sport and play; the youthful
sun joys like a hunter rouzed to the chace; he rushes up
the sky, and lays hold of the immortal coursers of day; the
sky glitters with the jingling trappings! Like a triumph,
season follows season, while the airy music fills the world
with joyful sounds." I answered, "Heavenly goddess! I am
wrapped in mortality, my flesh is a prison, my bones the
bars of death. . . ."

(*E* 442)

Wherever Blake himself stands in this debate in which the voice of
darkness has the last word, it is remarkable how the contrary vision of
Contemplation revives virtually the whole rhetoric of the poems in
the first half of the volume, with their anthropomorphic solar figures,
the metamorphic interchanges of man and nature, the profusion of
tropes, and the celebration of natural, sequential cycles. But this time
they are bracketed, as it were, enclosed in quotations, and qualified
by a counter-perspective that sees mortal time as a series of changes
from misery to misery in an inevitable course to the night of the grave.
A vision of visionary troping, meant to embody "magnificence" and
spiritual plenitude, is made to confront a vision of entropic desolation.
But to say this is not to award the palm to one side or the other in the
debate. The little unresolved dialogue in "Contemplation" mirrors a
larger one between prophetic, visionary, and millennial aspirations in
the series on the one hand and surrenders to the dark on the other.
That the balance seems to keep shifting toward the dark side of the
equation is only a testament to the strength of the splendor in which
the series begins in "To Spring" and "To Summer"; it takes more than
all the swerves toward night detailed above, more than the whole of
Burke's gravitational sway, to efface that splendor from our minds.

Yet the dark gravitational pull is there, and we have to account
for it. Of course there is no absolute need to invoke Burke here. In so
variously imitative a sequence as *Poetical Sketches,* it can scarcely be
accidental that the arrangement of the volume mirrors in miniature
the career arc, as it was traditionally conceived, of a great precursor,
one who began essentially as a poet in the pastoral mode and ended
by focusing on the darkly grand figure of Samon. Nor can we forget
that in *Samson Agonistes* Milton anticipates Burke's theorizing by
forging a strong connection between the sublime and a suggested final
entropy, a climactic "crouding after night" that includes the collapse

of great architectural structures, the confounding of multitudes, the eyeless hero's self-erasure, and the word "spent" at the conclusion of all. What was good enough for Milton's sublime surely is good enough for the young aspiring poet Blake. At the same time, however, there is much in the poetic and aesthetic environment of the late eighteenth century to turn Milton's conflation of gloom and Hebraic sublimity into an even more problematic and ambivalent sort of enterprise. If in "To Spring" the poet (to follow a common line of interpretation) invites the Hebraic style of poetry to "visit our clime" (8), in precursor works such as Macpherson's Ossianic poems the Hebraic style is boldly made to *suffer* "our clime," that is, it is subjected to all the gloom, damp, and storminess of an insistent northern setting; indeed the "northerliness" of these poems is virtually their only significant new point. This uneasy marriage of style and setting, drawn from the "indecorous" antipodal peripheries of mainstream European culture, has the odd effect of emphasizing their polarity while hinting at covert congruities of a subversive kind. The Nordic and native English pieces in *Poetical Sketches* partake of this tendency, as does the transformation of the Orientalized tropes of "To Spring" into the northern tropes for "To Winter," a poem that Geoffrey Hartman has read as "meaning there exists a genuine poetry of the North."[18] This poetry of the North is essentially the poetry of the Burkean sublime, the poetry of looming dark, of obscuring mists, of the strife of blood, and time's transformations. Just as Burke's theory of the sublime, with its dynamic of free-floating "terror," undercuts the older, religious grounding of the sublime experience, so the poetry of the North destabilizes the spiritual implications of the biblical style.

But this scheme of rival sublimities needs a further (albeit brief) explanation of its dynamics. Let us say that Blake begins with aspirations to a vision of a plenitude, immanent in the here and now of time and nature and expressible in a Hebraically based style of troping. He discovers that mythopoeic presences and a vision of all things identified can virtually be manufactured out of tropes alone. But tropes cannot intrinsically arrest the flow of time and the transformations of nature or create a factitious eternity, "an apocalyptic spring."[19] Intrinsically they are the stylistic mirror of outward change, and they form the rhetoric of instability, effacement, indeterminacy, and supersession. Ultimately they do Burke's work, not the visionary's. The mind is hurried in too many places, and sooner or later one of those places will be the dark, toward which, one soon notices, all mortal things, all temporal cycles, are also hurrying. One potent response to this melancholy situation is to court preemptively that which is feared and even glamorize it, to put a crown on the dark tyrant's head and a scepter in his hand. Even "when very young," part of Blake regards this psychological dynamic with "contempt and abhorrence," recognizes it as a kind of madness, and labels its most concentrated articulation a "Mad Song." Yet the dark attraction persists (a poet must be sublime *somehow*), and it will take a more severe, schematic, intellectual style than is available to Blake in the years before 1783 (or many years thereafter) to hold it at bay. In *Poetical Sketches* we are witnessing only the beginnings of an oscillation in Blake's poetry between the rival attractions of the northern spell and the biblical promise, between the "cliffs of Albion" ("Edward III" 6.55) and their separated emanative light, a rivalry that will not be reconciled until the closing plates of *Jerusalem.*

Notes

1. In these poems the personifications of the seasons derive their specific forms from what the seasons actually *touch* in the human and natural worlds; hence the fertile confusions between "our winds" and "thy morn and evening breath" in "To Spring" (8, 10) or the transformation of the solar deity in "To Summer" into bathers or sleepers in the shade seeking to escape the heat that deity has engendered. All quotations from Blake will be to *The Complete Poetry and Prose of William Blake,* ed. David V. Erdman, rev. ed. (Garden City, N.Y.: Anchor-Doubleday, 1982), cited as *E.*

2. Robert Lowth, *Lectures on the Sacred Poetry of the Hebrews,* trans. G. Gregory, 2 vols. (London: J. Johnson, 1787), I, 121.

3. Edmund Burke, *Philosophical Enquiry into the Origin of our Ideas of the Sublime and the Beautiful,* ed. J. T. Boulton (London: Routledge and Kegan Paul, 1958), p. 79, slightly misquoting Ecclesiasticus 50:5ff.

4. Robert F. Gleckner, *Blake's Prelude: Poetical Sketches* (Baltimore: Johns Hopkins, 1982), p. 64.

5. In his influential essay "The Rhetoric of Temporality," Paul de Man points out "the constitutive temporal element" in allegorical tropes and extends the simple diachronic succession suggested in my example into an infinite regress: "it remains necessary if there is to be allegory, that the allegorical sign refer to another sign that precedes it. The meaning constituted by the allegorical sign can then consist only in the *repetition* . . . of a previous sign with which it can never coincide since it is of the essence of this previous sign to be pure anteriority" (*Blindness and Insight: Essays in the Rhetoric of Contemporary Criticism,* 2nd ed. [Minneapolis: Univ. of Minnesota Press, 1983] p. 207).

6. Ibid., p. 93.

7. Ibid., p. 94.

8. *Philosophical Enquiry,* p. 57.

9. Ibid., p. 62.

10. Ibid.

11. L. C. Knights, *Sewanee Review,* 1971; quoted in Michael Phillips, "Blake's Early Poetry," in *William Blake: Essays in Honour of Sir Geoffrey Keynes,* ed. Morton D. Paley and Michael Phillips (Oxford: Clarendon Press, 1973), p. 11.

12. For useful remarks on this point, see Phillips, ibid., pp. 10–12.

13. See, e.g., Harold Bloom, *Blake's Apocalypse: A Study in Poetic Argument* (Garden City, N.Y.: Doubleday, 1963), pp. 19–20.

14. *Blake's Prelude,* p. 69.

15. For a similar position, although argued from a different perspective, see James McGowan, "The Integrity of the *Poetical Sketches:* A New Approach to Blake's Earliest Poems," *Blake Studies,* 8.2 (1979), 142. It must be clear by now that I subscribe to the view that Blake arranged these poems himself. This is not to deny that someone else (say, Flaxman) could have given them a satisfactory thematic arrangement. This becomes less likely, however (apart from other evidence one might cite), when it is observed how the thematic movement of the whole is reproduced not only in the movement of smaller internal clusters but also in that of individual poems themselves.

16. For the view that the arrangement is *inappropriate,* see Irene Chayes, "Blake and the Seasons of the Poet," *Studies in Romanticism,*" (1972), 225–240. By placing "To Spring" at the end of the series, Chayes would, among other things, deprive us of one of the most splendid choral openings in the history of English poetic sequences.

17. See McGowan, "The Integrity of *Poetical Sketches,*" p. 142, for a similar view that "Contemplation" represents "a reminiscence, a taking stock." McGowan precedes me in noting the confrontation of positive and negative visions in this prose poem. I differ from him, however, in regarding the "reminiscence" as one pertaining to the volume's range of poetic styles and moods, not, as McGowan would have it, to the poet's own past, outgrown attitudes (see p. 143).

18. Geoffrey Hartman, *Beyond Formalism* (New Haven: Yale University Press, 1970), p. 202.

19. See Michael J. Tolley, "Blake's Songs of Spring," in Paley and Phillips, p. 102.

The Rankest Draught

NELSON HILTON

Though unsigned, untitled, and undated, two short pieces of writing in Blake's hand have long been thought to stand in a significant relationship to *Poetical Sketches*. Both Geoffrey Keynes and David Erdman print them directly after the published collection, the latter under the heading of "Further Sketches." The first, longer, and more complicated of the two pieces, which contains two passages in common with one of the published "sketches," begins abruptly: "then She bore Pale desire." Erdman labels the autograph a fragment, observing and concluding at once that "[t]he first word is not indented or capitalized and was obviously not originally the beginning of the ms" (E 848). But as one never knows what was "originally the beginning" in a poet perceived increasingly as an inveterate drafter and grafter of fragments, and as the manuscript has its own adequately coherent genealogy, one may at least assume that nothing "of equal value was lost" (*MHH* 13).

With run-on sentences, erratic capitalization, ambiguous periods, ambiguous period-marks, and no paragraphing, the autograph would appear to test Blake's strategy of disseminating referential possibilities—loading every rift with "or." Indeed, the many periods from Blake's hand contrast so dramatically with the orderly syntax of the type-set sketches as to suggest a heavy editorial role on the part of those "friends" who arranged publication though "conscious of the irregularities and defects" in what they considered "the production of untutored youth." Perhaps such a betrayal of the manuscript of *Poetical Sketches* best accounts for the fact that Blake "never seems to have shown much interest in the little volume" (Bentley, *Records* 26)—the "sketches" as rendered in type weren't his work, in effect. A consideration, bit by bit, of what seems to be the earliest example of Blake's own irregular and defective writing may open some new possibilities even for the reader who feels familiar with it.

"[T]hen She bore Pale desire" seems to carry "irregularities and defects" to an extreme—in the commentary still included with the Erdman edition, Harold Bloom finds it "so slapdash" as to suggest "the most rapid kind of composition," one which "needs to be read as only a curiosity" (E 970). The truly curious reader will, however, soon discover that the composition offers a "blank-versed prose" (Saintsbury 22) and range of quotation and allusion that would suppose some degree of artifice and consideration. The metrical base, which it shares with the published prose sketches, is the most striking aspect of the piece, initially. Indeed, the manuscript was first presented to the public by William M. Rossetti in 1903 as "The Passions, An Unpublished Poem by William Blake," with the observation that "it is indisputably verse—lines in correct decasyllabic and other metre, intermixed with a few which cannot be reduced to regular scansion" (Rossetti 123). Rossetti refers to "another half-sheet of [Blake's] MS."—now apparently lost—which he obtained with "[T]hen She bore Pale desire" and in which Blake had "written out, as prose, the six lines of Shakespearean rhymed verse which begin, 'Orpheus with his lute made trees' ['/ And the mountain tops that freeze, / Bow themselves when he did sing. / To his music plants and flowers / Ever sprung, as sun and showers / There had made a lasting spring.' (*Henry VII* III.i)]" (Rossetti 123). This manuscript offers further evidence of an extraordinary concern with rhythm which has been emphasized by only a few critics, though as early as 1910 the historian of English prosody George Saintsbury noted "the extraordinary prosodic quality which, almost as much as his thought, his imagery, and his passion, distinguishes [Blake] as a poet" (9). In 1924, the ever-perceptive S. Foster Damon characterized Blake's metrical . . . 'polyphonic prose'" as "one form entirely his own, in which he made several experiments, whose true value could not be appreciated until the present day" (48–49). Blake's prose sketch "Samson" was, in particular, Damon suggests, an attempt "to improve on the broken, yet metrical cadences of Milton's *Samson Agonistes*" (49).

In order, then, to show how Blake's earliest rough draft may have been prepared—like his transcription from Shakespeare—to study the unifying effect of rhythm, one might return "[T]hen She bore Pale desire" to a form which highlights its metrical basis. Two such attempts by early editors have been generally and justifiably condemned: Edwin Ellis in his 1906 collection gratuitously mends, revises, and transposes the text; Rossetti, in the presentation already mentioned, follows the words more closely, but invents stanzas, punctuation, and capitalization to create "The Passions." What follows is the standard Erdman text (itself based on his exact transcription in *The Bulletin of the New York Public Library* [1958]) in a format whose lineation stresses the metrical base. The new form results largely from treating Blake's periods as line-endings. So the passage early on,

"But Pride awoke nor knew that Joy was born. and taking Poisnous Seed from her own Bowels" produces two lines of blank verse, and a number of similar lines supply a frame around which to organize the rest (the striking exception of the opening will be noted below). This hypothetical form is numbered by line for ease of reference in the extended commentary which follows it.

then She bore Pale desire father of Curiosity
a Virgin ever young.
And after.
        Leaden Sloth from whom came Ignorance.
who brought forth wonder.
5   These are the Gods which Came from fear.
for Gods like these.
            nor male nor female are
but Single Pregnate or if they list together
mingling bring forth mighty powrs[.]
She knew them not yet they all war with Shame
10   and Strengthen her weak arm.
But Pride awoke nor knew that Joy was born.
and taking Poisnous Seed from her own Bowels.
in the Monster Shame infusd.
forth Came Ambition Crawling like a toad
Pride Bears it in her Bosom.
15   and the Gods.
all bow to it.
        So great its Power.
that Pride inspird by it Prophetic Saw
the Kingdoms of the World & all their Glory.
Giants of Mighty arm before the flood.
Cains City.
20   built with Murder.
Then Babel mighty Reard him to the Skies.
Babel with thousand tongues
Confusion it was calld.
        and Givn to Shame.
this Pride observing inly Grievd.
        but knew not that.
25   the rest was Givn to Shame as well as this.
Then Nineva & Babylon & Costly tyre.
And evn Jerusalem was shewn.
        the holy City.

Then Athens Learning & the Pride of Greece.
and further from the Rising Sun.
30 was Rome Seated on Seven hills the mistress of the world.
Emblem of Pride She Saw the Arts their treasures Bring
and luxury his bounteous table Spread.
but now a Cloud oercasts.

and back to th'East.
to Constantines Great City Empire fled.
35 Ere long to bleed & die
a Sacrifice Done by a Priestly hand
So once the Sun his.

Chariot drew.

back.
to prolong a Good kings life.

The Cloud oer past & Rome now shone again
40 Miterd & Crown'd with triple crown.
Then Pride was better Pleas She Saw
the World fall down in Adoration [.]
But now full to the Setting Sun
a Sun arose out of the Sea.
it rose & shed Sweet Influence
45   oer the Earth
Pride feared for her City, but not long.
for looking Stedfastly She saw that Pride Reigned here.
Now Direful Pains accost her.

and Still pregnant.
So Envy came & Hate.

twin progeny
50 Envy hath a Serpents head of fearful bulk
hissing with hundred tongues,
her poisnous breath breeds Satire foul
Contagion from which none are free.
oer whelmd by ever During Thirst
55 She Swalloweth her own Poison.
which consumes her nether Parts.
from whence a River Springs
Most Black & loathsom through the land it Runs
Rolling with furious Noise.
60 but at the last it Settles in a lake called Oblivion.
tis at this Rivers fount where evry mortals Cup is Mix't

My Cup is fill'd with Envy's Rankest Draught
a miracle No less can set me Right.
Desire Still pines but for one Cooling Drop and tis Deny'd.
65   while others in Contentments downy Nest do sleep,
it is the Cursed thorn wounding my breast that makes me sing.
however sweet tis Envy that Inspires my Song.
prickt.
            by the fame of others how I mourn
and my complaints are Sweeter than their Joys
70   but O could I at Envy Shake my hands.
my notes Should Rise to meet the New born Day.
Hate Meager hag Sets Envy on
unable to Do ought herself.
but Worn away a Bloodless Daemon
75   The Gods all Serve her at her will
So great her Power is[.] like.
                 fabled hecate
She doth bind them to her law.
Far in a Direful Cave She lives
unseen Closd from the Eye of Day.
80   to the hard Rock transfixt by fate
and here She works her witcheries
that when She Groans She Shakes the Solid Ground
Now Envy She controlls with numming trance
& Melancholy Sprung from her dark womb
85   There is a Melancholy, O how lovely tis
whose heaven is in the heavenly Mind
for she from heaven came,
and where She goes heaven still doth follow her.
She brings true Joy once fled.
& Contemplation is her Daughter.
90   Sweet Contemplation.
She brings humility to man
Take her She Says & wear her in thine heart
lord of thy Self thou then art lord of all.
Tis Contemplation teacheth knowledge truly how to know.
95   and Reinstates him on his throne once lost
how lost I'll tell.
               But Stop the motley Song.
I'll Shew.
           how Conscience Came from heaven.

But O who listens to his Voice
T'was Conscience who brought Melancholy down
100   Conscience was sent a Guard to Reason.
Reason once fairer than the light
till fould in Knowledges dark Prison house.
For knowledge drove sweet Innocence away.
and Reason would have followed but fate sufferd not
105   Then down Came Conscience with his lovely band
The Eager Song Goes on telling
how Pride against her father Warrd & Overcame.
Down his white Beard the Silver torrents Roll.
and Swelling Sighs burst forth his Children all
110   in arms appear to tear him from his throne
Black was the deed.
                              most Black.
Shame in a Mist Sat Round his troubled head.
& filld him with Confusion
Fear as a torrent wild Roard Round his throne
115   the mighty pillars shake
Now all the Gods in blackning Ranks appear.
like a tempestuous thunder Cloud Pride leads.
                                        them on.
Now they Surround the God.
                              and bind him fast.
pride bound him, then usurpd oer all the Gods.
120   She Rode upon the Swelling wind
and Scatterd all who durst t'oppose.
but Shame opposing fierce and hovering.
over her in the darkning Storm.
She brought forth Rage.
125   Mean while Strife Mighty Prince was born
Envy in direful Pains him bore.
then Envy brought forth Care.
Care Sitteth in the wrinkled brow.
Strife Shapeless Sitteth under thrones of kings like Smouldring
fire.
130   or in the Buzz of Cities flies abroad
Care brought forth Covet Eyeless & prone to th' Earth,
and Strife brought forth Revenge
Hate brooding in her Dismal den grew Pregnant
& bore Scorn, & Slander.
                              Scorn waits on Pride.

but Slander.
135   flies around the World
to do the Work of hate her drudge & Elf.
but Policy doth drudge for hate as well as Slander.
& oft makes use of her.
                    Policy Son of Shame.
Indeed Hate Controlls all the Gods.
                              at will.
140   Policy brought forth Guile & fraud.
these Gods last namd live in the Smoke of Cities.
on Dusky wing breathing forth Clamour & Destruction.
alas in Cities wheres the man
whose face is not a mask unto his heart
Pride made a Goddess.
145   fair   or I mage rather
till knowledge animated it.
                       'twas Calld Selflove.
The Gods admiring loaded her with Gifts
as once Pandora She 'mongst men was Sent.
and worser ills attended her by far.
150   She was a Goddess Powerful & bore Conceit
and Shame bore honour & made league with Pride
& Policy doth dwell with her
by whom she [had] Mistrust & Suspition.
Then bore a Daughter called Emulation.
who.
            married.
155   honour
these follow her around the World[.]
Go See the City friends Joind Hand in Hand.
Go See.
            the Natural tie of flesh & blood.
Go See more strong the tie of marriage love
160   thou Scarce Shall find but Self love Stands Between

1   then She bore Pale desire father of Curiosity

    The first verb introduces the master trope of the piece, the con-
ception of lineage or the genealogy of mental states. For this reason
a recent book on "kinship as metaphor" considers the autograph
in some (highly selective) detail, arguing that the metaphor "is the
principal domain underlying [its] exposition of human psychology"
(Turner 108). But perhaps still more dominant, if far less accessible,

are the kinship and psychology of the narrator and the author so concerned with them: the domain of what Melanie Klein terms "splitting," or the infant's attempt to mark off a dependable, "good object" from more or less inevitable inadequacies in the prime shaper of its environment. The autograph's emphasis on "bringing forth" or, more graphically, "bursting forth" suggests something more profound and less rational than metaphorical parturition.

The capitalization throughout increases possible constructions of the text. To see "Pale Desire" (Turner 109), for instance, stresses "Desire" and leaves the adjective almost beyond the pale of due attention (or perhaps "the pale of love," as in *The Prelude* [1805] 10.760). An uncapitalized "desire" pulls more than a capitalized one toward the following lowercase word (so one may read, in several voices: "desire father"), while the thereby strangely emphasized "Pale" at the same time achieves enough charge to carry through the object ("Pale desire, [Pale] father"). This mention of such ghostly micro-effects at length will stand for many others.

1–5 then She bore Pale desire father of Curiosity
    a Virgin ever young.
    And after.
        Leaden Sloth from whom came Ignorance.
    who brought forth wonder.
    These are the Gods which Came from fear.

Damon's observation concerning "King Edward the Third," in *Poetical Sketches,* and "The French Revolution" pertains here: "Customarily poets begin with lines absolutely according to pattern, in order that the pattern may be established; but Blake, in direct defiance of this, is apt to begin with variations, so that the metrical basis may be less obvious" (58). And Alicia Ostriker, also considering Blake's early dramatic effort, notes how "[t]he trick of varying line-lengths . . . becomes absurdly exaggerated" and how "[o]dd-length lines . . . instead of being saved up for relief or dramatic effect, are cast about recklessly, and almost outnumber the pentameters." Blake, she concludes, seems "to feel that if a little freedom is good, a lot must be better" (32).

The psycho-theogony begins with fear, and so accords with "the common maxim" Edmund Burke cites in his treatise on "the Sublime and the Beautiful": *"primos in orbe deos fecit timor"* ("fear first in the world made gods" as Ben Jonson has it in *Sejanus*). Discussing what he sees as the crucial relation of power and the sublime, Burke goes on to qualify his quotation, arguing that "the notion of some great power must be always precedent to our dread of it," though, he concedes, "dread must necessarily follow the idea" (p. 70). "Mighty power," one might say in the language of the autograph, "brings forth fear," or the realization of power external to the self and, next, one's own powerlessness before such a potentially annihilating Other ("The fear of the LORD is the beginning of knowledge"; Proverbs 1:7). A decade before Burke's *Enquiry,* William Collins's popular "Ode to Fear" characterizes its object as the "Dark Pow'r," a description Blake perhaps remembers in conceiving Urizen as "the dark power" (*BU* 3.7) well-acquainted with "fear & pale dismay" (*FZ* 24.2). Urizen's subsequent involvement with the concept of futurity also invokes the origins of self-consciousness in fear, which Samuel Johnson in his *Dictionary* defines (quoting Locke) as "an unpleasantness of the mind, upon the thought of future evil likely to befall us." Blake does not see fear iconographically (with "bristled hair," for example) but psycho-dynamically, as the awareness of time and the accompanying knowledge of transience, separation, and loss: it is, foremost, "of Death" (*M* 38.38).

Fear's first act here bears Pale desire, sire of curiosity. "Pale" traditionally describes the effects of fear (Shakespeare's "Pale-hearted Fear," Milton's "pale fear," and Blake's own "paling fear"), so her offspring, desire, keeps the family resemblance ("Pale Avarice" and "Pale Envy" appear in Swift, "Pale Grief" in Gray, "Pale Melancholy" in Collins). Desire's virgin daughter, remaining within the family pale, must be not so much an inclination to enquiry, as the obsolescent "Curiosity," which denotes "undue niceness or fastidiousness" (*OED*)— the qualities of the experienced nurse, for instance, who turns "green and pale" when she remembers "desires of youth" (E 23, 709).

6–8   for Gods like these.
                            nor male nor female are
        but Single Pregnate or if they list together
        mingling bring forth mighty powrs[.]

An example of this text's mingling syntax: the first "These" points out "the Gods which came from fear," but immediately "Gods like these" slightly but decisively expands the demonstrative to include just-excluded fear, whose ability to "Single Pregnate" has been posited from the beginning. This grammatical glitch pricks the reader's sloth and ignorance and encourages continuing wonder at what Gods are like these. "List" activates another anomaly: on the one hand it refers to a lusty desire for "mingling" and carnal knowledge which saturates the text; on the other, following the brief list which suggests what's to come, this "list" comments on the mighty powers to be brought forth in the reader by its mingling catalogue ("Babel mighty," 21; "motley Song," 96; "Confusion," 113).

9–11 She knew them not yet they all war with Shame
and Strengthen her weak arm.
But Pride awoke nor knew that Joy was born.

Shame, like fear, is evidently an aboriginal presence: the "Keys" to *For the Sexes* imagines the newborn psyche "Naked in Air in Shame & Fear" (E 268). But the deletion of a sentence that followed "weak arm" (telling of "the Golden Sun" and his "beaming Joy") puts Pride in a conjunction with Shame which will soon intensify (13–14). The war with Shame is a vague affair, since she appears with "all the Gods" in the revolt (112ff) but only toward the very end "makes league" (151). Given the situation of the war, it would seem that Shame is strengthened by desire, Curiosity, Sloth, Ignorance, wonder, and fear—all perhaps to be considered as aspects of a quest for knowledge.

"I disdaine to have any parents," says Pride in Marlowe's *Dr. Faustus* (1. 723), and Blake's pride is similarly without family, save that its "awaking" links it to Milton's Eve *(PL* 4.449ff) and that heavy inheritance. As the principal protagonist in the autograph (the sixteen appearances of her name are twice those of her nearest competitor, Envy), Pride merits extended consideration. Her creator at times certainly evidences an assertive pride: "I, William Blake, a Mental Prince" (E 580) writes of "terrible Blake in his pride" (E 500), and in a letter refers to "my foolish Pride" as though it were common knowledge (E 732). One wonders how he related such a sense of pride to his "Nervous Fear" (E 708). Still more moving is Los's identification of the Spectre as "my Pride & Self-righteousness" (*J* 8.30). But the specific ontology of pride remains imponderable, a question Blake takes up in a few heavily scored notebook lines which leave the matter wholly unresolved: "How came pride in Man / From Mary it began" (E 472). As the mother of the man-god (to unpack one strand of Christian mythology), Mary so idolized her child and her position as its mother that she never sullied herself by engendering another through the usual means. Out of such devotion comes the old sad story made familiar by D. H. Lawrence and lurking behind *Jerusalem's* identification of "Self-righteousness: the proud Virgin-Harlot! Mother" (50.16). Pride's not knowing "that Joy was born" might suggest the lost possibility of a composite infant to be a positively cherished "Pride and Joy" (hence also the deleted "Golden Sun . . . with beaming Joy": in this piece the little boy Joy-son is lost in "poison"). In the famous letter of 23 October 1804 (E 756–57) reporting his victory over the "spectrous Fiend," Blake announces that he is now "proud of my work," a sensation he claims not to have experienced for the preceding twenty years. Some crisis in Blake's self-esteem would thus appear to date from the era of his marriage, the publication of *Poetical Sketches*, and the death of his father (August 1782; 1783; July 1784).

12–13   and taking Poisnous Seed from her own Bowels.
           in the Monster Shame infusd.

Who does what? The action centers on something "infusd," some sort of instilling or of fusing within. The verb usually denotes some kind of liquid mixing—semen "infused" in a body would violate ordinary usage—but at one time it also assumed the special sense of referring to the way in which God works spiritual grace. Here, though, the grace infused would be the spirit of Shame in the Monster, Pride; unless, alternatively, Pride infuses Seed in Monster Shame. This conceptual mingling of Pride and Shame persists in Blake's writing; a "Proverb of Hell" describes shame as "prides cloak," and the misguided speaker of "To Tirzah" proposes that "The Sexes sprung from Shame and Pride."

Besides suggesting semen, "seed" applies to offspring or posterity, as does "bowels," which also names the place from whence comes forth the desired seed (for the two senses of "bowels" see *Measure for Measure* 3.1.29–30 and 2 Samuel 7:12). "The Monster" cues an association to Spenser's figure of that name (six times in as many stanzas of *FQ* 5.11) which guards the "Idoll" to whom Gerioneo "for endlesse horrour of his shame" daily sacrifices "children and people." Suggestive of Blake's description, Spenser's Monster speaks "blasphemous words, which she doth bray / Out of her poysnous entrails, fraught with dire decay" (5.11.20.8–9). Following Luke 8:11, "the seed" is also "the word."

14–18   forth Came Ambition Crawling like a toad
           Pride Bears it in her Bosom.
                             and the Gods.
           all bow to it.
                   So great its Power.
           that Pride inspired by it Prophetic Saw
           the Kingdoms of the World & all their Glory.

Toads having been popularly imagined as being poisonous, the animal supplies an appropriate analogue for what may be the seed's developed form, a still infantile, crawling Ambition. Discovered in his attempt to taint Eve, Satan appears "like a Toad," not "infusing" but "inspiring venom" with the aim of "ingendering pride" (*PL* 4.800, 804, 809).

Squat in the center of "ambition" sits *it*: what men in women do require and vice versa (cf. E 474–75)—"Ambition's lust" (Dryden and Lee, *Oedipus* 4.1.387), the desire for something more valued than what one possesses at present. In "King Edward the Third," "ambition" figures as "a little creeping root" that "grows in every breast; / Ambition is the desire or passion that one man / Has to get before another, in any pursuit after glory" (4.11–4: "to get" is also "to beget," "to bear"). Directly following the inspiration of Ambition the text dramatically bares an extended graft from Milton: an entire line of *Paradise Regained* which relates a temptation offered the Son, "The Kingdoms of the world, and all thir glory" (4.89; Milton's version of Matt. 4:8: " . . . the kingdoms of the world, and the glory of them").

19–23 Giants of Mighty arm before the flood.
    Cains City.
         built with Murder.
    Then Babel might Reard him to the Skies.
    Babel with thousand tongues
    Confusion it was calld.
         and Givn to Shame.

Blake builds here with Milton's vision of "Giants of mightie Bone" (*PL* 11.642 ["Arms" appears in both immediately adjacent verses]; cf. the LORD's "mighty arm," Ps. 89:13) "Before the Flood" (*PR* 2.178) and "that proud Citie . . . Left in confusion, *Babylon* thence call'd," "Confusion nam'd" (*PL* 12.342–43, 62). Added are the elements of using murder as mortar (unless Murder is an assistant giant) and Babel as another God "rearing" himself (or Ambition or Cain) skyward. This mighty city's being "Givn to" or prone to Shame suggests that Shame's weak arm (10) is already considerably strengthened. The flood and confusion will return.

24–28 this Pride observing inly Grievd.
         but knew not that.
    the rest was Givn to Shame as well as this.
    Then Nineva & Babylon & Costly tyre.
    And evn Jerusalem was Shewn.
         the holy City.
    And Athens Learning & the Pride of Greece.

Observing inly leaves Pride, like Adam, inly "Griev'd" ("Griev'd at his heart," *PL* 11.887) at a vision of the shameful world before the flood, but Shame is given rest until line 112, while Pride's labors are just beginning. "Costly tyre" anticipates Blake's later pun utilizing Ezekiel's description of the King of Tyrus as the "Covering Cherub" (Ez. 28:14, *Milton* 37.8): attire at such cost—work of satin, perhaps (cf. *M* 18.30)—manifests the "sin" that "covers" a narrator in *Poetical Sketches* "as a cloak" ("The Couch of Death") and which, as "Shame," is also "Prides cloke." *Paradise Regained* takes us, with the Son, to "*Jerusalem, / The holy city,*" after its vision of "*Athens* the eye of *Greece*" (4.544–45, 240).

29–32 and further from the Rising Sun.
   was Rome Seated on Seven hills the mistress of the world.
   Emblem of Pride She Saw the Arts their treasures Bring
   and luxury his bounteous table Spread.

Geographical orientation supplies a new figure who would leave behind the text (as he will by line 71); the Athens of *Paradise Regained* is similarly "much nearer" to its rising Son than the "great and glorious *Rome,* Queen of the Earth," "elevate / On seven small hills" (4.237, 45, 34–35).

33–36 but now a Cloud oercasts.
         and back to th'East.
   to Constantines Great City Empire fled.
   Ere long to bleed & die
   a Sacrifice Done by a Priestly hand

G. E. Bentley, Jr., finds this passage "apparently echoing similar assertions in Gibbon's *Decline and Fall of the Roman Empire* (Vols. I-III, 1776, 1781)" (Bentley, *Books* 439). The curious diction of "and back to th'East" might recall the speaker of "Mad Song," who has his "back to the East" (E 415).

37–38 So once the Sun his.
      Chariot drew.
         back.
   to prolong a Good kings life.

The classical conception of the sun's having a chariot makes a splice—perhaps via the Son's "Chariot of Paternal Deity" (*PL* 6.750)—with the Hebrew Bible's story of the LORD's adding fifteen years of life to the dying King Hezekiah, the "sign" of this gift being that "the sun returned ten degrees by which degrees it was gone down" (Is. 38:8; also 2 Kings 20:11, and 2 Chr. 32:32, which tells of Hezekiah's "goodness"). Just as unsettling and so compounding the effect is the introductory conjunction and the setting off, by punctuation, of the single word, "back" ("back to th'East"?). "So" implies some logical or causal or consequential or comparative connection, absent which, as here, one might posit a psychological connection: something concerning an artistic Blake son's drawing "back" (cf. Blake/black, 111), or repressing the "Chariot of his Contemplative Thought" (E 560) or his "chariot of pride" (*FZ* 65.4), so to preserve the image of a "goodly king" like Hamlet, or Laios, or the God the good Father, the King of Glory. But soon enough he will back the revolt (106ff).

39–42   The Cloud oer past & Rome now Shone again
         Miterd & Crown'd with triple crown.
         Then Pride was better Pleasd She Saw
         the World fall down in Adoration[.]

Lost from view when a Cloud "oercast" (33), Rome is shown again, shining with the Primacy of the Holy Father, when the dark age of the clouded past "oerpast." "Adoration," according to the initial definition in Johnson's *Dictionary*, denotes the "external homage paid to the Divinity"—here, evidently, Pride herself.

43–47   But now full to the Setting Sun
         a Sun arose out of the Sea.
         it rose & shed Sweet Influence
                           oer the Earth
         Pride feared for her City, but not long.
         for looking Stedfastly She saw that Pride Reignd here.

More orientation relative to a Sun, though the two suns and the expression "full to" instead of the usual "full in" complicate mundane geography. Milton puts "Shedding sweet influence" in conjunction with "the Moon" (*PL* 7.375), a body which might suit the Sun rising here, to the east of a still westering Sun. By the same token, Pride's City would now become "the City" (of London)—"here" where the author writes, a son arising out of what he sees in the city (cf. 157: "Go See the City").

48–51   Now Direful Pains accost her.
                           and Still pregnant.
         so Envy came & Hate.
                       twin progeny
         Envy hath a Serpents head of fearful bulk
         hissing with hundred tongues,

Direful Pains seems a new character with the audacity to seduce Pride (and her still pregnant; " 'Accost' is front her, board her, woo her, assail her," by the interpretation of Sir Toby Belch in *Twelfth Night*, 1.3.59). As for the "twin progeny," the "Imitation of Spen[s]er" in *Poetical Sketches* links "Envy and Hate, that thirst for human gore," and in the description of "The Last Judgment" the terms appear to be almost interchangeable (E 564–65). Envy's head is of fearful size (like Spenser's monstrous *Echidna*, "so huge her hed"; *FQ* 6.6.10.3) or, reflecting Pride's fear (46), bulks fear as its freight; her song (?self-reflexively of the wily author, his-sing-ing his tongues) accomplishes a ten-fold reduction of "Babel with thousand tongues" (22).

52–53   her poisnous breath breeds Satire foul
          Contagion from which none are free.

While her mother Pride possessed "Poisnous Seed" (12), the spirit of "poysonous Envy" (*FQ* 3.5.54.5) "breeds" or breathes social dis-ease, like Spenser's "old woman," *Sclander*, whose

> . . . words were not, as common words are ment,
> T'expresse the meaning of the inward mind,
> But noysome breath, and poysnous spirit sent
> From inward parts, with cancred malice lind,
> And breathed forth with blast of bitter wind;
>
>   (*FQ* 4.8.26.1–5)

or like another of his monsters, cited above (at 12–13), which perishes "Breathing out clouds of sulphure fowle and blacke, / In which a puddle of contagion was" (*FQ* 5.11.32.2–3). The self-reflexive judgment on "Satire" (in Blake's only use of the term) invokes the autograph's final line of defense, ironic aporia—for if "none are free," then one must suppose that this too is sick satire, especially considering the author's impending satire on the audience and supporters of *Poetical Sketches* in *An Island in the Moon*. Evidently Blake mocks in anger or disgust the snarling muse of the great age of English satire, and his evaluation of what it had to offer governs the first allusion to one of the autograph's crucial contexts, "Lycidas" 125–27 (italics added):

> The hungry sheep look up and are not fed,
> But swoln with wind, and the *rank mist* they *draw*,
> Rot inwardly, and *foul contagion* spred.

Littleton's 1760 *Dialogues of the Dead* similarly links contagion of
satire to the rank draft of envy as it equates Swift's "satire" with
"rank poison" (quoted in Tannenbaum 92).

Such sweeping cultural judgments, however, usually reflect the
projection of inner states, and here one might return to the work
of Melanie Klein, with its focus on the genesis of envy. Using her
rich speculations one might imagine a Blake extremely conflicted as
a result of inadequate maternal nourishment (evident in the mostly
female, negative cast of the autograph), and, in particular, deeply envious of the breast which, keeping its good for itself, long ago generated
a poisonous situation. According to Klein, envy is at bottom "directed
against creativeness," the breast and its milk offering the unconscious
prototype of creativity. As an example of the "envious and destructive
attitude towards the breast" and creativity, Klein cites lines from
Spenser which neatly round out the consideration of Blake's passage
here. *Envie,* she quotes (p. 41), "hated all good workes and vertuous
deeds" as well as (apropos of "Lycidas," above) "who with gracious
bread the hungry feeds":

> And eke the verse of famous Poets witt
> He does backebite, and spightfull poison spues
> From leprous mouth on all that ever writt.
>
> (*FQ* 1.4.32.6–8))

Drayton confirms that the "calumnious Critick" "blasteth all things
with his *poys'ned breath,* / Detracting what laboriously we doe" (*Moses
his Birth and Miracles* 2.165–68). Envy, to iterate, can occasion extremely conflicted (ambivalent, split) states, as the dim awareness of
its spoiling effects generates guilt (shame) and hence resistance to
insight. Poetic texts offer one way to attempt to work through or at
least temporarily externalize such conflicts.

54–56   oer whelmd by ever During Thirst
         She Swalloweth her own Poison.
         which consumes her nether Parts.

Envy's "ever During Thirst" seems an improbable echo of Milton's "ever during Gates" of Heaven (*PL* 7.206), but that context
seems to resurface when, in Luvah's history of the phallus, Vala
becomes a "Serpent" (cf. Envy's "Serpents head," 50) "poisonous"
for whom open "all the floodgates of the heavens to quench her
thirst" (*FZ* 26.9, 13, 14). Thirst also denotes "vehement desire" (Johnson), which, via the self-produced "poison" Envy swallows (following

Spenser's *Envie, FQ* 5.12.31), relates the thirst to Pride's "Poisnous Seed," Ambition (14). Robert Burton's *The Anatomy of Melancholy* nicely sums the mix in describing "Ambition" as "a dry thirst, a great torture of the mind, composed of envy, pride, and covetousness . . . a pleasant poison" (I.280). The archaic verbal ending for the third-person singular of "swallow," however, together with the ingestion of the poison, can invoke "Death" and thus prime (again à la Melanie Klein) some son's phantasy of a mother's devouring him, or, more conventionally, Sin's womb incestuously swallowing (cf. *PL* 2.149–50) the poisonous seed of a son who would consummate their relation by consuming her transforming "nether Parts" (cf. *PL* 2.777ff). Dryden and Lee's version of *Oedipus* comments that "Nature would abhor / To be forced back again upon herself / And like a whirlpool swallow her own streams." Yet again, it may be that—almost as in these images themselves—the poison apparently, temporarily, purges Envy's "shame" (?infused at 13) or "what one should be ashamed of ": *pudendum* (cf. Spenser, "Her neather parts, the shame of all her kind" [*FQ* 1.8.48.11]).

57–60   from whence a River Springs.
          Most Black & loathsom through the land it Runs
          Rolling with furious Noise.
          but at the last it Settles in a lake called Oblivion.

From the part or rift in the nether world a riv-er springs, assimilating various characteristics of the infernal streams. It suggests "Sad Acheron of sorrow, black and deep" (*PL* 2.578) with its "poisonous exhalation" (according to Burke in *OED*) and, perhaps more phallically, that "blacke flood . . . the river of *Cocytus*" (*FQ* 2.7.56.7–8). Though "*Lethe* the River of Oblivion rouls," in Milton, "silent" (*PL* 2.583, 582), it to "disgorges" in "the burning Lake"; the Blake River settles, swallowed, at "the last" ("the end," according to Johnson) in a Black lake (i.e., a Blake; see also 111). One might also hear, with the last, a lack called Oblivion and its envy at being passed over and forgotten, its anger at repressing and forgetting.

61–63   tis at this Rivers fount where evry mortals Cup is Mix't
          My Cup is fill'd with Envy's Rankest Draught
          a miracle No less can set me Right.

Like Comus, the autograph offers a "cup, / With many murmurs mixt" (525–26), and one doesn't have to listen very closely to hear its obscenity. The "fount" is in "her nether Parts": the term the author can't write initiates "Contagion" (53) and "Contentments downy Nest" (65), and overdetermines the reading of "rankest" (as in Dryden's "rankest harlot" or Shakespeare's "rank sweat of an enseamed bed"). Less allusive is the evocation of Jove's good and evil urns in the *Iliad*, from whence "the cup of mortal man he fills," even the happiest of whom finds "the cordial draught is dash'd with care" (Pope's version, 24.665, 672). Like thirsty Envy, "oer whelmed" and consuming her own poison, so evidently the narrator—now directly entering his text—drinks or drafts (or, poetically, sketches) "Envy's Rankest Draught." Envy entails ranking oneself against other sketchers (poetic and graphic), and for those who fall short, "the rank mist [/missed—] they draw." In Blake's next autograph such ranking becomes a source of satiric (or manic?) amusement as Quid argues that "Homer is bombast . . . & Milton has no feelings they might be easily outdone"; still later, to the unsympathetic Dr. Trustler, Blake asserts that he shares in the power that "sets Homer Virgil & Milton in so high a rank of Art" (E 702). One wonder is that it takes no less than the rankest draft to set the narrator down to write (cf. E 501).

64–66   Desire Still pines but for one Cooling Drop and tis Deny'd.
         while others in Contentments downy Nest do sleep,
         it is the Cursed thorn wounding my breast that makes me sing.

The narrator's Desire, now capitalized and unqualified, continues quietly to languish and to pine, like Tantalus or the fallen angels (*PL* 2.612–14, 606–7), or Faustus (*Dr. Faustus* 1433), or Lazarus's rich man (Luke 16:24), not "for" but "but for" one Drop. The particular formulation Blake uses recalls Isaac Watts's song for children "Against Swearing, and Cursing, and Taking God's Name in Vain," which consoles that to those who "treated thee with such disdain," "never shall one cooling drop / To quench their burning tongues be given" (13–14).

Another association leads to *The Rape of Lucrece*—which also bulks large throughout—and Tarquin, *in flagrante*, "Cooling his hot face in the chastest tears" (682), though the narrator evidently respects denial. But the quasi-pornographic focus remains as he recalls Spenser's "neast of love, the lodging of delight: / The bowre of blisse, the paradice of pleasure" (*Amoretti* 76.2–3) and Shakespeare's "nest of spicery" (*Richard III* 4.4.425) to imagine "others" sleeping "in Contentments downy Nest." The narrator's "thorn in the flesh" (2 Cor. 12:7) or "prickle" (Johnson's definition) is "it" (cf. 9–11), and he uses it to become a Poetic Melancholy Bird who, à la Giles Fletcher's Philomel,

> . . . leaning on a thorn her dainty chest,
> For fear soft sleep should steal into her breast,
> Expresses in her song grief not to be expressed.
>
> ("Christ's Triumph over Death," 66.6–8)

or Richard Barnfield's Nightingale,

> . . . poor bird, as all forlorn
> Lean'd her breast up-till a thorn,
> And there sung the dolefull'st ditty
> That to hear it was great pity.
>
> (N. Ault, *Lyrics* 248–49)

Young's *Night Thoughts*, however, shifts the conceit to first-person:

> Grief's sharpest Thorn hard-pressing on my breast,
> I strive, with wakeful Melody, to chear
> The sullen Gloom.
>
> (1.437–39)

One can find it odd almost to psychopathology to see this singer curse the thorn in the flesh that pricks him on, but perhaps such unyielding irony and self-satire suggest a subtle yet massive defense against the conscious articulation of psychic traumas.

67–71   however sweet tis Envy that Inspires my Song.
       prickt.
             by the fame of others how I mourn
      and my complaints are Sweeter than their Joys
      but O could I at Envy Shake my hands.
      my notes Should Rise to meet the New born Day.

But turning momentarily to his psychology, the narrator reveals that Envy (however sweet) inspires his song (however sweet)—a significant change on the "Song" in *Poetical Sketches* where the young lover concludes that "more than mortal fire / Burns in my soul, and does my song inspire" (E 416). All of which might suggest that even the seemingly artless songs of an early adolescent, like "How sweet I roamed," should be studied as envious attempts at envisioning, if not appropriating, the genius of others. So, in addition, the singer's being "prickt" can mean, "dressed for show" (cf. Johnson and *OED*) "by the fame of others," as well as goaded by their "prick-songs" (vocal music written with notes) and (as always) potency. Nonetheless, he claims that even his (loverly) "complaints" are more filled with sexual pleasure or are "Sweeter" than their "Joys"—or, at lest, he complains in ecstasy, sweeter than all their joys except the big "O" ("O was no deny," E 467).

"But O could I at Envy Shake my hands," the narrator mocks in a comical image which gives the reader increasing pause. Will the left hand finally meet the right, showing that the narrator can congratulate himself and feel proud of his work? Or does this notorious wag wish to flourish at himself and other envious detractors his many "forms or casts of writing" (Johnson, s.v. "hand")? Then his "notes" (like these hand-written papers), his "Song. prickt.," would "Rise to meet the New born Day" of himself ("I mourn"), and so become "the Rising Sun" that "rose & shed Sweet Influence" (29, 45). His other notes evidently included extracts from bombastic Homer (to "be easily outdone"), like the formula that opens three books of Pope's translation:

> The saffron Morn, with early blushes spread,
> Now rose refulgent from *Tithonus'* bed;
> With *new-born day* to gladden mortal sight,
> And gild the courts of heav'n with sacred light.
>
> (*Iliad* 11.1–4; 19.1–4; *Odyssey* 5.1–4; second italics added)

72–75   Hate Meager hag Sets Envy on
unable to Do ought herself.
but Worn away a Bloodless Daemon
The Gods all serve her at her will

The "New born Day" is suddenly "Worn away" by the reappearance of Hate and Envy, whose twinned identity asserts itself through the possible double predication of the pronoun. This spiritual leader seems the fury or ghost of someone old or dead ("worn away," idiomatically), like Milton's "Blue meager hag, or stubborn unlaid ghost" (*Comus* 434) or Shakespeare's "timely-parted ghost . . . meager, pale and bloodless" (*2 Henry VI* 3.2.162). Hate or Envy now replaces or joins Ambition as a power the Gods "all" acknowledge (see 15–16). The first of two appearances of the author's given name (cf. "Printed by Will: Blake"; E 60), this "will" can remind the reader that all these Gods serve at a certain will, and a certain image of will (cf. Will's "great ambition" in "King Edward the Third" 4.17). More at 139.

76–77 So great her Power is[.] like.

fabled hecate

She doth bind them to her law.

"Bloodless" Hate literally expands to "fabled hecate," and Blake seems to recall Hesiod's statement (in Thomas Cooke's version) that "Great is her power" and "her decrees irrevocable stand" (*Theogony*, 653, 650). Hecate stands out, however, as the first of only two figures the text cites from classical mythology; perhaps—especially after the mention of "her will" (75)—the name has special resonance for an author whose immediate feminine Other took the triple form of Kate (mother, sister, wife [to whom he was bound in law]; Female Will? He Kate).

78–82 Far in a Direful Cave She lives
unseen Closd from the Eye of Day.
to the hard Rock transfixt by fate
and here She works her witcheries
that when She Groans She Shakes the Solid Ground

Much like Ovid's Envy (*Metamorphoses* 2.760ff), Hate/Envy lives in a far cave unseen by "the Eye of Day" (not to mention "conscious me," the waking I) and "transfixt" by yet another link in the "-ate" sequence, "fate" (cf. "vengeful *Ate*" in Pope's *Iliad* 19.92). Fate would thus seem to be the mightiest power of all, except for the fact that it goes unpersonified (unless, along the lines of Hate's literal expansion to *Hecate*, "fate" takes the form of the "*fat*her" all will soon war against). Envy/Hate's condition, at any rate, brings to mind rebels like Prometheus, Orc, Ajax (not the hero but the plunderer whom Virgil has Athena bind, in Dryden's version, "Transfix'd and naked, on a rock" [*Aeneid* 1.69]), and Milton's Belial, who fears that the fallen spirits may be "Each on his rock tranfixt" (*PL* 2.181). Note, however, that one is usually "transfixed on," not, like Hate, "to."

Perhaps she is held motionless to a different kind of rock, like that which Blake's Samson desires to engrave "with iron pens" (E 443) or that of the first "Memorable Fancy" of *The Marriage of Heaven and Hell*, which also evokes the copperplate of the trade Blake was bound to. "Here," reports the narrator with typically enchanting ambiguity (hear!), "She works her witcheries that when She Groans She Shakes the Solid Ground"—which might be to say that when she works her wit, the earth moves. The sexual denotation of "groan" occurs most famously in *Hamlet* (3.2.249). And why, one may wonder aside, does a pun typically elicit a groan? is the solidity of one's "ground" shaken by "groaned"? Does it so shake spheres?

83–88   Now Envy She controlls with numming trance
        & Melancholy Sprung from her dark womb
        There is a Melancholy, O how lovely tis
        whose heaven is in the heavenly Mind
        for she from heaven came,
        and Where she goes heaven still doth follow her.

"Now" begins a passage of some 350 words written in a different color of ink with a different nib, and the evidence for an insertion is strengthened by removing the entire passage (ending at 132 with "Revenge."), which restores an unimpeded flow to Hate/Envy's development. The interpolation, almost one third of the autograph, seems to offer a somewhat distinct unit concerning memory, contemplation, and, at its center the Revolt Against the Father (the infant's envy of the breast evolves into heightened oedipal conflict). It opens with the formulation that Hate "controlls" Envy, or that Envy by herself "controlls," with a trance reminiscent of *Comus*'s "numming spell" (853—note that Blake follows the archaic spelling, already corrected in Johnson's *Dictionary* quotation of it). The first Melancholy, it would seem, is sprung like the Black River (57–58) from "earths dark womb" (Milton, "On the Death of a Fair Infant Dying of a Cough," 30), and one can recall that elsewhere in Blake "trance" evokes erotic rapture.

    Apparently in contrast with the first, the narrator introduces Melancholy again—though the issue is complicated if "There" also refers locationally to the "dark womb" and "melancholy" is glossed as "black bile" (evoking the black river) or, multi-lingually, "black hole." The labored association of Melancholy with "heaven" suggests the erotic euphemism (as in Keats' "I'll feel my heaven anew" ["unfelt, unheard, unseen" 17]), and Blake later writes of "the whole [/hole-]heaven of [Vala's] boson & loins" (*J* 70.29) and of the "Heavens" into which the Daughters of Albioan take "whom they please" in "intoxicating delight" (*M* 5.9–10). If there are to be different Melancholies, one might suppose as well a heaven "where more is meant than meets the ear" ("Il Penseroso" 120). Milton imagines "heav'nly minds" as being clear from "distempers foul" (*PL* 4.118), and such, like "the fixed mind" of "Il Penseroso," best appreciate the "divinest Melancholy" which is "higher far descended" than the classical pantheon (21).

89–90   She brings true Joy once fled.
         & Contemplation is her Daughter.
                              Sweet Contemplation.

This comment may say more about the wished-for departure of, or from, a "once fled" Melancholy than about Joy, whose flight has nowhere been reported. *Twelfth Night*'s pun on the "cont-" in "Contemplation" (2.5.30ff) perhaps helps to expose the Malvolio-like sententiousness of the (immediate) narrator in these lines and to confirm the developing "cont-" concern ("Contagion" 53, "Contentments downy nest" 65). Joy, as in Shakespeare and elsewhere in Blake, can denote pleasure in sexual intimacy and so stand as strongly against "vain deluding joys" as the Melancholy of "Il Penseroso" and its "Cherub Contemplation" (1, 54).

91–93   She brings humility to man
         Take her She Says & wear her in thine heart
         lord of thy Self thou then art lord of all.

Contemplation turns spiritual pander as she turns over humility "to man" with a potentially bawdy instruction ("take her": e.g., Shakespeare, *King Richard III*, 1.2.231) and echoing Hamlet's declaration, "Give me that man / That is not passion's slave, and I will wear him / In my heart's core" (3.2.76–78). Humility, it would seem, offers freedom from secular contemplation, and with that a solipsistic fantasy which echos Sir Henry Wotton's "Character of a Happy Life"—reprinted in Percy's 1765 *Reliques of Ancient English Poetry*—and the idea that the man free "Of hope to rise, or fear to fall" is "Lord of himself, though not of lands, / And having nothing, yet hath all" (Ault, *Lyrics* 459–60; the commonplace goes back to Horace and, supposedly, Pythagoras).

This passage is one of two which directly tie the autograph to *Poetical Sketches,* for in "Contemplation" the protagonist, foregoing any rank possibilities, says to "vain foolish man," "Lo then, Humility, take it, and wear it in thine heart; lord of thyself thou than art lord of all"; she also exclaims over the "humble garb true Joy puts on!" (E 442).

94–96   Tis Contemplation teacheth knowledge truly how to know.
         and Reinstates him on his throne once lost
         how lost I'll tell.

The underlying steady sexual regard of Contemplation appears in her ability to teach "truly how to know," and perhaps her intimate acquaintance with the loins or seat of the feelings—the "reins," in the archaic term Blake sometimes uses—"reinstates" knowledge "on his throne" ("Reason," not knowledge, possesses a throne in popular idiom). The regret-filled reading of "how lost[!]" perhaps cues the narrator's announcement of an overtly confessional mode.

96   But Stop the motley Song.

Instead the narrator stops himself and trivializes what has come thus far. The narrator of *An Island in the Moon* similarly breaks the frame to report, "I was only making a fool of you" (E 453), and the patchwork incoherences of this piece suggest that the truth in the jest will be hard to gauge. Again, however, one might consider these stops and turns, nearly-concealed double-entendres and self-mockeries as instances of the narrator's increasing resistance to what he has to reveal.

97–99   I'll Shew.
                   how Conscience Came from heaven.
          But O who listens to his Voice
          T'was Conscience who brought Melancholy down

Where before Melancholy "from heaven came" (85ff), now Conscience shares the distinction; to preserve the contrary reading of "heaven," one might invoke Shakespeare's pun that "con[-]science is born of [sexual] love" (*Sonnets*, 151.2). Melancholy and Conscience are thus linked, with the suggestion that the tale of "how" knowledge lost his throne parallels that of "how" Conscience came and "brought down" or "overthrew" (in one reading) Melancholy. "But O," the teller interjects, stopping himself once again with a general disparagement which asks the reader to attend more closely and to suspect that this confused raconteur is himself troubled by a voice we do not listen to:

> And I will place within them as a guide
> My Umpire *Conscience,* whom if they will hear,
> Light after light well us'd they shall attain
>
> (*PL* 3.194–96)

100–105 Conscience was sent a Guard to Reason.
          Reason once fairer than the light
          till fould in Knowledges dark Prison house.
          For knowledge drove sweet Innocence away.
          and Reasons would have followed but fate sufferd not
          Then down Came Conscience with his lovely band

The narrator's tactics are exemplified in the confused temporal sequence and ambiguous semantics which mark the brief tale of Conscience, and they repay slow reading. Indeed, Robert Gleckner has suggested that the passage might be seen as a rewriting of *Paradise Lost,* or at least a preliminary take on the version in *The Marriage of Heaven and Hell* (personal communication). Having brought down, or in order to bring down, Melancholy, Conscience "was sent"—by whom one knows not—"a Guard to Reason." Reason then appears "fould in Knowledges dark Prison house," where, it seems logical, Conscience would be stationed. "For," the narrator continues, implying some causal explanation, "knowledge [?foreknowledge] drove sweet Innocence away." "Reason would have followed but fate"—again (as before with Hate, 80) evidently the final authority—"sufferd not": did not permit or was unaffected by the departure of Innocence. "Then down Came Conscience with his lovely band," concludes the interlude, and considering the earlier assumption that Conscience was already descended or descending when he "brought Melancholy down" (the only member of this "lovely band" in evidence), this suggests a general collapse of Conscience, including its "banned"'s and "bonds."

Reason's being "fould" in "Knowledges dark prison house" offers a curious gloss on the standard *soma/sema* equation made by the speaker of "Contemplation" ("my flesh is a prison," E 442) and draws attention again to the nature of the "Knowledge" under discussion. Perhaps the text again breathes that "fould Contagion from which none are free" (53), Satire (popularly derived from *satura,* a "medley" of dishes: motley song). The adjective "dark" reaches back to its single other occurrence, the "dark womb" which forms the site of foul carnal knowledge to a certain psychopathology, while the "Prison house" stitches together Milton's' Samson in "this loathsom prison-house" (*SA* 922) and—anticipating what will unfold next—King Hamlet's spirit and the "secrets" he cannot tell of his "prison-house" (1.5.14).

106   The Eager Song Goes on telling

The "motley Song" had been restrained while the narrator gave expression to Conscience, but that qualm dispatched, the now irrepressible, even sexually "Eager" Son/g gets the upper hand and as it were with a will of its own moves toward the climatic account of the Revolt Against the Father. Johnson's primary definition for "eager" is "Struck with desire; ardently wishing; keenly desirous; vehement in desire; hotly longing."

107   how Pride against her father Warrd & Overcame.

Pride at the beginning "awoke"; the belated introduction of her sire entails reconceiving Pride and opens the question of what fate her father desired. "Her father" turns out to be the general father as "his Children all" (109) join Pride to become "all the Gods" (116). His identity goes unrevealed, though his "throne" links him to knowledge (95), who lost his, and to Milton's "mightie Father Thron'd / On high" (*PL* 6.890–91); Milton also refers to a daughter's revolt using Blake's verb: "*Titanian, or Earth-born, that warr'd on Jove*" (*PL* 1.198). The omission of any possible mother of Pride reasserts her connection to Eve and to Sin (whose preeminent form was Pride).

108   Down his white Beard the Silver torrents Roll.

"Pity not honor'd age for his white beard," says Shakespeare's Timon, mocking Alcibides' plans to "war against" their fatherland (*Timon of Athens* 4.3.112, 103) and supplying a proverbial identification. Dalila's "false tears" in Blake's published sketch, "Samson," make her seem "a silver stream" (E 443), opening a slight outline of association involving a tearful father (like Phoenix in Pope's *Iliad,* down whose "white beard a stream of sorrow flows," 9.559). Rolling torrents suggest something more like a river (like the "Rolling" Black River of 58–59), perhaps the traditional "silver Thames" which appears in *Poetical Sketches* (E 425). Following the famous classical sculptures of Nile and of Tiber, personified rivers have "flowing" beards such as Blake supplies in depicting Gray's "Father Thames" ("Ode on a Distant Prospect of Eton College," no. 4). This popular image of "Old Father *Thames*" (in Pope and Dryden, for example)—"parent stream" (*J* 53.3)—may be as close as the text dare come to encrypting the name of Blake's old father, *James* (close enough, it would seem, to be itself displaced).

109–10   and Swelling Sighs burst forth his Children all
           in arms appear to tear him from his throne

Torrents swell rivers; incipient birth/burst swells the pa-rent; the sighing heart bursts too, like Caesar's at the betrayal of "well-beloved" Brutus (*Julius Caesar* 3.2.176 ff). "A Sign is the Sword [the S-word] of an Angel King" (E 202, 489), perhaps manifest in melancholy stabs of conscience at recalling sighs of the departed Good king (38), "The King my father" (*Hamlet* 1.2.192; *The Tempest* 1.2.390). Here, however, the appearing of children (James Blake, Sr., apparently fathered seven) "in the Arms of their Father" (E 559) itself tears him ("Do they hear their father sigh"? E 16) from his throne; or the children appear with his weapons to do so; or perhaps they only appear to do so, since, according to Milton, "th' Omnipotent / Eternal Father from his Throne beheld / Thir multitude" (*PL* 7.136–38). The initial speaker in Cowper's *Olney Hymns* (first printed in 1772) hopes for "a closer walk with God," and sorrows over the sweet memory of "peaceful hours I once enjoy'd"; "I hate the sins that made thee mourn," he laments to the Holy Spirit, and concludes:

> The dearest idol I have known,
>   Whate'er that idol be;
> Help me to tear it from thy throne,
>   And worship only thee.

111   Black was the deed.
              most Black.

The "deed" entails a dead dad. In *Poetical Sketches* the word denotes the murder of fair Elenor's husband and Dalila's fantasied murder at the hand of Samson (E 411, 443); Oothoon's vision of the family romance combines death and the little death to foresee "the child dwell with one he hates. and do the deed he loaths" (*VDA* 5.30). Objecting to the deposition of Richard II, the Bishop of Carlisle in Shakespeare's play speaks "boldly for his king" and characterizes the action as "so heinous, black, obscene a deed" (4.1.131). What's Black is at least in part Blake, an association so pronounced in Blake's work that one wonders how, precisely the name was actually vocalized; in "Blind-Man's Buff," for example, "bear-ey'd Will the black lot holds" (and soon has "titt'ring Kate . . . pen'd up"; E 422). The archaic adjective "black" denotes "pale," and the *OED* observes how this "added to the formal confusion with Black," since "black" also means "absence of color"—so the "Pale desire" which initiates the autograph may be the contemporary form of an older "Blake desire."

112   Shame in a Mist Sat Round his troubled head.

Absent since line 14, Shame is revived by the naming of the Black deed and, reminiscent of the "black mist" Satan sat in (*PL* 9.180, 75), becomes a type of crown. Aeneas sees the ill-fated Marcellus in the underworld and wonders why "hov'ring mists around his brows are spread / And night with sable shades involves his head" (*Aeneid*, Dryden trans., 6.1198–99).

113   & filld him with Confusion.

Confusion is "putting to shame" as well as "ruinous destruction" as well as the state manifest by Bable (22–23: Babel . . . Confusion . . . Shame) and by this motley babbling, this "tumultuous medley" (Johnson, s.v. "Confusion," 1).

114–15   Fear as a torrent wild Roard Round his throne
         the mighty pillars shake

Blake's rough verse does, following Pope's dictum in *An Essay on Criticism*, "like the *Torrent* roar," perhaps even suggesting "the *wild Torrent* of a *barb'rous Age*" (369, 695). Fear, later for Blake "a living torment" (E 821), roars round the father's throne, or his own, and the pillars shake; or just roars, and the pillars round his throne shake. In Milton's memorable image, cannon are "Pillars" which "roar" (*PL* 6.572, 586), but Blake seems closer here to Watts's popular hymn stanzas which ask "for a strong, a lasting faith":

> Then should the earth's old pillars shake,
> And all the wheels of nature break,
> Our steady souls should fear no more
> Than solid rocks when billows roar.
>
> ("The Truth of God the Promiser," 33–36)

116–17   Now all the Gods in blackning Ranks appear.
         like a tempestuous thunder Cloud Pride leads.

                                        them on.

When last seen, "the Gods all" were serving Envy/Hate "at her will" (73); now, like the father's "Children all," they "appear" and show a blackning family resemblance. In *Poetical Sketches* the "sons of blood" in revolt are likened to "tempests black," and as "nations black" they "Like clouds, come rolling" toward Gwin and his chiefs, each of whom is also "like an awful thunder cloud" (E 418). If not in heaven, then war in "the heavenly Mind" (86).

118–19   Now they Surround the God.
                              and bind him fast.
         Pride bound him, then usurpd oer all the Gods.

This single mention of "the God" evidently invokes the father. Blake's anxiety-provoking precursor reports that "cloud . . . and ever-during dark / Surrounds me" (*PL* 3.45–46), and in the "bind . . . bound" sequence one might hear Samson, "bound and blind" (438).

But the emphatic action suggests more the binding of Proteus as related in Dryden's translation of Virgil's *Georgics*, Book 4. Aristaeus is told by his mother of "a prophet and a god" whom the "river gods adore," and that "Proteus only knows / The secret cause, and cure, of all they woes" (569–70). Once having surprised "the wayward sire," she says, "bind him fast. / Thus surely bound, yet be not over bold" (584–85)—since Proteus will try to escape by assuming various forms (Blake uses the story again in *Tiriel* 4.49ff). The idea of usurpation swerves toward another story however, as evident in Blake's later reference to the mythological account that "Jupiter usurped the Throne of his Father Saturn" (E 555).

120–14   She Rode upon the Swelling wind
          and Scatterd all who durst t'oppose.
          but Shame opposing fierce and hovering.
          over her in the darkning Storm.
          She brought forth Rage.

Pride also denotes sexual heat (Tarquin's veins "Swell in their pride" in Shakespeare's *The Rape of Lucrece* 432), which readies her to ride (nb.: P/ride Rode) "the Swelling" and, swelling, bring forth lust, or, "amorous rage" (Dryden, trans., *Georgics*, 3. 433—the context is Virgil's account of mares and the impregnating "parent wind, / [Which] Without the stallion, propagates the kind"). The "Swelling wind" of Pride recalls the "hungry sheep" of "Lycidas" "swoln with wind" (see discussion of 52–53) and the "vain foolish man" of "Contemplation," whose garments "are swoln with wind" (E 442). Shame opposes such tumescent display and, in one reading, hovers or broods over, incubates Pride, and herself brings forth Rage ("to swell" is "to be inflated with anger," notes Johnson); in another reading, Shame wavers uncertainly, like Lucrece who "prepares to write, / First hovering o'er the paper with her quill," but finds that "What wit sets down is blotted straight with will" (1296–97, 1299).

Freud's first case in *Studies in Hysteria* presents a patient who describes as "'storms in her head'" her many confusing "fits of despair" (p. 80). The image seems to bear comparison here, and more strikingly in the separate fragment two pages further on in the autograph. "What does this mean," cries the narrator of "Woe cried the muse," seeing that in the midst of "Buxom Joy" (as per M. Klein) he is struck with Grief and his "Nerves with trembling": "how soon the Winds Sing round *the Darkning Storm* ere while so fair" (E 448, emphasis added). Another fragment refers to "the Mental Storm"

(E 482), and the Spectre or feeling of shame evidently is followed "in a Storm" (E 477). As Albion faces Eternal Death ("Envy hovers over him!"), the narrator sees his body "Torn with black storms, & ceaseless torrents of his own consuming fire" (*J* 36[40] 14, 39).

125–27   Mean while Strife Mighty Prince was born
        Envy in direful Pains him bore.
        then Envy brought forth Care.

The opposition of Pride and Shame appears as/in Strife; but at the same time the text revels in the "aspectual interconnection" (Donald Ault's term) of these states: Strife was born (as) Envy who in turn bore him, and with "Direful Pains" like those which saw Envy herself come from Pride (48–49). In the midst of all these bearings, one recalls that "to bring forth" also means "to express, or utter," as in Isaiah 42:22, "bring forth your strong reasons."

128–30   Care Sitteth in the wrinkled brow.
        Strife Shapeless Sitteth under thrones of kings like Smouldring fire.
        or in the Buzz of Cities flies abroad

The "wrincled Care" of Milton's "L'Allegro" (31) joins his picture of Satan with "Pride" in his "Brows" and "Care" sitting ("Sat") on his cheek (*PL* 2.601–3). In *For the Sexes: The Gates of Paradise,* "Fire" is glossed as "That End in Endless Strife" (E 262), an anagrammatic association (*fire/strife*) which perhaps here draws on Donne's "shapelesse flame" ("Aire and Angels," 3) to qualify Strife and join it to Dryden's description of the "smould'ring" beginnings of the City's Great Fire ("Annus Mirabilis," 870). Sitting, as he may, in the "Buzz of . . . flies," Strife can double for the Lord of the Flies, Beelzebub. "Buzz" also denotes "rumour, ferment" which "flies abroad" through the great hive of the city.

131–32   Care brought forth Covet Eyeless & prone to th' Earth
        and Strife brought forth Revenge

The *OED* does not document a single instance of "covet" as a substantive, and it is disconcerting to imagine exactly how those "that covet such eye-glutting gaine" (*FQ* 2.7.9.8) would function without sight, but Blake likes the formulation enough to join "Eyeless Covet" with the more stereotypical "Thin-lip'd Envy," "Bristled Wrath," and "Curled Wantonness" in *The Book of Los* (3.10). Perhaps, as with strife-ridden Samson "Eyeless in *Gaza*" (Milton's only use of the word), the coveted object is revenge. Almost subliminal disruptions continue with the preposition "to," the semantics of which the reader may be prone *to* neglect in favor of a more physical, down-to-earth association with "prone"—Milton's Satan in the Serpent, for instance (who is, in the usual idiom, not "Prone *on* the ground, as since" [*PL* 9.49, emphasis added]); "earth," as in Shakespeare's Sonnet 146 and many hymns can denote the body ("my sinful earth"; and, e.g., Cowper, who in the *Olney Hymns* writes of a "grovelling creature" who "basely cleaved to earth"). These curiosities ask for closer consideration even if they cannot be resolved. In *Poetical Sketches*, for instance, Blake's Samson states "for care was I brought forth," while Fair Elenor laments that her husband was " 'Drawn down to earth"; and in *Songs of Experience*, "EARTH'S Answer" equates that speaker with "free Love." Whether or not or in what way slight idiomatic discrepancies ("to" for "on") or conceptual anomalies (eyeless covet) can be the cue for, or trace of, greater liberties undisposed remains: but perhaps in this text which bears with such labored care so many bringing-forths (or, "emanations"), the narrator reports that "care brought forth" and then jumps to the rhetorical comment that he doesn't covet anything less ("covet I less?") even if his care is not really for airy nothings but (like the covert blind mole or eyeless worm) partial to "th'Earth." Great poets can be blind and covet still treasures for th' ear. Care having elicited such a display, Strife continues and produces "Revenge" to terminate the lengthy insertion which began back at 83 with "Now Envy."

133–34   Hate brooding in her Dismal den grew Pregnant
       & bore Scorn, & Slander.
                    Scorn waits on Pride

Hate here fulfills Milton's type of the "Spirit" which "from the first / Wast present" and "satst brooding on the vast Abyss / And mad'st it pregnant" (*PL* 1.19–22), except that the abyss, seen before as Hate's "Direful Cave" (78) and "dark womb" (84), becomes the Serpent's "dismal Den" (*PL* 9.185), never occupied in the Garden.

135–39   but Slander.
             flies around the World
      to do the Work of hate her drudge & Elf.
      but Policy doth drudge for hate as well as Slander.
      & oft makes use of her.
                    Policy Son of Shame.
      Indeed Hate Controlls all the Gods.
                 at will.

Like Strife before (132), Slander "Rides on the posting winds and doth belie / All corners of the world," frequently to the poisoning of sexual trust (as in the context of the quotation, *Cymbeline* 3.4.36–37). An underlying context of sexual relationships includes the repeated term "drudge," which can denote, as in Shakespeare and Dryden, "male sexual servicer/servicing." In Sonnet 151, for example, the speaker remarks his flesh "rising at thy name" and comments, "Proud of this pride, / He is contented thy poor drudge to be" (10–11); Dryden's translation of Juvenal's sixth satire urges the (evidently male) reader to let his eunuch "drudge for" his lady (496), that is, "make use of her" (cf. "Take her," 92). Policy as "cunning" continues the sexual reference but also seconds the re-emerging focus on "man politic." For, as "Blind-Man's Buff" concludes, the state came into existence to structure sexual desire, the "will" by which and "at" which hate "Controlls all the Gods" in deed (on "will" as sexual desire, sexual organs, and personal name, see especially Shakespeare's *Sonnets* 135 and 136).

140–42   Policy brought forth Guile & fraud.
        these Gods last namd live in the Smoke of Cities.
        on Dusky wing breathing forth Clamour & Destruction.

The "Smouldring fire" of 129 here generates more obscurity: "Smoke" is traditionally "Dusky" ("duskish . . . smoke," Spenser; "smoke and dusky vapours," Shakespeare; "smoke . . . in dusky wreaths," Milton). If these Gods live "in the Smoke" (like Strife "in the Buzz of Cities" [130]) and "on . . . wing," then they must be, like Shame, "hovering . . . in the darkning Storm" (123), while their black pall sounds a bit like Saul, "breathing out threatenings and slaughter" (Acts 9:1). In a published sketch, Contemplation reports, "Clamour brawls along the streets, and destruction hovers in the city's smoak" (E 442). London, one recalls, centered on "the City," and owing to its atmosphere was known in the nineteenth century as "the Smoke"; the harlot's cry seems to have been an aspect of the clamour (c[see] l'amour?) which greatly affected Blake (E 492, 27).

143–44   alas in Cities wheres the man
        whose face is not a mask unto his heart

Samuel Palmer called Blake "a man without a mask" (Gilchrist 301), and the phrase has enjoyed some prestige in the history of Blake criticism; but like *Poetical Sketches*, this text displays one mask after another, and here the mask of pointing to itself. Such a world of masculine masquers—whose "observing inly" only leads to Grief (24)—suggests two particular applications: where's the father whose deep emotions are evident to his son? where the great poet who does not raise *A Mask* before his heart's desire? And lastly, "where's the Man, who counsel *can* bestow. . . . a *Soul* exempt from *Pride* . . . ?" (Pope, *An Essay on Criticism* 631, 641).

145–46   Pride made a Goddess.
                          fair   or I mage rather
       till knowledge animated it.
                   'twas Calld Selflove.

A mage, like a magician or magus, has great knowledge, so the two odd spacings in the autograph here (the second not recorded by any editor but suggested in the manuscript [Berg Collection, New York Public Library]) can reinforce the intensifying sense of an authoring conflict even as the "images" proliferate:

    . . . the dreadful Mage there found
Deep busied bout worke of wondrous end,
And writing strange characters in the ground,
With which the stubborn feends he to his service bound.
                          (*FQ* 3.3.14.6–9).

Pride makes the masked man's heart a "Goddes fair" (like Milton's "Mirth," "L'Allegro," 11) or, rather, it was an image I, mage, enjoyed until carnal knowledge, displaced, returned to animate the displacement as selflove, the defensive posture to which "I" is now devoted ("Self-love each jealous Writer rules" [Pope, *An Essay on Criticism* 516]). "Knowledge" has, evidently, no truck with a hypothetical "self-knowledge." "General Knowledge is Remote Knowledge; it is in Particulars that Wisdom consists & Happiness too," Blake writes later (E 560), but the manuscript refuses such particulars, masking a heart one can only hear in the remote depths of its abstract conjurings with vague, general names of Pride, Envy, Selflove, knowledge, Emulation and the rest.

147–50   The Gods admiring loaded her with Gifts
       as once Pandora She 'mongst men was Sent.
       and worser ills attended her by far.
       She was a Goddess Powerful & bore Conceit

Blake again loads his rifts with Milton, here the description of Eve "in naked beauty more adorn'd, / More lovely than *Pandora,* whom the Gods / Endowd with all thir gifts" (*PL* 4.713–15). The comparison to Pandora—like Eve for Milton, the first woman according to Hesiod—would seem to lend an exclusively masculine cast to "men" and confirm the unthinking sexism of the autograph. As Pandora's box brought labor, old age, disease, misery, and care, Selflove's "worser ills . . . by far" seems quite a conceit on the narrator's part. The meanings of "Conceit" over-determine its appearance at this point: as "imagination" it develops logically from an "image animated"; as "an overweening opinion of oneself" it embodies "Selflove"; and as "something conceived" it reflects something conceived and born.

151–54   and Shame bore honour & made league with Pride
           & Policy doth dwell with her
           by whom she [had] Mistrust & suspition.
           Then bore a Daughter called Emulation.

From her beginning, Shame has been warring with all the Gods (9) or "opposing fierce" (122); now, after the advent of Selflove, she is evidently strong enough to change policy and, marrying her interest with Pride, express herself through an increasingly socialized progression of offspring. Emulation, however, still remains marked by the world of its forebears, like *Hamlet*'s "most emulate Pride" (1.1.83) or the "envious fever / Of pale and Bloodless Emulation" of *Troilus and Cressida* (1.3.133–34).

155   who.
                married.
                      honour

William Blake and Catherine Butcher (or Boucher) married on 18 August 1782. Gilchrist reports that "[t]o his father, Blake's early and humble marriage is said to have been unacceptable" (Gilchrist 37; cf. Bentley's objection, *Records* 24).

156   these follow her around the World[.]

As Slander drudges for hate "around the World" (135), so now do Policy, Mistrust, Suspition, Emulation, and "honour" work for Shame.

157–59   Go see the City friends Joind Hand in Hand.
           Go See.
                the Natural tie of flesh & blood.
           Go See more strong the tie of marriage love

The Hand-in-Hand was a noted fire insurance office in the City (London): its plaques on protected houses representing the work of "Policy" and the kind of mutual ties one might see in cities (as Cowper wrote in 1781, "Hand-in-Hand insurance plates / Most unavoidably creates / The thought of conflagration"; "Friendship," 106–8 [published 1800]). "Hand in Hand" also recalls Milton's repeated description of Adam and Eve, whose "Link of Nature" and "wedded Love" (*PL* 9.914, 4.750) occasion such woe. The use of the imperative, quaint expression, and following second-person familiar pronoun suggest that the narrator may be addressing someone familiar ("Go see, love"). These insistent lines of blank verse coming at the end of the piece can serve to alert the reader to the metrical variations that have been offered along the way.

160   thou Scarce Shall find but Self love Stands Between

"Such is self-love that envies all! a creeping skeleton / With lamplike eyes watching around the frozen marriage bed," laments Oothoon (*VDA* 7.21.22), hinting, perhaps, at a much earlier scene with a child's lamprey eyes frozen to the image on the marriage bed, emblem and generator of its outcast condition. Perhaps only some such perception of real or imagined rejection primes a sight such as that which "often" struck Blake: "a Dog will envy a Cat who is pamperd at the expense of his comfort as I have often seen" (E 565—shades here of Will "Quid the Cynic" on sister or wife Cate?). As the hurt drive for "comfort" experiences intensifying conflict and lack of fulfillment in sexual relations (since sex doesn't answer the drive's imaginary goal of permanently annihilating its ambivalent self, and self-knowledge—of one's split-off hatred, for example—feels too genuinely annihilating), sexuality itself comes under rejection as the occasion of "Self-love / The Rocky Law of Condemnation & double Generation, & Death" (*J* 44[30].36–37). The autograph may be seen to announce such psychic disturbance and the pale desire to set things right by sketching in hopes of the scarce find: the rankest draught.

Works Cited

Ault, Donald. *Narrative Unbound: Re-Visioning William Blake's* The Four Zoas. Clinamen Studies Series. Barrytown, N.Y.: Station Hill Press, 1987.

Ault, Norman, ed. *Elizabethan Lyrics.* 4th ed. London: Longmans, 1966.

Bentley, Gerald E., Jr. *Blake Books* [etc.]. Oxford: Clarendon Press, 1977.

———. *Blake Records.* Oxford: Clarendon Press, 1969.

Blake, William. See Erdman, David V., ed.

Breuer, Josef and Sigmund Freud. *Studies on Hysteria*. Trans. James Strachey et al. [Volume 2 of the Standard Edition of the Complete Psychological Works of Sigmund Freud.] New York: Basic Books, n.d.

Burke, Edmund. *A Philosophical Enquiry into the Origin of our Ideas of the Sublime and Beautiful*. Ed. w. intro. by James T. Boulton. South Bend and London: University of Notre Dame Press, 1968.

Burton, Robert. *The Anatomy of Melancholy*. Everyman's Library. Vol. 1. London: Dent; New York: Dutton, 1964.

Cooke, Thomas. *The Works of Hesiod. Translated from the Greek*. In *The Works of the British Poets*. Ed. Robert Anderson. Vol. 13. London, 1795.

Cowper, William. *Poetical Works*. Ed. H. S. Milford. 4th ed. w. corrections and additions by Norma Russell. Oxford Standard Authors. Oxford: Oxford University Press, 1971.

Damon, S. Foster. *William Blake: His Philosophy and Symbols*. 1924. Rpt. Gloucester, MA: Peter Smith, 1958.

Drayton, Michael. *The Poetical works of Michael Drayton*. In *The Works of the British Poets*. Ed. Robert Anderson. Vol. 3. London, 1793.

Dryden, John. *The Poetical Works of John Dryden*. Ed. George R. Noyes. Cambridge Edition. Boston: Houghton Mifflin, 1909.

——— and Nathaniel Lee. *Oedipus*. In *The Works of John Dryden*, vol. 13. Ed. Maximillian E. Novak. Berkeley, Los Angeles, London: University of California Press, 1984.

Erdman, David V. "A Blake Manuscript in the Berg Collection: 'then She bore Pale desire' and 'Woe cried the muse.'" *Bulletin of the New York Public Library* 62:4 (April 1958): 191–201.

———, ed. *The Complete Poetry and Prose of William Blake*. Commentary by Harold Bloom. Newly Revised Edition. Berkeley and Los Angeles: University of California Press, 1982. Cited throughout as E.

Fletcher, Giles. *The Poetical Works of Giles Fletcher*. In *The Works of the British Poets*. Ed. Robert Anderson. Vol. 4. London, 1795.

Freud, Sigmund. See Breuer, Josef.

Gilchrist, Alexander. *The Life of William Blake*. Ed. Ruthven Todd. Everyman's Library. London: Dent, 1945.

Gleckner, Robert F. *Blake's Prelude:* Poetical Sketches. Baltimore: Johns Hopkins University Press, 1982.

Johnson, Samuel. *A Dictionary of the English Language* [etc.]. 1755. Facsimile reprint [2 vols. in 1]. London: Times Books Limited, 1979.

Keats, John. *Complete Poems*. Ed. Jack Stillinger. Cambridge: Harvard University Press, 1982.

Klein, Melanie. *Envy and Gratitude: A Study of Unconscious Sources*. New York: Basic Books, 1957.

Milton, John. *The Complete Poetry of John Milton*. Ed. John T. Shawcross. Revised edition. The Anchor Seventeenth-Century Series. Garden City, NY: Anchor Books (Doubleday), 1971.

Ostriker, Alicia. *Vision and Verse in William Blake*. Madison: University of Wisconsin Press, 1965.

Pope, Alexander. *The Works of Homer. Translated into English Verse*. In *The Works of the British Poets*. Ed. Robert Anderson. Vol. 12. London, 1795.

Rossetti, William M., ed. "The Passions: An Unpublished Poem by William Blake." In *The Monthly Review* 12 (August 1903).

Saintsbury, George. *A History of English Prosody from the Twelfth Century to the Present Day.* Vol. 3. London: Macmillan, 1910.

Shakespeare, William. *The Riverside Shakespeare.* Ed. G. Blakemore Evans. Boston: Houghton Mifflin, 1974.

Spenser, Edmund. *Poetical Works.* Eds. J. C. Smith and E. De Selincourt. Oxford Standard Authors. Oxford: University Press, 1979.

Tannenbaum, Leslie. "Blake's News from Hell: *The Marriage of Heaven and Hell* and the Lucianic Tradition," *ELH* 43 (1976): 74–99.

Turner, Mark. *Death is the mother of beauty: Mind, Metaphor, Criticism.* Chicago and London: University of Chicago Press, 1987.

Watts, Isaac. *The Poetical Works of Isaac Watts.* In *The Works of the British Poets.* Ed. Robert Anderson. Vol. 9. London, 1795.

Young, Edward. *Night Thoughts.* Ed. Stephen Cornford. New York: Cambridge University Press, 1989.

Obtuse Angled Afterword

ROBERT F. GLECKNER

To offer a "response" to this remarkably varied group of essays would not only be a daunting task, but in one sense would also be a usurpation of the prerogatives of a reviewer. Perhaps only so brash a writer as Byron would dare take up his "own especial pen" when he was "juvenile and curly" both to "pour along the town a flood of rhyme" to "show [his] wrath and wit" and to "make [his] own review." In any case, with little wrath and no doubt less wit, my prosy muse would inspire little more than niggling "buts" in my retreat to cover my *Blake's Prelude* flanks—something like Byron's defense of his in *English Bards and Scotch Reviewers* (from which the above quotes also come):

> "But hold!" exclaims a friend, "here's some neglect:
> This, that, and t'other line seem incorrect."
> What then? the self-same blunder Pope has got,
> And careless Dryden—'Ay, but Pye has not:'—
> Indeed!—'t is granted, faith!—but what care I?
> Better to err with Pope than shine with Pye.
>
> (ll. 97–102)

And so I retreat to safer ground all round, from which vantage point I may add an afterword in the afterward of my own foray into the thicket that is *Poetical Sketches*.

One way or the other all Blakeans have implicitly argued for Blake as an *avant-garde* artist, if not, in fact, an artist *sui generis*. After all, his Hebraic/prophetic "originals" neither painted nor etched nor literally *made* books. Least of all did they, even more self-generationally, combine several arts—including those of the book—into an indissoluble "composite" adamantly resistant to paraphrase, a powerful paralogos in the Greek-root sense. I prefer, however, to suggest here Blake's *avant-gardism* in somewhat different terms, terms that seem to me not only to incorporate much of what the authors in this collection have to say about *Poetical Sketches* (especially Vogler, Wolfson, and Peterfreund), but to acknowledge that the *Sketches* is of course not an example of Blake's composite art—except in the ways

Wolfson shrewdly reveals in her focus on the extraordinary visualness of that unpretentiously thin, "merely" verbal, anthology. And so I borrow my operative sense of avant-garde from a recent essay by Martin Price on Thomas Gray.[1]

Like the Wartons and Collins, Price argues, Gray sought "for a new idiom," one forged in the course of his trying "to define himself against" the poetry of, especially, Pope and Dryden—that is to say, by opposition to a reigning (or otherwise powerful) "taste or tradition." In so doing, the belated poet "elects a new canon of ancestors, uncles rather than fathers, the knight's move rather than direct descent" as in the line of the rook or bishop (pp. 46–48). These terms are Victor Shklovsky's (*The Knight's Move*, 1923); but while they have a certain attractiveness and provocativeness, they beg the entire question of "descent" or genealogical succession— and hence of allusion, involuntary allusion, echo, as well as assorted variations, degrees, and overlap of these, not to say the question of the certain identifiableness of any of these deprived of self-confessional quotation marks. Vogler's formulations of the question are elegant:

> How can the moment of origin for an "original" genius occur in a belated scene of copying or imitation? . . . How can we grant Blake a distance from the conventions he seems to invoke, granting him that ORIGIN-ality that means being present at the time and place of a *new* beginning?

Vogler's early answer to the question is also elegant, though it is Blake's cryptic and wry elegance that he appropriates to speak *for* him: "In the *Sketches* Blake may be read [indeed, of course, has been read] as trying on a variety of voices, not in the superficial manner that one can try on a suit of clothing [does anyone now *really* argue for that trying-on?], but in the manner of his advice to God: 'If you have formd a Circle to go into / Go into it yourself & see how you would do.'" Thus we, as readers, must "locate" the poems in *Poetical Sketches* in a context of discourse mapped by codes of literary practices.

Gray, of course, never formed a circle, so that Vogler's formulation here can hardly be seen as commensurate with Price's point about Gray's progress. But what Vogler suggests is not entirely irrelevant to that "progress." In Price's words, Gray's early odes bespeak his "self-conscious use" of a "new language of poetry" that "brings the literariness of the language to the fore, recognizes the precariousness of its hyperbolic power, and falls often into an irony that resists control." The idiom, in other words, "draws upon the funded meaning of terms, but they can take an interesting and surprising turn" (p. 55), a turn that often leaves us uncertain as to "how to take Gray's tone" (p. 54). I doubt that that helps us much in characterizing Blake's achievement in *Poetical Sketches*, though the delicate issue of "tone" has yet to be much discussed with respect to that volume. But if we superimpose on Price's provocative vagueness Bakhtin's argument for the heteroglossia of the novel (something Price reserves for the "idiom of the Augustans" *against* which Gray strives to define himself), we may come closer to Blake's avant-garde stance. Here is Bakhtin, summarized by Gary Morson: the novel

> represents the drama of speech reacting to speech, of words struggling to answer, paraphrase, or even deliberately ignore each other—and of words anticipating how they themselves will be answered, paraphrased, or ignored. (Quoted in Price, p. 46)

Even if that is not precisely (or solely) what Blake is "doing" in *Poetical Sketches,* my conflation (or misconflation) of two parts of Price's case may suggest an ideological (social, political, religious/doctrinal) "play of voices" in the volume that has little to do with the burden of the past but much to do with the troping focused on in different ways by Vogler and De Luca. And it may have even more to do with the wonderful play of verbal/spatial form illuminated by Wolfson, in which "irregularities and defects" are seen to constitute a "visual rhetoric" of "visually charged deformations" that speaks as eloquently to the eye as the ear, enunciating (or rather enacting) an extraordinary "poetics of form." Yet "Blake's formalism is no static aesthetic," she introductorily concludes. "It is an action that calls readers into a critical awareness of the work of form [including what she calls later the "radical antiform(s)" of the three prose sketches] not only in poetic, but also in cognitive, social, and historical processes."

The grandness of the claim is, to me, neither grandiose nor misplaced. The essays in this volume bear eloquent testimony to Blake's ambitiousness of enterprise, to what I called in *Blake's Prelude* its radical expansiveness—all of the essays, that is, except perhaps Hilton's. De Luca's essay may seem to be another candidate for exclusion in its suggestion that Blake's reach exceeded his grasp—an all too rare reservation in my judgment, whether or not one agrees with his precise formulation of that reservation as the absence of a sufficiently "severe, schematic, intellectual style." In fact, however, De Luca's analysis of the volume's falling-short emerges out of an admiration (largely unexpressed) for Blake's daring to aspire, even this early, to visionary power "in the sublime mode"—rather than his settling for what Vogler calls (in reference to misreadings of the seasons poems) "eminently simple and comprehensible . . . representations of a human voice, changing and developing in an on-going relationship with an external Nature," readable only "in the most banal sense." Blake's "daring," in De Luca's terms, involves his knowingly courting the "dangers of [his own] aspiration." If the "splendor" of the seasons poems inheres in their "vision of a plenitude, immanent in the here and now of time and nature . . . expressible in a Hebraically based style of troping," that very troping is "the stylistic mirror of outward change" and as such paradoxically forms a "rhetoric of instability, effacement, indeterminacy, and supersession."

What might well be argued here, of course, and in effect is argued in other terms elsewhere in this collection (notably by Vogler and Hilton), is the effective, and affective, power of instability and indeterminacy, if not effacement and supersession. If, as De Luca argues, Blake's quadrilateral rhetoric "hurries" the "mind . . . in too many places" until it ultimately, inevitably "crouds after night" as "Mad Song" puts it, isn't Blake's very inability (or perhaps disinclination) in the *Sketches* "to hold . . . at bay" this ever-threatening entropic slide into places of darkness in itself constitutive of remarkable power? Surely much of the rest of his poetry is in some sense a herculean effort to hold back the dark and hail (or hurl in its face) his "version" of Milton's "holy Light,"

> of Heav'n first-born,
> Or of th' Eternal coeternal beam

that

> Dwelt from eternity, dwelt then in thee,
> Bright effluence of bright essence increate—

that light/sun that he (Blake) eternally ("really") sees as "an Innumerable company of the Heavenly host crying Holy Holy Holy is the Lord God Almighty."[2] While such a seeing/hearing is of a different order, functioning in a different register, from that of most if not all of the *Poetical Sketches,* that volume's seeing/hearing/singing in days "Too, too late for the fond believing lyre" reflect a will to self-empowerment not entirely unlike Keats's "I see, and sing, by my own eyes inspired," to be not merely a "voice," a "lute," a "pipe," but a "choir" and "oracle" *(Ode to Psyche).*

Hardly Blake's voice or lute or pipe or choir or oracle, of course, Keats's formulation is nevertheless an implicit program something like the one announced by Blake in the "Introduction" to *Songs of Innocence:* Piping songs of pleasant glee, piping "a song about a Lamb," singing the same song, and finally writing songs either in invisible ink ("water clear") or in watercolors ("stain") on no apparent paper but rather in the consciousness of "Every child" who both sings and hears: "Songs *of* Innocence and *of* Experience" sung chorally to Innocence and to Experience. Oracularity, of course, is not so easily achieved. But out of the cacaphonous din of the early prophecies, forged in the preludic and epic struggle of *Milton,* it is ringingly enacted in the encyclopedic, Hebraic, Revelationary prophetic mode of *Jerusalem,* "The Song" (to end all songs) "*of* Jerusalem" (of the end of "the Sleep of Ulro" and "the awakening to Eternal Life"). *Jerusalem* is, then, an avant-gardism that is a retrogardism, a resurrection of the origins of voice and language itself. Vogler's formulation, not of what *Jerusalem* (or Blake's career) is and does but of *Poetical Sketches,* has a kind of uncanny resemblance to my point, which is far less pointedly and elegantly made. *His,* however, just may be too grand for that volume to support—though I like his courage:

> After the sterility of a debased, rhetorically wintry age [even the age of the sleep of Ulro?], Blake's voice seems to call out and by its power transform the wintry "climate" of English [*only* English?] poetry into the spring of Romanticism. The imputed power of his authentic word not only names being as a presence, it *calls itself into being* as the authentic utterance of a subject, William Blake, so says (i.e., writes) "Sing *now*" and whose voice becomes one with nature, present to us as the natural emanation of a transcendental principle higher even than nature, an epiphany of a permanent presence ordinarily hidden from "vision," which can be revealed through the poetic word.

What Vogler calls my "rhapsody in the verb-mood of Truth, the indicative," on pages 67–68 of *Blake's Prelude,* can't hold a candle to that—with all *its* indicatives hurrying after the seeming tentativeness of "seems" in the preliminary sentence.

The seasons poems, "To the Evening Star," and "To Morning," on the first of which Vogler concentrates exclusively, *can* bear the weight of such critical (uncritical?) rhapsodizing. Indeed, as Vogler himself suggests in quoting mine, such acknowledgement of what De Luca calls their "splendor" is well nigh irresistable. The *Sketches* volume as a whole, in fact, has elicited a whole range, and various degrees, of irresistableness to the urge to find reasons to praise. I am clearly as guilty as everyone, perhaps more so—though I did try on occasion to separate *my* sense of the wheat from my sense of the varying degrees of chaff.

But now, even "then She bore Pale desire" has been brought into the canon of irresistableness—as a test of "Blake's strategy of disseminating referential possibilities" and (or?) an "announce[ment]" of "psychic disturbance and the pale desire to set things right by sketching in hopes of the scarce find." Moreover "Mad Song," as widely admired and commented upon as it is, is now further elevated to the status of "the crucial poem" in the entire volume, its last stanza in fact "briefly reenact[ing] the movement of *Poetical Sketches* as a whole." And the heretofore largely neglected "Contemplation" has now become "a clearly delineated retrospective summary of Blake's ambiguous posture as a poet" in the *Sketches,* and his "Imitation of Spen[s]er" not only "shows the extent to which Blakean imitation is criticism" but actively "correct[s] Spenserian delusions." I do not single out these particular instances meanspiritedly to pillory their respective authors (Hilton, De Luca, Peterfreund) for rummaging in the dustbin and discovering the gems the rest of us missed. Rather, I cite them as, if not typical, at least not untypical symptoms of the quite extraordinary, perhaps even unique, mesmerizing power of virtually anything William Blake wrote (and, of course, graphically created) to galvanize critical acumen (not to say ingenuity) also to write. "Admire me I am a violet! dote upon me I am a primrose" (Keats's 3 February 1818 letter to J. H. Reynolds), the poems seem to cry. And we do admire, even dote. Nothing is read "in the most banal sense," to steal Vogler's phrase. *Is* there nothing banal—or even mediocre, or (God forbid) uninteresting? No weeds in the garden? No "possibility," in Hazard Adams's words, "that things might have gone wrong here and there" or, less gently in W. J. T. Mitchell's words, that "incoherence, nonsense, failure to communicate, . . . accident, random sloppiness, lack of facility" are *really* all there, perhaps even embarrassingly often to "the Blake Mafia that regards their Prophet as above reproach, . . . achieving [always] a rhetorical and formal mastery of language that anticipates the great experimental texts of modernism"?[3]

Mitchell's call is for the defamiliarizing of the Blake we have all made "safe for modern consumption" by way of our assorted critical strategies—and ingenuities—for at least entertaining the supposition "that Blake, like the rest of us, is a weak vessel, a flawed instrument" who "nods as often as he awakens us or himself."[4] I still like that idea, though this call, voiced ringingly ten years ago, has fallen on (willfully?) deaf ears. Let me try again, on a somewhat different though related tack—one that relates, less sweepingly than Mitchell's supposing, only to *Poetical Sketches*. What if that collection constituted the only Blake poems known to be extant? Or, even better, what if the *Sketches* and *An Island in the Moon* were all? Would we, any of us, read the poems and the "prose-poems" the way we do now, even in this critically enlightened and sophisticated age? Suppose he died young: would he have emerged as the new Chatterton, his "testing [of] possibilities, projecting schemes with a few strokes" recognized immediately as the work of a poet eager to define or establish his own poetic identity by "manipulating the inventories of various conventions to authorize individual performance, and distinguishing this with the energy of particular variations on and resistances to cultural norms"? Maybe so—but I doubt it. I have been quoting Wolfson, of course, mainly because I admire her essay enormously but also, in the context of my present ruminations, because her approach to the *Sketches* implicitly nominates her as the ideal candidate for answering my not entirely rhetorical what-ifs. In fact, what she writes of the efforts to determine meaning in the volume's order may give us a clue as to how she might respond:

> Blake's formalist poetics gain semantic value not only in these turns with tradition but also in the way they compel a reader's involvement in the play of forms. This intertextual field of activity—both across literary history and within the volume's field of repetition, echo, and parody—is more important than the question of Blake's actual ordering of the sketches.[11] For rather than yielding a stable, unified image of the cryptic sketcher, "W. B.," the volume sketches various interactions. The correlative to this unnamed and unfixed authorial form is the sketcher's production of his

reader, the intelligence in which these formal actions are registered and received.

That is to say, finally it does not matter whether W.B. is William Blake or Walter Bagehot or Wilford Brimley or Willy Boy? Or, is that a non-question—hence unanswerable by definition? Or just not interesting even if raised?

In fact, Wolfson seems to go beyond my question by suggesting that what we do know of Blake's composite verbal/graphic art "has tended to obscure attention to the way [he] generates meaning from the material presence of language itself and the graphic resources" of that medium alone, its "lines, words, and even syllables." And, moreover, whether or not she had in mind Blake's outrageous claim in *Jerusalem* that "Every word and every letter is *studied* and put into its *fit* place" (Erdman 146; my italics), her own minute and shrewd analyses of *Poetical Sketches* amply demonstrates the power of such studied "fitting" and "fitness," even if W.B. did not indeed *studiously* fit each word and letter in its "place." In fact, even if the printed "pattern" of lines (such as that of the run-over word or words) "exceeds what can be assigned to authorial intention, that very independence," Wolfson argues, "suggests the generativity of Blake's formalism, its verging on a Barthesian poetic of textual 'productivity.'"

Perhaps. Indeed it is very difficult not to nod assent to most, if not all, of Wolfson's discoveries. Yet, her own method prompts other eyes to see other minute particulars that she does not address, even as one grants her inability to "cover" everything in all the poems in an essay. For example, how does a perception of Summer's passing "thro' our vallies," yet being halted three lines later by his pitching his tent and sleeping beneath the oaks, "cohere" intelligibly, not to say dovetail with or corroborate, her overall analysis of the poem's progress? Blake's tense-shifts point us to some past when Summer did pitch a tent, did sleep, and we did behold and hear. Is the rhetorical thrust of these past tenses implicitly reflective of the possibility that the apostrophes are vain, that though "with the year / Seasons return," not to the speaker returns

> Day, or the sweet approach of ev'n or morn,
> Or sight of vernal bloom, or summer's rose,
> Or flocks, or herds, or human face divine;
> But cloud instead, and ever-during dark,

"a universal blank / Of Nature's works to [him] expunged and razed"? Only Autumn responds and appears and even sings ("Thus sang the jolly Autumn as he sat")—though the moment of his presence is but the moment of a nine-line song that yields immediately to the past tense of "sang," "rose," "girded," "fled," and "left," as well as to the coinstantaneous suddenness of "bleak / Hills" being thrust before the speaker's eyes. And what do we do, or what would Wolfson do, with the intertextual resonance of the progression from Spring's "golden crown" to Summer's "golden tent" to Autumn's "golden load" to Winter's "iron" (cf. Vogler's interpolated mini-essay on gold/golden)? And what about the comparable progression from Spring's "holy feet" and Summer's (noon's) "fervid car" drawn by "fierce steeds" riding "o'er the deep of heaven," to the parallel construction of Autumn's Spring-like pedestrian progress and Winter's "iron car" that "Rides heavy" "o'er the yawning deep"—though he seemingly coinstantaneously *strides o'er the groaning rocks*" withering all, silencing all, unclothing all, freezing all, and *sits* "upon *his* [not our?] cliffs"? Are there other, as yet unexplored, ramifications, then, of this seemingly neat alignment of Spring and Autumn, Summer and Winter?

And why do Summer, Autumn, and Winter sit but Spring does not, instead merely "visit[ing] our clime"? That is, here and gone in the blink of an eye—or maybe not here at all but in the love-sick fervor of willed imaginative presence? Is there some reason for, some formal function in, having Spring and Autumn walk but Summer and Winter ride? And why is Summer's person and vehicle conflated in threatening terms seemingly more appropriate (albeit in a different register) to Winter: "strength," "fierce[ness]," "flames," "fervid car"; and how does the echo of Summer-Noon's car riding "o'er the deep of heaven" in "To Winter" (riding heavy "o'er the yawning deep") lend itself to Wolfson's readings? Perhaps, indeed, rather than Blake's conceiving in "To Winter" the "power of the imagination to cancel itself, to project its undoing in the ruin of everything it has brought into play in the field of forms," Winter itself may be the bleak and barren season of the present, from which the isolated imagination of the speaker recoils in visions of fancied presence (Autumn) or desperate supplications of presence. Perhaps, then, rather than "To Winter" "figuring the dark, deep-founded habitation of an audience moving without regard for how it is called" (or even for the fact of its *being* called), Winter figures the would-be poet not only cut off from "the cheerful ways of men" (cheerful only in their obliviousness to their withered world and selves) but "Presented with a universal blank" that he must somehow fill. Is he but a "poor little wretch!," Crying in vain Cassandra-like precisely as "The Voice of one crying in the Wilderness" of *All Religions Are One* (dated only on the grounds of "internal evidence of themes and style" and Blake's 1822 [!] reference to his "Original Stereotype . . . 1788")[5]

I shall not cite again here the elaborate tissue of allusions, near-allusions, echoes, and the like that I marshal in my somewhat different reading in *Blake's Prelude* of the final impact of "To Winter" on the seasons poems as a whole—though many of them may be applicable here as well. Rather I cite another possible allusion, Gray's "Hymn to Ignorance," a fragment that Mason suggested was to be a "Satire upon false Science and scholastic Pedantry." Whether his guess is sound or not, the thirty-eight lines we have are suffused with allusions to Milton's Satan, Death, and Sin (along with *The Dunciad, Night Thoughts, Macflecknoe*), and in themselves constitute an apostrophe to Ignorance to "awake, arise!" and once again ride "High on her car . . . / . . . with barbaric pride," "triumphant o'er the vanquished world" as she did of yore when "all was Ignorance, and all was Night." Leading up to this mock-prophetic call to action are a series of rhetorical questions:

> Oh say, successful dost thou still oppose
> Thy laden aegis 'gainst our ancient foes?
> Still stretch, tenacious of thy right divine,
> The massy sceptre o'er thy slumbering line?
> And dews Lethean through the land dispense
> To steep in slumbers each benighted sense?
> If any spark of wit's delusive ray
> Break out, and flash a momentary day,
> With damp, cold touch forbid it to aspire,
> And huddle up in fogs the dangerous fire.

"Oh say," Gray then begins again, but abruptly breaks off: "she hears me not, but, careless grown, / Lethargic nods upon her ebon throne." For Blake, of course, neither "science" nor "scholastic pedantry" is to his point—though clearly "benighted sense" is, as well as the snuffing out of (or already snuffed-out) "dangerous fire" of the human imagination: all *is* Night, Winter, Sleep, Death. If the lingering remnant of the dangerous fire is figured in Blake's mariner (and, of course, in himself as poet), he "Cries in vain" precisely as the poet in propria persona must confess, "He hears me not." And if mariner/poet conflates, as it does syntactically, with "wretch" (from Old English *wrecca,* meaning "exile" as well), that composite persona only vaguely "deal'st / With storms" with no indication from Blake as to whether "heaven['s] smiles" do anything for *him* even if and when (the "till" irresolvably suspending everything) "the monster / Is driv'n yelling to his caves beneath mount Hecla." And even if the smiles *do* do "*something,*" the monster clearly will again ride his car heavy "o'er the yawning deep" into which all wretches are driven.

Something too much of this no doubt, especially my seeming to quibble only with Wolfson's essay alone. My bottom line is, if it is not already clear, that we all (and they all), one way or the other, succumb to the temptation to regard anything and everything Blake wrote as faultless, the product not of "untutored youth" but rather of untutored original genius whose very "irregularities," not to say "defects," bespeak a constitutional incapacity for klutziness of any sort or degree. "Does a firm perswasion that a thing is so, make it so?" the awestruck speaker of *The Marriage of Heaven and Hell*'s second "Memorable Fancy" asks. "All poets believe that it does," responds Isaiah blithely; "& in ages of imagination this firm perswasion removed mountains; but many are not capable of a firm perswasion of any thing." Do all critics, interpreters, believe that it does? my Obtuse Angled persona might ask; do we *re*move, if not mountains, what Wordsworth in the "Preface" to the *Lyrical Ballads* called "real defects," however variously they may be defined from age to age? Or are such "real defects" critically rationalizable into accidental poetic virtues if only seen via the proper, or appropriate critical/interpretative perspective?

Just asking, of course, despite the apparent rhetoricalness of my questions. Nevertheless, I am perfectly willing to admit that I welcome the *implication* of Peterfreund's more-or-less minority report on the otherwise universally lauded seasons poems. While I, personally, find much to debate in his elaborate build-up to this judgment, the fact of the judgment is salutarily provocative: "There is no apocalypse in 'To Spring,'" he writes (as if there should be or might have been), and as a consequence of that absence "originality suffers accordingly." Then, more sweepingly, the "three seasonal poems that follow are derivative poems—'copies' in the negative sense, rather than 'imitations' in the positive sense"—the latter sense one that Peterfreund is at great pains to define by reference to an army of others, including the later Blake we all know and love. And, finally, because these poems

> do not emphasize each of the steps in the sequence [of poetic process suggested by Blake's remarks in plate 11 of *The Marriage of Heaven and Hell*] equally, the poems are skewed or incomplete visions. Moreover, they begin from wrong initial premises—not absolutely wrong, but premises that can only follow from a suppressed initial premise. "To Spring" begins correctly with a recognition of the fundamental "thou-ness" or otherness of the object of address, but neither the speaker nor any of his companions is able to move toward the Apocalypse that such a recognition should set in motion.

"To Summer" "suppresses such a recognition," "To Autumn" in turn suppresses the "animation" "To Summer" favors, and "To Winter" suppresses the activity of naming that "To Autumn" favors.

There is more, but I leave that to the reader's re-reading (if necessary) of Peterfreund's argument. My point of quoting as much as I have is to congratulate him on his willingness and critical courage to *de*value (though not to disparage) Blake's achievement in the *Sketches*—even if, as I confessed earlier, I have strong misgivings about his sense of Blake's "classicizing" tendencies in the seasons poems as the basis for devaluation. They are at least analogous to my earlier-voiced misgivings about De Luca's conclusion that "the dark attraction" of the Burkean sublime for Blake (who is said to have thought "a poet must be sublime *somehow*") necessitated his development of "a more severe, schematic, intellectual style," unavailable to Blake before (and "many years" after) 1783, "to hold it at bay."

But De Luca prompts a few other "what-ifs" to go with my earlier, broader ones. "Mad Song," which he argues is "the crucial poem" in the "volume" (a word he regularly synonymizes with "the series"), is crucial for three reasons: (1) its last stanza "briefly reenacts the movement" of the entire volume; (2) it "shows Blake turning his back to the East, where the series began . . . and choosing to go with the epic chants of warfare and death" that "dominate" the latter half of the volume; and (3) it is the thirteenth of the volume's twenty-six poems and hence is "Situated at the center" of it. But what if we read the volume from the perspective of the fourteenth poem, "Fresh from the dewy hill," which is also at the center of the volume and picks up and redeploys many of the details and much of the language and phrasings of the first three seasons poems? Is this a "new beginning" of some sort, especially given its unique (in the *Sketches*) locution "more than mortal fire / Burns in my soul, and does my song inspire," as well as such strange linguistic sprinklings as "the music of angel's tongue," "the voice of Heaven," "laurel wreath[e]s," and "rising glories beam[ing] around [his] head"? And if indeed the latter half of the volume is far more suffused with "warfare and death" than the first half, what do we "do" with "An Imitation of Spen[s]er" or, more especially, "Blind-Man's Buff" (a poem virtually no one ever talks about, an unfortunate embarrassment perhaps)? And, finally, to return to my earlier what-if (*Poetical Sketches* as all we have from the hand of W.B.), can we even then suppose that Blake's "aspiration" was "to become a poet in the sublime mode"?

I fear that much of what I have had to say above may appear to participate in a conversation distressingly reminiscent of the wonderful comic debate in *An Island in the Moon*, ostensibly about whether Chatterton was a mathematician but far more profoundly about how we know anything. To Aradobo's (whose name in reverse is of course a coordinate signifier) assertion that Chatterton was a mathematician, Obtuse Angle (no doubt the benighted brother of the enlightened Right Angle) replies,

> No . . . how can you be so foolish as to think he was. Oh I did not think he was I only askd said Aradobo. How could you think he was not, & ask if he was said Obtuse Angle.—Oh no Sir I did think he was before you told me but afterwards I thought he was not.
>
> Obtuse Angle said in the first place you thought he was & then afterwards when I said he was not you thought he was not.—Oh no sir I thought that he was but I askd to know whether he was.—How can that be said Obtuse Angle how could you ask & think he was not—why said he. It came into my head that he was not—Why then said Obtuse Angle you said that he was. Did I say so Law I did not think I said that—Did not he said Obtuse Angle Yes said Scopprell [no doubt an Anglo-Saxon minstrel]. But I meant said Aradobo I I I cant think Law Sir I wish youd tell me, how it is

In fact Aradobo "really" does know how it is: "Chatterton was clever" at *everything*, "Fissic Follogy, Pistinology, Aridology, Arography, Transmography, Phizography, Hogamy HAtomy, & hall that."

And so say all of us—of Blake. He *is* irresistible in his endless challenging of our critical, interpretive faculties. Moreover there is little doubt, happily, that no savior will arise, as one of some self-appointed sort does at the end of *An Island*, to "fall into such a passion . . . hollow and stamp & frighten all the People . . . & show them what truth is."

Notes

1. "Sacred to Secular: Thomas Gray and the Cultivation of the Literary," in *Context, Influence, and Mid-Eighteenth Century Poetry*, ed. Maximillian E. Novak (Los Angeles: Clark Memorial Library, 1990), pp. 41–78.

2. *Paradise Lost*, III, 1–6; *A Vision of the Last Judgment*, Erdman, p. 566.

3. Adams, "Post-Essick Prophecy," *SiR* 21 (1982), 401; Mitchell, "Dangerous Blake," ibid., pp. 414, 411.

4. "Dangerous Blake," pp. 415, 414.

5. *The Complete Poetry and Prose of William Blake*, ed. David V. Erdman (Berkeley and Los Angeles: University of California Press, 1982), p. 790. References to "Erdman" in my text and notes are to this edition.

Index

Aaron, 86
Abrams, M. H., 100
Accioli, Joseph, 64
Achilles, 93
Adam, 93
Adams, Hazard, 139, 145, 208, 216
Addison, Joseph, 134
Aikin, John, 77–78, 101
Alpers, Paul, 119
Apollo, 91
Appleton, Jay, 123
Artaxerxes, 81
Ault, Donald, 194
Ault, Norman, 183, 187
Austin, J. L., 101

Bacon, Francis, 81
Bagehot, Walter, 210
Bakhtin, Mikhail, 205
Barnfield, Richard, 183
Barthes, Roland, 30, 210
Bate, Walter Jackson, 19, 81, 101
Beattie, James, 76, 101, 106
Bedingfield, Edward, 146
Bentley, G. E., Jr., 25, 32, 64, 65,
  165, 177, 199
Berkeley, George, 32, 137–38, 141
Bible, 19, 24, 106
Blake, James, Sr., 190
Bloom, Harold, 13, 19–20, 45, 65,
  100, 102, 106, 113, 132, 164, 165
Borges, Jorge Luís, 106
Boucher, Catherine Sophia, 198
Brimley, Wilford, 210
Bronowski, Jacob, 101
Brooks, Cleanth, 46
Bryant, Jacob, 95, 101
Buber, Martin, 102
Burdett, Osbert, 32, 63

Burke, Edmund, 122, 131, 154,
  156–58, 161–63, 173, 181
Burns, Robert, 14, 116
Burton, Robert, 181
Butcher, Catherine. *See* Boucher,
  Catherine Sophia

Carr, David, 101
Cervantes Saavedra, Miguel de, 106
Chartier, Roger, 17
Chatterton, Thomas, 19, 52, 71, 72,
  95–96, 99, 106, 209, 215
Chayes, Irene, 164
Christ, Jesus, 80, 82–83, 87–88
Claude Lorrain, 123
Cohen, Ralph, 114
Coleridge, Samuel Taylor, 14, 126,
  128, 135, 147
Collins, William, 24, 77, 95–96, 103,
  106, 155, 173, 204
Cooke, Thomas, 185
Cowper, William, 14, 114, 191, 199
Culler, Jonathan, 33, 64
Cunningham, Alan, 13
Cyrus, 81

Damon, S. Foster, 56, 103, 166, 172
Darius, 81
De Luca, Vincent A., 11, 19, 23–24,
  28, 54, 205–6, 208, 214
De Man, Paul, 119, 122, 126–27,
  141–42, 163
Dennis, John, 147
Derrida, Jacques, 30, 75, 79, 101,
  108–9, 115–17, 123, 137, 146–48
Descartes, René, 123–25, 142, 147
Dictionary of the English Language,
  24
Donne, John, 194
Drayton, Michael, 180

Dryden, John, 44, 55, 65, 72, 81, 101,
176, 182, 185, 190–91, 193–94,
196, 203–4
Duff, William, 76, 101, 146

Easthope, Anthony, 66
Eaves, Morris, 73, 55, 99–100, 109,
Edward, King, 56, 65
Ehrstine, John, 64–66
Eliot, Thomas Stearns, 30, 32, 62,
116, 146
Ellis, Edwin J., 166
Epicurus, 144
Erdman, David V., 13, 24, 29, 51, 61,
63–66, 100, 163, 165–66, 210, 216
Essick, Robert N., 18, 29
Ezekiel, 91
Ezra, 82

Ferber, Michael, 101–2
Fisch, Harold, 73, 100
Fish, Stanley, 120
Flaxman, John, 13, 25, 63, 71, 81
Fletcher, Giles, 182
Fogle, Aaron, 63
Foster, Hal, 108
Freemason, 81
Freud, Sigmund, 193
Frye, Northrop, 13, 57–58, 62–63,
99–100
Fuseli, Henry, 72

George the Third, King, 54
Germ, The, 15
Gibbon, Edward, 177
Gilchrist, Alexander, 13–15, 18, 32,
40–41, 99, 196, 198
Gleckner, Robert F., 11–13, 19, 22,
24, 39, 45, 49, 53, 62, 65, 74, 81,
85, 87, 95–96, 99, 101–3, 105–6,
110, 114–16, 131–34, 138, 143–44,
146, 148, 155–56, 159, 163, 189
Glen, Heather, 66
Gödel, Kurt, 78

Goethe, J. W. von, 146
Graves, Robert, 32
Gray, Thomas, 24, 76, 77, 95–96,
103, 106, 119, 129–30, 144, 146,
190, 204–5, 212, 216
Greenberg, Mark L., 11, 25

Hagstrum, Jean, 63
Hart, Clive, 149
Hartman, Geoffrey, 19, 33–34, 41,
64, 66, 107, 162, 164
Hayley, William, 13
Hector, 93
Hendrickson, J. R., 103
Henry the Fifth, King, 55
Herodotus, 148
Hesiod, 77
Hilton, Nelson, 11, 18–19, 24, 63,
146, 206, 208
Hobbes, Thomas, 124
Hollander, John, 28, 34, 42–43, 45,
63, 65–66
Holloway, John, 65
Homer, 77
Horace, 144, 149
Hubbard, Margaret, 149
Hughes, Merritt Y., 65, 102
Husserl, Edmund, 78, 79, 101

Isaiah, 82, 145
Israel, 94, 99

Jacob, 93–94, 99
Jakobson, Roman, 63
Jameson, Fredric, 108
Jeshurun, 93–95
John of Patmos, 87–88
Johnson, Dr. Samuel, 24, 31, 44, 49,
63, 65, 72, 77, 173, 178, 180–82,
186, 189, 192–93
Jonson, Ben, 19
Joseph of Arimathea, 80
Joyce, James, 105, 128, 146

Kames, Henry Home, Lord, 55